T0291238

Blue Shark Team-Building

Blue Shark Team-Building

Leading High-Performance Teams
during a Crisis

Rizwan Amin Sheikh, Ph.D.

CRC Press
Taylor & Francis Group
Boca Raton London New York

CRC Press is an imprint of the
Taylor & Francis Group, an **informa** business
AN AUERBACH BOOK

First edition published 2022
by CRC Press

6000 Broken Sound Parkway NW, Suite 300, Boca Raton, FL 33487-2742
and by CRC Press
2 Park Square, Milton Park, Abingdon, Oxon, OX14 4RN

ISBN: 978-1-032-08105-2 (hbk)
ISBN: 978-1-032-06295-2 (pbk)
ISBN: 978-1-003-21671-1 (ebk)

Typeset in Minion
by KnowledgeWorks Global Ltd.

DOI: 10.1201/9781003216711

Contents

PART II   Case Study

Acknowledgments

I want to dedicate this book to my parents (M. Amin Sheikh and Nasira Amin Sheikh), who left this world too early. Whatever success I have achieved in my career is because of them. They supported me through the thick and thin of life. They worked hard so that I could go to school, be successful in life, and achieve the American dream.

My wife, Dr. Huma Sheikh, provided me the motivation and support to write this book. The book would also not exist without my three children's encouragement: Dr. Marryum Sheikh, Dr. Omar Sheikh, and Sana Sheikh (currently in medical college). Sana inspired me because she also wants to be a writer when done with the medical school. My two brothers (Imran Amin Sheikh and Zeeshan Amin Sheikh) always stood by me. My brother (Zeeshan) and nephew (Haaziq Sheikh) were kind enough to accompany me to the Golf course and brainstorm the book ideas. They were always with me when I missed the par shot on the 3rd hole at the Bridle Wood Golf course. Also, I want to thank my nephew (Sheharyar Amin Sheikh) niece (Khadija Amin Sheikh) for checking up on me and make sure I was on track to finish the book. I could not go without thanking my niece Isra Sheikh and her cat (Lilly) for their support. Isra always brought me the cookies from the Great American Cookies shop. Special thanks to my sisters: Samina Sheikh, Tayyaba Imran Sheikh, Saima Pirzada, Ayesha Afzal, Sumaira Afzal, and Beenish Afzal for their support. Also, I would like to thank my nephew (M. Ali Pirzada) and nieces (Rukhsar Pirzada and Hira Pirzada). Besides, thanks to my brothers-in-law Aamir Pirzada and Imran Ahmed for their support.

A book is never ready until it goes through a critique. I want to offer my special thanks to Faiza Jawad (Head of Global Programs at ISBE USA) for challenging my ideas. She provided excellent constructive feedback and made me re-think and re-write many sections of this book. Faiza was very meticulous in reading, deciphering each chapter's theme, proofreading, and providing precious input. I would not have been able to finish this project without her continuous support. Also, I would like to thank Haider Iqbal for his timely support.

My Ph.D. supervisors, Professor Dr. Ralf Müller, Professor Dr. Rodney Turner, and Professor Dr. Azhar Khan, deserve a standing ovation for preparing me to conduct the research and write this book. I'm enormously grateful to them for providing me the necessary training on research and academic writing during the Ph.D. program at Skema Business School (Lille, France).

I would also like to thank my friends and colleagues, Dr. Ted James at Harvard Medical School, Dr. Dan Shapiro at Harvard Law School, Jeremiah Whitehall (Founder and Partner Liberum), and Dr. Khalid Ahmad Khan (CEO of Expert Systems), for their encouragement and support.

At the Public Transportation Division (PTD) of Washington State Department of Transportation (WSDOT), I would like to thank everyone for providing their support and encouraging me to pen the Grants Management System (GMS) project's success story during COVID-19. I hope the lessons learned mentioned in this book will help future projects in the public and private sector companies.

Finally, I want to thank John Wyzalek and everyone at Taylor & Francis Group for helping me to edit and publish the book. It was not possible to bring this book to life without their professional help and support.

Part I

There are two parts to the book. Part I (Chapters 1–6) of the book describes theories of leadership, team-building, and emotional intelligence that social scientists and researchers have developed after decades of research. It further discusses the challenges faced by organizations and projects during a national crisis and pandemics like COVID-19. We also describe ten strategies to lead high-performance teams. In addition, we explain *The Blue Shark Model of Leading High-Performance Teams,* which has been developed by the author based on Daniel Goleman's Emotional Intelligence (EQ) and Bruce Tuckman's team-building model.

DOI: 10.1201/9781003216711-1

1

Introduction

We have written the book on the foundation of the last 70 years of studies conducted by many researchers on leadership, emotional intelligence, and team-building. It shows you, with real-life case studies, how to create and lead high-performance (The Blue Shark) teams and manage Fortune 500 companies, mid-to-small businesses, and deliver projects successfully around the world during a global crisis such as COVID-19.

The author has devised *The Blue Shark Model of Leading High-Performance Teams* based on Daniel Goleman's emotional intelligence model[1] and Bruce Tuckman's team-building model (forming, storming, norming, performing, and adjourning)[2,3]. It shows you how to apply these models to large companies, small-to-medium size businesses, and projects during a crisis. Besides, it explains how you can develop your leadership style[4] and lead high-performance teams. In addition, a real-life case study, which was a success story during COVID-19, is discussed to elaborate the team-building and emotional intelligence models. The lessons learned can be applied to any crisis and industries across the spectrum, including healthcare, IT, telecom, construction, manufacturing, oil and gas, airlines, financial services, retail, public sector, consulting, public sector, and others.

And Part II describes a real-life case study that shows you how to implement the Blue Shark, Goleman, and Tuckman's model to lead high-performance teams and deliver projects successfully worldwide, especially during a crisis such as COVID-19.

For those of you who are not familiar with theories of leadership, emotional intelligence, and team-building or looking for a quick refresher, you can read Chapter 2 on theoretical frameworks and models. Others can skip

DOI: 10.1201/9781003216711-2

to the case study in Part II of the book or the chapters on organizational challenges during global emergencies and pandemics like COVID-19. We recommend reviewing the *Blue Shark Model of Leading High-Performance Teams* in Chapter 6.

The book is written in a manner whereby each chapter has its own set of lessons learned and key takeaways. You can read any chapter or just the real-life case study in Part II of this book and learn a few tips that can help you succeed during a national or global crisis. The lessons can help you in leading and managing companies and projects globally during turbulent and volatile times.

In Part II, we describe a case study about an IT project that was successfully executed at the Public Transportation Division (PTD) of the Washington State Department of Transportation (WSDOT) in the US during COVID-19.

The book answers the five key questions that CEOs, CFOs, CIOs, CMOs, CXOs, directors, leaders, managers, senior managers, project managers, and executives can find immensely helpful during national and global emergencies. Answers to the five questions can help you lead teams, organizations, and projects effectively and successfully worldwide during a national crisis and global emergency such as COVID-19. Below are the five questions answered in the book from a practical and real-life perspective.

1. Does the Tuckman model of team-building (forming, storming, norming, performing, and adjourning) work[2,3]? Can it be applied to Fortune 500 companies, mid-to-small size businesses, or projects during a national crisis or global emergency such as COVID-19? If yes, how?
2. Does Daniel Goleman's model on emotional intelligence work[1]? Can it be applied to Fortune 500 companies, mid-to-small size businesses, or projects during a national crisis or global emergency such as COVID-19? If yes, how?
3. As a leader, how can you develop your leadership style to create and lead a high-performance (Blue Shark) team and cope with a national crisis or pandemic?
4. Can leaders create and lead high-performance (Blue Shark) teams using emotional intelligence to lead Fortune 500 companies, manage

small-to-medium businesses, and deliver projects successfully during a national crisis or pandemic? If yes, how?

5. What are the tools and techniques that leaders can use to successfully lead their companies and projects during a national crisis, emergency, or pandemic?

If you are a CEO, CIO, CTO, or CXO of a Fortune 500 company, a mid-to-small size business owner, project manager, or a senior executive facing a crisis, this book is for you. It describes real-life case studies and projects and shows how the theoretical frameworks and models developed by researchers like Tuckman and Goleman can be applied successfully to companies and projects, especially during a crisis and pandemic like COVID-19.

BACKGROUND AND GLOBAL CRISIS OF 2020

News started to flow out of Wuhan, China, in December 2019, some flu had been spreading. Nobody knew what it was? The World Health Organization (WHO) started to follow it and declared it a "Public Health Emergency of International Concern" on January 30, 2020[5]. On March 11, 2020, the Director-General of WHO stated:

> There are now more than 118,000 cases in 114 countries, and 4,291 people have lost their lives…. We have therefore made the assessment that COVID-19 can be characterized as a pandemic[6].

The coronavirus (COVID-19) was also known as severe acute respiratory syndrome coronavirus 2 (SARS-CoV-2). The disease attacked a human being's respiratory tract and lungs, causing death due to the lungs' dysfunction and inability to breathe.

There were two waves of COVID-19 in the US, and in some countries, there were three. The first wave started in March 2020 and peaked in July 2020. The second wave was even more deadly, started in October, and kept going well into December 2020. By December 05, 2020, COVID-19 had caused more havoc in the entire world than World War II. Some of the stats and news headlines are shown in the following pages to show the readers the devastation that COVID-19 caused globally.

The first case of coronavirus was reported on January 20, 2020, in the US. The US President declared the coronavirus as a public health emergency on January 31, 2020. The situation got so bad that some states in the US had to implement lockdowns and curfews.

Almost everything was disrupted globally by April 2020, including human life, businesses, hospitals, airlines, government operations, hotels, travel, financial markets, and other daily lives. It almost seemed like the world had turned upside down. Nobody knew what to do and how to put a lid on the coronavirus. Many theories started to circle around, such as the virus would go away automatically during summer due to the heat. Unfortunately, by the end of November 2020, the virus got more deadly than it was from March to July 2020. The number of infections and deaths skyrocketed in the US, Europe, Asia, and other regions around the world.

Schools, colleges, restaurants, bars, gyms, parks, hotels, cruises, and all recreational activities were shut down worldwide. Some countries, including the US, implemented lockdowns, stay-at-home orders, and curfews due to the surge in coronavirus infections. Imagine not being able to go to school, work, gym, restaurant, or other places with public gatherings. The entire world went into shock and depression. People were losing jobs, businesses were filing bankruptcies, and individuals were dying all over the world. No vaccine was available until December 08, 2020. The coronavirus did not discriminate. It hit everybody, the rich and poor, black and white, Americans, Europeans, Asians, Africans, Middle Eastern, and everybody else globally.

COVID-19 caused a global social, healthcare, and economic crisis, which became the largest crisis since the Great Depression of the 1930s. The International Monetary Fund (IMF) called it "The Great Lockdown: Worst Economic Downturn since the Great Depression" in its blog on April 14, 2020[7]. It further stated:

> This is a crisis like no other … the cumulative output loss over 2020 and 2021 from the pandemic crisis could be around 9 trillion dollars … many countries now face multiple crises – a health crisis, a financial crisis, and a collapse in commodity prices.

GLOBAL CORONAVIRUS INFECTION CASES AND DEATHS

According to WHO, as of February 28, 2021, globally, 113,466,558 cases of coronavirus infections were confirmed; 2,520,537 deaths were confirmed; and 223 countries, territories, or areas had been affected by the coronavirus[8,9]. Details are shown in Table 1.1.

Unfortunately, the US was hit with the highest number of COVID-19 infections and deaths among the world's countries. According to WHO, there were 28,174,978 confirmed cases of COVID-19 infections, with 506,706 deaths in the US as of February 28, 2021[10]. More Americans died due to COVID-19 than World War II.

States throughout the US issued lockdown and stay-at-home orders from March to July 2020, and in some states, curfew was ordered. The situation went from bad to worst in July and then in November–December 2020, especially after the Thanksgiving holidays. Below are some of the headline news related to COVID-19 during March–December 2020:

World Health Organization Declares Coronavirus A Global Pandemic.

Forbes, March 11, 2020

NYC declares state of emergency, de Blasio says Coronavirus could easily be a 6-month crisis.

CNBC, March 12, 2020

TABLE 1.1

Global COVID-19 Infection Cases and Deaths

Situation by WHO Region	Confirmed Cases of Infection	Deaths
Americas	50,426,060	1,205,245
Europe	38,674,452	861,803
South-East Asia	13,517,009	208,013
Eastern Mediterranean	6,388,249	144,479
Africa	2,840,208	71,991
Western Pacific	1,620,580	29,006
Total	113,466,558	2,520,537
United States	28,174,978	506,760

Source: World Health Organization; February 28, 2021.

National Guard to deploy against Coronavirus in NY, California, Washington.

ABC News, March 23, 2020

New York to impose curfew on restaurants, bars and gyms as Covid worsens across the US

CNBC, November 11, 2020

The Virus Is Devastating the US, and Leaving an Uneven Toll.

The New York Times, Dec 04, 2020

COVID-19 has already exhausted the US. And it's only the start of a dark and deadly winter.

CNN, December 05, 2020

US sets new single-day record with 227,885 coronavirus cases Friday, according to Johns Hopkins University

Fox News, December 06, 2020

New COVID-19 stay-at-home orders set to take effect Sunday night for millions of Californians … roughly 33 million of California's 39 million residents, about 85% of the nation's most populous state, will be under the orders beginning Sunday evening

CNN, December 06, 2020

Europe in meltdown as Covid death tolls soar and progress unravels. Russia and Germany reported record daily COVID-19 deaths on Friday, and October was Russia's deadliest month in a decade. Stockholm's intensive care units hit 99% capacity as Sweden proposed a spring "pandemic law" to potentially force closures of certain public spaces.

CNN World, December 11, 2020

ECONOMIC IMPACT OF COVID-19

The unemployment rate and overall economic situation were quite dismal during March–April 2020. According to various reports published by the Congressional Budget Office (CBO)[11] and the US Bureau of Labor Statistics[12] in May 2020, the US's unemployment rate jumped from 3.5% in February to 14.7% in April 2020, which was the worst since World War II.

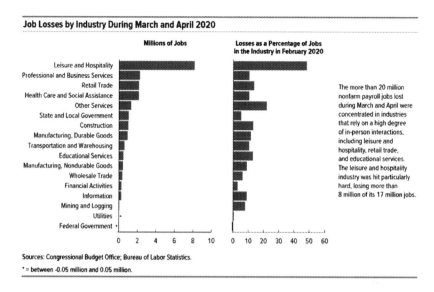

FIGURE 1.1
US job losses by industry during COVID-19.

More than 25 million got unemployed, and another 8 million exit the job market. By the end of April 2020, almost 33 million people were unemployed in the US As shown in Figure 1.1, the leisure and hospitality industry was hit the hardest, and 8 million people lost jobs in the hospitality industry during this time, followed by professional and business services, retail, healthcare, and others[11,12].

The Unemployment Rate in the US

The US unemployment rate jumped to 14.7% in May 2020, which was the highest in the last 40 years. Companies lost money, layoffs were rampant, and people filed unemployment claims at unprecedented levels. Figure 1.2 shows the 40-year unemployment rate since 1980.

Interest Rate on the US Treasury Bills

The 10-Year US Treasury notes' interest rates were about 0.5%, and the 3-Month Treasury bill rate was almost 0%. These numbers were mind-boggling and unprecedented in recent memory. Figure 1.3 shows the interest rates on the US Treasury notes and bills since 2016. These figures are as of May 2020.

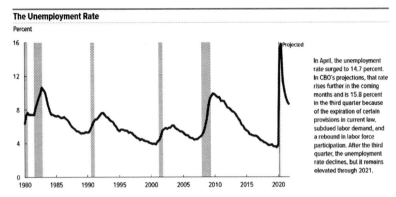

FIGURE 1.2
The unemployment rate in the US since 1980.

Just so that you understand the magnitude of the situation and enormity of the global crisis, here's a summary of the economic and social impact of COVID-19 during March–April 2020 as reported by CBO[11], US Bureau of Labor Statistics[12], and USA Facts[13]. In the US, during March–April 2020:

- 24.9 million unemployment claims were filed.
- The Stock Market S&P 500 Index closed at 2,237 points on March 23, 2020, compared to 3,338 points on February 21, 2020.

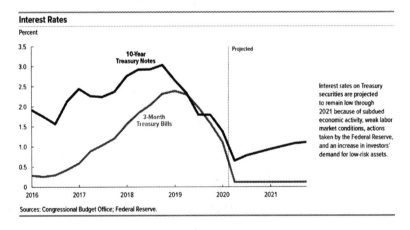

FIGURE 1.3
Interest rates on the US treasury notes and bills.

- On April 16, 2020, only 95,500 airline passengers traveled in the US, compared to about 2.0 million passengers on March 08, 2020.
- On April 01, 2020, household spending was down by 20% as compared to January 2020.
- In April 2020, car and light truck sales were 49% below the late 2019 monthly average.
- Mortgage applications fell 30% in April 2020 versus April 2019.
- The CBO projected that the federal budget deficit would be $3.3 trillion for the fiscal year 2020, which would be the largest and worst since 1945.

COVID-19 had a devastating impact on the overall global economy, healthcare systems, and social life. Schools, colleges, parks, gyms, restaurants, and other public places were shut down. For example, I went for a walk at the beautiful Puget Sound Community College campus in Olympia, Washington, in April 2020, and I could not find a soul at the campus because everything was shut down. It seemed like I was part of a horror movie and in a ghost town.

Depression, anxiety, and uncertainty in communities increased due to the loss of 33 million jobs in the US The business atmosphere and economic outlook in the entire US, Europe, and other regions were immensely somber and depressing during March–July 2020. As economies around the world had started to pick up some pace in September, then the second or in some regions and countries, the third wave of the coronavirus hit in November 2020. These waves were deadlier than the first wave. They broke all the previous records of infections and deaths. Hospitals in the US, Europe, and other territories came under severe pressure and began to choke.

COVID-19 IMPACT ON HOSPITALS AROUND THE WORLD

As of December 08, 2020, with 67.21 million confirmed cases of COVID-19 infections and 1.54 million deaths globally, hospitals in the US, Europe, Asia, and other regions were severely strained and operating at more than their capacity. Doctors, nurses, and staff were exhausted, over-worked, and devastated. Some of them caught the coronavirus while treating patients and died. All these stories and scenes were heartbreaking, depressing, and nerve-wracking. Below are some of the headlines to give you an idea of how dire the situation in hospitals worldwide was.

COVID-19 surges across US as some hospitals stretched.

Reuters, October 22, 2020

Europe's Hospital Crunch Grows More Dire, Surpassing Spring Peak.

The New York Times, November 6, 2020

Europe's Hospitals near COVID-19 Capacity. Hospitals in several parts of Europe, from the Midlands of England to Ukraine, are warning their intensive care units are reaching full capacity as a second wave of coronavirus sweeps across the continent.

VOA News, November 13, 2020

European countries believed that Germany would always have spare ICU beds for them. Now they're almost full.

CNN, November 22, 2020

Coronavirus: Indian hospitals run short of intensive care beds.

Deutsche Welle (DW), November 23, 2020

Japan's COVID-19 third wave clogs hospitals' capacity for care.

Nikkei Asia, December 04, 2020

The US Has Passed the Hospital Breaking Point. A new statistic shows that health-care workers are running out of space to treat COVID-19 patients.

The Atlantic, December 5, 2020

Hospitals in crisis mode as US coronavirus deaths top 283,000.

CNBS News, December 08, 2020

Imagine waking up in the morning and reading the headline news mentioned above. Depression and anxiety among people were rampant during March–December 2020. Nobody knew when this crisis would be over, even though some drug companies had announced that a vaccine would be available in the coming weeks and months. As mentioned earlier, the IMF estimated the total economic loss of about 9 trillion dollars during 2020 and 2021. The COVID-19 global crisis was like no other, and it brought the entire world to a halt.

In light of the facts mentioned above and the global crisis, we decided to write this book to help leaders, managers, project managers, and organizations worldwide build high-performance teams to cope with the challenges caused by an unprecedented global crisis. Based on my 30-year experience in the industry and academia, I have shared the real-life case studies, strategies, tools, and techniques that would not only help you get through the COVID-19 challenges but are also applicable to any national or global crisis. The lessons learned described in the book will help leaders, project managers, and organizations to recover from the colossal healthcare crisis, social disruption, and economic loss caused by a pandemic or global emergency such as COVID-19.

2

Theoretical Frameworks and Models on Leadership, Emotional Intelligence, and Team-Building

This chapter talks about the theoretical frameworks and models on leadership, emotional intelligence, and team-building that are the foundation of the practical implications and the case study described in this book. For the readers who are already familiar with these definitions and frameworks, this might be a refresher. Those who are relatively new to the topic can learn about these models and understand how they are applied to real-life projects and situations, especially during national or global emergencies such as COVID-19.

Various research studies have been conducted in the last few decades on leadership, but researchers have not agreed on a single definition of leadership. There are perhaps as many definitions of leadership as there are authors and research groups. And the debate among the research community continues on the question: Are leaders born or made? You will find arguments on both sides of the fence. The consulting answer is "leaders are born and made."

WHAT IS LEADERSHIP?

John Kotter[14] defines leadership and management in his HBR article *What leaders really do* as:

> Leadership and management are two distinctive and complementary systems of action. Management is about coping with complexity. Leadership, by contrast, is about coping with change.

DOI: 10.1201/9781003216711-3

Warren Bennis and Burt Nanus[15] make an important distinction between management and leadership in their book *Leaders: The strategies for taking charge*[2] and say:

> To manage means to bring about, to accomplish, to have responsibility for, and to conduct. Leading is influencing, guiding in direction, course, action, and opinion. This distinction is crucial. Managers are people who do things right, and leaders are people who do the right things.

A 10-year research study called Global Organization Behavior Effectiveness (GLOBE) explored the leadership theory factors, traits, and links to national culture. During the GLOBE research conference held in Calgary (Canada) in 1994, 54 researchers from 38 countries agreed to the following definition of leadership, which was defined by Robert House and his colleagues in their book "Culture, Leadership, and Organizations: The GLOBE Study of 62 Societies:[16]" as:

> It is the ability of an individual to influence, motivate, and enable others to contribute toward the effectiveness and success of the organization of which they are members[16].

According to the International Project Management Association's (IPMA) Competencies Baseline:

> Leadership involves providing direction and motivating others in their role or task to fulfill the project's objectives. It is a vital competence for project managers.
>
> *(IPMA, 2007, p. 86)*[17]

Rizwan Sheikh and Ralf Müller said in their research study[18]:

> Leadership can be important on projects because project managers have to deal with multiple facets of change on projects (i.e., employee turnover, economic conditions, environmental changes, organization change, and others)[18].

There are hundreds of definitions of leadership that can be found in the literature. The readers might be wondering which definition of leadership is right or wrong. Based on my 30-year experience in the industry and academia, I say that all leadership definitions are correct. Leadership is situational, so leaders and professionals have to adapt their leadership style according to the situation, organization, or project they are executing.

In the HBR article *What makes an effective executive?*, Peter Drucker mentioned that you should not worry about the kind of leader you are[19]. It does not matter whether you are an extrovert, easygoing, visionary, or numbers-oriented. Drucker argues that you, as a leader, need to get the right things done, in the right ways, and by following the eight simple rules[19]:

1. *Ask what needs to be done.*
2. *Ask what's right for the enterprise.*
3. *Develop action plans.*
4. *Take responsibility for decisions.*
5. *Take responsibility for communicating.*
6. *Focus on opportunities, not problems.*
7. *Run productive meetings.*
8. *Think and say "We," not "I."*

Every time I teach a leadership course or deliver a keynote speech, people ask me: what is your leadership definition? My definition of a leader is someone who has the necessary intellectual quotient (IQ), emotional intelligence quotient (EQ), and decency quotient (DQ). Most of the executives and participants are familiar with IQ and EQ, but they are not aware of DQ because it is a relatively new term.

WHAT IS DQ?

Decency Quotient (DQ) goes one step beyond the EQ as it implies that a leader not only has empathy for his colleagues and team members but he/she genuinely cares about them and their well-being. It means that a leader, manager, or project manager cares about his team and employees and explores ways to help them succeed.

Most of us have been quite familiar with IQ and EQ. However, the DQ might be new to some of us, but it is one of the traits that all transformational leaders must possess to successfully lead organizations and projects. We are not trying to undermine the importance of IQ and EQ. Successful leaders must have the necessary intellect (IQ) and emotional intelligence (EQ) to build and lead organizations and teams. However, the decency (DQ) element can enhance leaders' ability to lead people and organizations. In his article, Bill Boulding argued that we need more leaders with triple-threat leadership capability: IQ+EQ+DQ[20]. As a leader, if you deploy the combination of IQ+EQ+DQ, you will develop a high-performance organization and team. We have discussed practical examples of DQ in Chapter 6 as part of the Blue Shark Model.

Unfortunately, there are many examples where organizations failed because leaders did not have the DQ capability. For example, the 2007–08 meltdown of the financial markets brought the public and retirees to its knees. Financial services are one of the least trusted industries. Only 57% of the people surveyed showed trust in the industry. It has gone a couple of notches up, but it is still the least trusted industry[20]. If leaders can bring the DQ to the financial services and other industries across the board, our societies and the world can be better and happier.

WHAT IS EQ?

Various research studies have been conducted on emotional intelligence (EQ) in the last few decades. Researchers and authors have offered different definitions of EQ. Here are some of the definitions of EQ that I find relevant for creating and leading high-performance teams.

Salovey and Mayer[21] define EQ as:

> An ability to monitor one's and others' feelings and emotions, to discriminate among them and to use this information to guide one's thinking and actions.

Mayer et al.[22] have defined EQ as:

> The ability to be aware of, to utilize, to understand, and to manage emotions in self and others.

Van Rooy & Viswesvaran[23] have defined EQ as:

> the set of abilities (verbal and non-verbal) that enable a person to generate, recognize, express, understand, and evaluate their own and others' emotions in order to guide thinking and action that successfully cope with environmental demands and pressures.

We have focused on the research conducted by Daniel Goleman and his colleagues because it is most relevant to our topic of creating and leading high-performance teams. Boyatzis, Goleman, and Rhee[24] have defined EQ as:

> Emotional intelligence is observed when a person demonstrates the competencies that constitute self-awareness, self-management, social awareness, and social skills at appropriate times and ways in sufficient frequency to be effective in the situation.

DANIEL GOLEMAN'S EMOTIONAL INTELLIGENCE (EQ) MODEL

You might already be familiar with Daniel Goleman's model[1]. In case you are not or need a refresher, here are five components of Goleman's EQ model: self-awareness, self-regulation, motivation, empathy, and social skills that are summarized in Table 2.1.

Self-Awareness

Self-awareness is knowing and understanding your strengths and weaknesses. Most readers might have conducted SWOT (strengths, weaknesses, opportunities, and threats) analysis for our businesses or companies. I ask executives during my lectures and programs: have you conducted a SWOT analysis on yourself? Most of the executives answer it in the negative.

You must assess and understand your professional strengths, weaknesses, opportunities, and threats. For example, you might be very good at looking at the big picture, but you might not be good at figuring out the details of a project or situation. Understanding your weaknesses is equally important. You can either improve or delegate the responsibilities to a colleague who is better than you in some of the tasks. As Steve Jobs said, "It does not make sense to hire smart people and then tell them what to do. We hire smart people so that they can tell us what to do." Once you understand your weakness, you can either hire somebody or assign a teammate who can fill in that gap. As a leader, you don't have to do everything by yourself. You have to find the right person to do the right job.

Once you understand your professional strengths and weaknesses, the next step is to assess the opportunities and threats to your profession and career. Look for opportunities to lead, build teams, and expand your

TABLE 2.1

Emotional Intelligence (EQ) Components of Daniel Goleman's Model

EQ Component	Definition	Hallmarks	Example
Self-awareness	Knowing one's emotions, strengths, weaknesses, drives, values, and goals—and their impact on others	• Self-confidence • Realistic self-assessment • Self-deprecating sense of humor • Thirst for constructive criticism	A manager knows tight deadlines bring out the worst in him. So he plans his time to get work done well in advance.
Self-regulation	Controlling or redirecting disruptive emotions and impulses	• Trustworthiness • Integrity • Comfort with ambiguity and change	When a team botches a presentation, its leader resists the urge to scream. Instead, she considers possible reasons for the failure, explains the consequences to her team, and explores solutions with them.
Motivation	Being driven to achieve for the sake of achievement	• A passion for the work itself and for new challenges • Unflagging energy to improve • Optimism in the face of failure	A portfolio manager at an investment company sees his fund tumble for three consecutive quarters. Major clients defect. Instead of blaming external circumstances, she decides to learn from the experience—and engineers a turnaround.
Empathy	Considering others' feelings, especially when making decisions	• Expertise in attracting and retaining talent • Ability to develop others • Sensitivity to cross-cultural differences	An American consultant and her team pitch a project to a potential client in Japan. Her team interprets the client's silence as disapproval, and prepares to leave. The consultant reads the client's body language and senses interest. She continues the meeting, and her team gets the job.
Social Skill	Managing relationships to move people in desired directions	• Effectiveness in leading change • Persuasiveness • Extensive networking • Expertise in building and leading teams	A manager wants his company to adopt a better Internet strategy. He finds kindred spirits and assembles a de facto team to create a prototype Web site. He persuades allies in other divisions to fund the company's participation in a relevant convention. His company forms an Internet division—and puts him in charge of it.

Source: Adopted from Daniel Goleman.[1]

social network. Also, beware of the threats to your profession and career. You must be proactive in exploring the environment and figuring out the threats to your career. For example, if you are an IT professional, you must stay abreast of the latest tools, technologies, and platforms. Otherwise, your skills might get obsolete and that can become a threat to your career.

Self-Regulation

It is also called self-discipline. Controlling yourself is one of the crucial factors in leading and building high-performance teams. The real test of your leadership skills would come at a time of crisis. Most of us do fine during a normal situation, but when a crisis arises, that's when executives and leaders tend to falter.

I remembered a few years ago, one of my colleagues, Joe Espinosa, gave a presentation to the Board of Directors of a Fortune 500 company. Everything looked fine in the presentation, except he had accidentally put in the wrong dates for the key milestones; the month and year were off. It was such a turn-off during the meeting that the client almost canceled our contract. Of course, I was quite upset, but I also knew that I had to stay calm to rectify the situation. My instincts worked, and before too many noticed the wrong date in the boardroom, I asked Espinosa to fix the dates. One of the board members had caught the wrong dates, but the situation was kept under control as I had already requested Espinosa to fix them.

After the meeting, instead of yelling and screaming at Espinosa, I sat with him and tried to figure out how he got the wrong dates. It was a cut-and-paste from an older presentation, and he forgot to update them. The lesson learned was to double and triple-check every word, especially the dates, before the final presentation. Ever since that incident, every time I received the presentation from Espinosa, I joked with him and asked him in a lighter way to make sure that the dates were correct.

Motivation

As per Goleman, motivation is *being driven to achieve for the sake of achievement.* Motivation can be divided into two categories: intrinsic or extrinsic. Intrinsic motivation is defined as a desire and energy that emanates from within a person. For example, he/she is motivated for a cause such as "mothers against drunk driving." They do it for humanity and to save lives, and not for any monetary rewards. On the other hand, extrinsic motivation is related to external factors such a financial reward, promotion, recognition, and other factors.

While both forms are necessary to achieve excellence in organizations and teams, intrinsic motivation is crucial during a crisis. Based on our experience and research, high-performance teams are more intrinsically motivated than extrinsically. They fight for a cause and purpose. Once they are clear on the purpose or mission, they don't necessarily need any extrinsic rewards to achieve success. Therefore, whenever you are building a high-performance team, look for intrinsically motivated individuals.

Empathy

Empathy is defined as *considering others' feelings especially when making decisions.*[1]. As a leader, you must care for your employees and teammates. You must show respect and appreciation for the team members and solicit their input and feedback while making decisions. The hallmark of successful and transformational leaders is that they can attract talented team members and develop leaders for the next generation. They are sensitive to diversity and cross-cultural differences. These traits are highly desirable during a crisis, as evidenced by all of us during the COVID-19 pandemic.

Social Skills

Goleman has defined it as *managing relationships to move people in desired directions.*[1] One of the critical traits of a leader is to persuade and influence people to move in his direction. He/she sets the vision and direction for the organization and team. And then everybody follows the path. Having social skills is essential in creating and leading high-performance teams. It requires persuasion and extensive networking skills. The hallmark of leaders with extraordinary social skills is that the ability to build and lead high-performance teams.

HOW CAN YOU IMPROVE YOUR EQ?

I'm often asked this question by executives and leaders around the world: "how can I improve my EQ?" Daniel Goleman and Michele Nevarez, in their HBR article (2018) *Boost Your Emotional Intelligence with These 3 Questions*[25] provided the three questions. Answering these three questions can help you improve your EQ.

What Is the Difference between How You See Yourself and How Others See You?

Understanding the difference between how you see yourself and how others see you is the first step to improve your emotional intelligence. It's quite common to give yourself high marks on leadership characteristics. For example, you might think you are a great listener, but you might be surprised after seeking feedback from your colleagues, teammates, customers, and supervisor.

Also, EQ is not a binary, yes or no answer. It's not like either you have it or not. As Goleman and Nevarez have pointed out in the HBR article[25], there are four aspects that you need to consider while assessing and improving your EQ: self-awareness, self-management, social awareness, and relationship management. It would help if you ascertained external feedback or 360 degrees feedback on all these four aspects to assess and enhance your emotional intelligence.

You can also find a well-trained coach to help you assess and improve your emotional intelligence. It's crucial to know where you stand on the EQ, and your qualified coach can help you do that. Also, the coach can help you create a plan to improve your EQ.

What Matters to You?

When you work with a coach to enhance your EQ, you need to synchronize the external or 360-degree feedback with your long-term goals and objectives. Simply improving your EQ based on your customers, colleagues, or boss's feedback might not be helpful for your career. It would be best if you informed your coach about your vision, goals, and objectives so that he/she can customize the plan for you. There has to be an intrinsic motivation to achieve your objectives and enhance your EQ. Otherwise, this might be a mechanical exercise like learning how to use a project management tool like MS Projects.

There has to be an integration of what matters to you and what the external feedback says about you. All these aspects must meet an intersection to enhance your EQ and achieve your goals and objectives. As suggested by Goleman and Nevarez[25], you should ask yourself these types of questions: Do you want to improve your capacity as a leader so that you can take a leadership position? Do you want to enhance your team-building skills? Do you want to be a better professional? Answering these questions and devising an integrated plan will help you improve your EQ.

What Changes Will You Make to Achieve These Goals?

Once you understand the areas you focus on, you need to create an action plan and execute it. For example, if you have identified that you need to improve your listening skills, you should focus on that and look for opportunities to practice those skills. For example, I was coaching a newly appointed project manager (call him Mike) during my tenure at Deloitte Consulting. I noticed that Mike had an issue with listening to the customers. He was a young, bright, and highly energetic project manager. The problem that he had was that we would not let the customer finish his/her thought and would interrupt in the middle of the conversation.

One day, I took Mike out for a coffee and showed him how he interrupted the customer multiple times. He realized the challenges that he had, and we put together an action plan for him. In the next several weeks, Mike joined me in multiple meetings with the customers, watched how I listened to the customers, did not interrupt them, and took notes while the customers talked. He started to practice, seek my feedback after the meetings, and overcame his problem in about three-to-four months. As they say, the devil is in the details. In this case, the devil is in the execution of the action plan. You must practice and execute your action plan and continuously seek feedback from your coach, customers, and teammates.

You might struggle initially, but you will train your brain repeatedly to listen and not interrupt others during conversations or discussions. It's just like learning how to drive. When you first hold the steering wheel, you feel like you would never be able to steer it. Once you start practicing and get the feel of the steering wheel, brakes, and other instruments, you get comfortable with them. Improving your EQ skills can be similar to learning how to drive.

You can practice at home with your spouse, children, and others. And then you can apply these skills at work. When it comes to listening skills, there is no difference at home or work. You can use these skills in all settings. You must keep in mind that it's okay to struggle initially, but you must stay motivated and keep practicing until you feel comfortable listening to others. With practice and effort, it will come naturally to you. That time will come; you have to be patient and persistent. For some people, it might happen in two-to-three months, and for others, it might take several months. The key is to stay focused, keep practicing, and execute your action plan.

TUCKMAN'S TEAM-BUILDING

Bruce Tuckman, a psychological researcher conducted a research study on group dynamics and team-building in 1965[2]. He came up with a group development theory that described four stages of team-building or group development: forming, storming, norming, and performing (Tuckman, 1965)[2]. His team-building model is known as Tuckman's stages of group development. Later on, in 1977, he added the fifth stage to the model called "Adjourning" (Tuckman & Jensen, 1977)[3]. All five stages are shown in Figure 2.1 and explained in the following pages.

Forming

This is the initial stage where uncertainty is high as team members do not know each other. It is also known as the "orientation" stage. They go through an orientation and getting acquainted stage. The team members have lots of questions, and they look for a leader who can help, guide, and lead them. Team members ask questions like: What are the goals and objectives of the team? What are the expectations from me? Will I be a good fit for the team? At this stage, team members interact informally, and they are generally nice to each other.

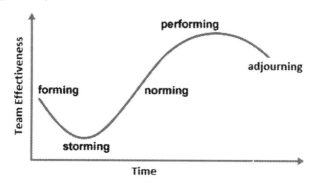

FIGURE 2.1
Tuckman's team-building model.

Source: Adopted from Tuckman Model[2,3] and Lumen Learning[26].

Team members try to avoid any conflict, misunderstanding, or controversy during the *forming* stage. Everybody desires to be accepted in the team, so the relationships are collegial. As a leader, you need to make sure that the team's charter, scope, mission, goals, objectives, and communication policies are clearly defined.

The outcome of this stage is that the team members will:

- Get to know each other's professional background, work habits, style, and other aspects.
- Understand team's purpose, goals, and objectives.
- Determine who will be responsible for what?
- Understand the tasks, deliverables, and milestones.
- Get to know the team norms and rules.

Storming

This is the most challenging and toughest stage of team-building. It is also known as the "power struggle" stage. Individual personalities of team members get exposed or highlighted during this stage. A power struggle erupts between team members with strong personalities. I consider this stage as a very "delicate" stage that requires the most attention. The team's morale and productivity are at the lowest levels during this stage due to conflicts, lack of trust, and power struggles.

A leader must pay a lot of attention to the details, and he/she must listen to all the members. Storming is the stage where people can develop conflicts that can last for a very long time or till the end of the project. Sometimes people would take things personally, which might cause irreparable damage to their relationship. That can be immensely detrimental not only for the team members involved in the conflict but also to the team's overall mission. Therefore, a leader must have a very high level of emotional intelligence to get through this team-building stage.

This stage requires structure, discipline, agility, and empathy because most of the conflicts will occur at this stage. The leader must step up and ensure that all team members' voices are heard, especially those with introverted personalities. The extroverts or people with dominating personalities will try to take over. Usually, a tug of war also erupts at this stage. Therefore, as a leader, you must step in and ensure that the team stays focused on its mission, goals, and objectives. This stage is also a real test for a leader's ability to resolve conflicts, negotiate, empathize, listen, and respond to the team's concerns and issues.

The team's productivity is lowest during this stage because personal and professional conflicts reach their peak at this stage. During my 30-year career, I have seen that most teams and projects fail during this stage. Projects or groups that can come out of this stage relatively unscathed have a very high chance of success. And leaders that can manage this stage adequately can be successful as well.

Norming

The norming stage is also called the cooperation and integration stage. This is the stage where harmony, happiness, and collegiality prevail. Team members understand each other's strengths and weaknesses. They leverage their strengths and downplay the weaknesses. As a leader, you need to guide the team and help them to resolve conflicts as they arise.

Here are the key characteristics of a team that goes through the norming stage.

- Team members respect each other.
- Communication amongst the team members is open and collegial.
- Bonding and cordial relationships develop amongst the team members.
- Conflicts are resolved in an amicable manner.

Performing

This stage is also called the "synergy" stage because team members have developed synergy amongst themselves, and they have started to work as a cohesive and collegial team. I'm sure you all have heard of the phrases like "the team is gelling together" or "the team has been running like a well-oiled machine." Phrases like these are applicable to the performing stage. As a leader, you need to empower the team members to make day-to-day decisions and perform their tasks.

Some of the key characteristics of a team that has reached the performing stage are as follows. Team members:

- Are united, cohesive, and collegial.
- Acknowledge skills, talents, and experience that each team member brings to the team.
- Focus on the mission, goals, and objectives of the team.

- Produce high-quality deliverables and achieve the milestones.
- Are flexible and trust each other.
- Have developed a synergy and perform like a "well-oiled machine".

Adjourning

This stage is also called the "closure." Meaning, the project has achieved its objectives and has reached the end. The team has achieved its mission, goals, and objectives. It is time to dismantle the team and move on to the next mission or project. As a leader, you must appreciate, acknowledge, and recognize team members' efforts, achievements, and contributions. And don't forget to celebrate as this is the most fun and essential part of adjourning. The team members will remember how they were treated when the team adjourned, so it's your responsibility, as a leader, to make their final moments as cheerful as possible.

LEADERSHIP THEORIES AND COMPETENCIES

The six schools of leadership theories, which have been around for the last 70 years, as summarized by Rodney Turner and Ralf Müller (2005)[27] are:

- Trait school
- Behavior school
- Contingency school
- Visionary school
- Charismatic school
- Emotional Intelligence school

Rizwan Sheikh and Ralf Müller summarized various leadership schools in their research study[18]: the trait school focuses on the leadership traits people are born with, such as their physical appearance, personalities, and capabilities. Behavior school focuses on leadership behavior and styles adopted by leaders while getting the tasks completed. Contingency school deals with the leadership styles that leaders adopt in different situations. Visionary and charismatic schools focus on organizational change. Emotional intelligence focuses on social management, interaction with people, and self-management.

According to the various schools of thought mentioned above, leadership is considered as a combination of competencies and personal traits. As mentioned by Linda Geoghegan and Victor Dulewicz[28], leadership is seen as a combination of knowledge and skills, such as achievement and empowerment, with personal traits, such as conscientiousness, which makes a leader[28].

As John Kotter[14] explained, we live in an immensely dynamic and volatile world and business environment. The world as a whole is going through an unprecedented change phenomenon. The coronavirus, commonly known as COVID-19, has changed the global landscape. Companies, governments, and individuals need to think of new and innovative ways to do business and cope with uncertainty. We need both leaders and managers to deal with various challenges and situations.

During a global crisis like COVID-19, organizations and businesses need more leaders and managers to overcome the new world order's challenges. Therefore, we need to create a leadership-centered culture to produce more leaders that can lead companies, teams, communities, and societies around the world[14]. The same is true for projects where we need project managers with leadership capabilities to deliver projects successfully[18].

As various definitions of leadership indicate, leaders and managers must have the ability to influence, motivate, guide, set the course and direction, cope with the change, and enable team members and followers to contribute to the team's successful organization. This implies that a leader or manager must establish a shared vision, goals, and objectives that team members can pursue and achieve together. What can a leader do to influence, guide, motivate, set the direction, and enable the team? This question is answered in the next few pages while we discuss transactional and transformational leadership and the emotional intelligence framework and model.

Transactional and Transformational Leadership

There are two broad categories within leadership: transactional and transformation leadership. An operational manager generally exercises transaction leadership during day-to-day operations, where they have to lead teams and get the tasks completed. Some operational projects can also fall into the transactional leadership category. That's why sometimes project managers also get an extra reward, compensation, or promotion to complete an operational project. Transactional leadership is practiced by middle management. The focus is on performance, supervision, and organization of the tasks. Day-to-day management and small-to-midsize projects require transactional leadership.

On the other hand, transformational leadership encompasses the vision for the next 10, 20, or 30 years. This leadership style is practiced by leaders that can influence, motivate, and strengthen organizations, communities, societies, and countries. They can build the foundation for the next generation. Some large-scale and mega projects also need project managers with transformational leadership traits because they can also significantly impact the community, society, or country. For example, Nelson Mandela was a transformational leader because he transformed South African society when he was released from jail after 27 years.

Victor Dulewicz and Malcolm Higgs[29], in their article "Leadership at the top: The need for emotional intelligence in organizations," identified 15 leadership competencies, which affect the performance of leaders. The competencies have been grouped into three types: intellectual (IQ), managerial (MQ), and emotional (EQ). The Fifteen Leadership Competencies of Dulewicz and Higgs are shown in Table 2.2[29].

The literature on leadership shows that leadership is an integral part of managing organizations and people[27]. Since a project is considered a

TABLE 2.2

Fifteen Leadership Competencies by Dulewicz and Higgs

Group	Competency
Managerial (MQ)	Managing Resource
	Engaging Communication
	Empowering
	Developing
	Achieving
Intellectual (IQ)	Critical Analysis and Judgement
	Vision and Imagination
	Strategic Perspective
Emotional (EQ)	Self-Awareness
	Emotional Resilience
	Intuitiveness
	Sensitivity
	Influence
	Motivation
	Conscientiousness

Source: Adopted from Dulewicz & Higgs.[29]

temporary organization and it entails managing tasks and people, it also requires leadership capabilities and skills[27].

DEVELOPING YOUR LEADERSHIP STYLE

We can continue to argue whether the leaders are born or made, but the latest research reveals that you can develop your leadership style[4]. Based on Peterson and her colleagues' research and engagement with over 12,000 leaders, they have created markers that can help you develop your leadership style. They have called it *A Guide to Leadership Markers*[4]. They have put these markers into three categories: status markers, nonverbal style, and verbal style. If you want to develop or enhance your leadership style, the guide can be a beneficial tool.

Whenever we interact with people at work, we send signals about our power and status. It is quite natural that leaders want and enjoy power and status. Therefore, when we interact with customers, colleagues, and others at work, we send signals related to our leadership style: verbal, nonverbal, or status markers[4]. Peterson and her colleagues have categorized these markers into two broad categories: power and attractiveness[4].

We cannot say those power markers are better than attractiveness markers or vice versa. Both can be good and needed depending on the situation. For example, powerful markers are related to competence, self-confidence, and influence. But, powerful markers are also associated with harshness, arrogance, and intimidation[4]. Examples of powerful markers include:

- Interrupting others during meetings.
- Cutting people off in conversations.
- Grabbing a notepad off someone's desk without permission.

On the other hand, attractiveness markers are associated with: amicability, cordiality, friendliness, lack of confidence, obedience, and compliance. For example, if you hold the door for somebody, it shows humbleness and kindness. Other examples include asking questions as opposed to making powerful statements. Leaders or project managers with powerful styles often view teammates or colleagues with attractive styles as weak. In contrast, leaders with an attractive style view their colleagues and teammates with powerful style as impolite and discourteous.

If you consistently use any of the markers outlined in Table 2.3, people will tend to associate you with either powerful or attractive leadership style[4]. For example, if you consistently talk over people or do not bother to take any notes during meetings, your colleagues will associate you with

TABLE 2.3

Leadership Styles Defined by Peterson

	Powerful	Attractive
Status Markers	More formal	More informal
	Nondeferential address	Deferential address
	Detached responses	Empathetic responses
	Expanded personal space	Respectful of others' personal space
	Interruptions and talk-overs	Respectful conversational turns
	Abrupt topic shifts	Gradual topic shifts
	Directive gestures (finger- pointing, head-shaking)	Acceptance gestures (head-nodding, shoulder-dropping)
	Less polite	More polite
	Little to no note-taking	Extensive note-taking
	Inattentiveness (ignoring others, wandering eyes)	Attentiveness (engaging with all senses, especially eyes)
Nonverbal Style	Backward leans	Forward leans
	Physical distance	Physical closeness
	Eye contact when speaking	Eye contact when listening
	Averted gaze when listening	Averted gaze when speaking
	Tendency to stare	Tendency to break eye contact
	Serious expressions	Happy expressions
	Controlled movements	Natural movements
	Talking while moving away	Body square while talking
Verbal Style	Longer speech duration	Shorter speech duration
	Faster speech rate	Slower speech rate
	Louder volume	Softer volume
	More direct	More indirect
	Declarative statements	Questions
	Fewer nonfluencies (um, well, you know)	More nonfluencies and pauses
	Intense words	Everyday words
	Technical Jargon	Personal idioms
	Careful pronunciation	Relaxed pronunciation
	Fewer hedges and qualifiers (I guess)	More hedges and qualifiers
	Exclusive language (I, me, my)	Inclusive language (we, ours)
	More humor/sarcasm	Less humor/sarcasm

Source: Adopted from Peterson et al.[4]

the powerful leadership style. On the other hand, if you are consistently polite, take extensive notes, or give empathetic responses during meetings, people will relate you to an attractive leadership style.

There are times when someone would adopt the powerful or attractive leadership style naturally. For example, highly educated people, more senior than others on the team, or experienced tend to adopt a powerful leadership style. On the other hand, teammates who are junior or less experienced would tend to adopt an attractive style.

As a leader, you might have to switch gears multiple times during the day, depending on the situation. You might have to lead a meeting where you have to exhibit your experience and technical expertise. Thus, you would have to adopt a more powerful leadership style because that's what people expect from a leader in that situation. In contrast, you might be called into a meeting where people expect you to be more collaborative and polite. Therefore, you would have to adopt an attractive leadership style.

STEPS TO ADOPT A BLENDED LEADERSHIP STYLE

Ideally, you would want to have a blended leadership style to switch back and forth between power and attractiveness based on the situation. It might take you a while to achieve the blended leadership style, but it is possible to get to that point with practice and experience. Below are the steps that Peterson and her colleagues have suggested[4]. Some advice and examples on how to adapt your leadership style are mentioned in Table 2.4.

TABLE 2.4

Sample Advice on Adapting Leadership Styles

Comment Given	Problem	Sample Advice
"You're not senior enough"	Too attractive	Use declarative statements
"You're intimidating"	Too powerful	Speak less, listen more
"You don't have enough gravitas"	Too attractive	Dress more formally for the context
"Your team is afraid of you"	Too powerful	Use more questions, fewer statements
"You're boring"	Too Attractive	Use more-intense words
"You're overbearing"	Too powerful	Shift topics more gradually
"You're too nice"	Too attractive	Minimize deferential address

Source: Adopted from Peterson et al.[4]

Know Yourself

The first thing is to understand where you stand on the leadership spectrum. As mentioned earlier, you must solicit feedback from your colleagues, customers, boss, and others. You might have heard of comments like "you are intimidating" or "your team is afraid of you" Comments like these suggest that you have a powerful leadership style and people are looking for an attractive leadership style in that situation. You can adopt the markers that are associated with an attractive leadership style. Similarly, you might receive feedback such as "you are too nice" or "you are too boring" These comments suggest that you have an attractive leadership style, but your teammates or the situation requires a powerful leadership style.

Test Various Markers

Once you figure out where you stand on the leadership spectrum and know the areas you want to improve, you should experiment and test various markers. It would be best if you tried to move towards a blended style of leadership. You should pick one verbal and one non-verbal marker and try to utilize them in a meeting or situation. You should assess the results after you have used those markers. If need be, you can tweak them in the next interaction until you feel comfortable and satisfied.

Initially, you might feel challenged or overwhelmed when mixing and adopting various markers, but you will get comfortable with them after a while. You can continue to experiment and add the markers to your repertoire as you progress in your career. Eventually, you will achieve a blended leadership style that you can adopt comfortably depending on the situation.

Read the Situation

As suggested by Peterson and her fellow researcher[4], you should assess the room or situation when leading a team. When it comes to adopting a leadership style, there are no such things as "one-size fits all." Figure out whether you should lean toward a powerful or attractive leadership style depending on the situation.

Once you enter a situation or start a new project, you should try to figure out other people's leadership styles. Do they lean toward powerful or attractive markers? Before adapting your leadership style, you should first assess the situation and then adopt an appropriate leadership style. For example, when you join a company or project and see people being very polite, cordial, and friendly to each other, it should tell you that people lean towards attractiveness. Therefore, you should adopt an attractive leadership style.

Leaders often mistake using a powerful leadership style with the subordinates and an attractive style with their bosses. It should be the other way around. It would help if you used a powerful style with your boss and executives in your company. And it would be better if you used the attractive leadership style when interacting with junior staff and subordinates because this approach is more effective, according to the research conducted by Peterson[4].

3

Ten Strategies of Leading High-Performance Teams during a Crisis

Companies, organizations, employees, communities, and societies around the globe were affected by COVID-19. No country in the world escaped from it. Employees and team members were separated from their workplaces, office space, coworkers, friends, morning rituals, and daily routines. It created havoc on peoples' lives around the world. All of this led to stress, anxiety, uncertainty, a drop in morale, and fragmentation of teams, which caused suboptimum performance and productivity across the private and public sector organizations. Layoffs, furloughs, and salary reductions exacerbated the situation. That's why creating and leading high-performance teams was critical for everybody's survival, including small businesses, big corporations, employees, teams, projects, and public sector organizations. Companies must figure out a better way to create high-performance teams to overcome the challenges posed by a global crisis such as COVID-19. And that's what we explore in the next few pages. We are going to answer the following two questions:

1. What are the challenges and strategies of creating and leading high-performance teams during a pandemic or global crisis such as COVID-19?
2. What strategies, tools, and techniques can be used to overcome those challenges and create high-performance teams?

DOI: 10.1201/9781003216711-4

STRATEGY 1: APPRECIATION AND RECOGNITION OF TEAM MEMBERS

Most of us want to be valued and appreciated. In his article, Mike Robins said, appreciation was one of the things that Oprah Winfrey mentioned in one of her commencement speeches[31].

She said that she had interviewed hundreds of leaders and celebrities in the last 30 years and they all had one thing in common: they all wanted to be appreciated[31].

The desire to be appreciated and valued is human nature. All of us don't crave financial or other rewards. Still, as human beings, we all have the longing to feel valued and appreciated by our families, siblings, loved ones, employers, teammates, communities, and the society that we live in.

As mentioned above, people's lives went upside down during COVID-19. Research studies have shown that employees and teams need appreciation and recognition more than financial rewards, especially during a pandemic or global crisis like COVID-19. Wei Zheng, an Associate Professor at Stevens Institute of Technology, surveyed in April 2020 after COVID-19 had entered the initial months of the devastation[30]. Zheng surveyed 187 people in New York and New Jersey across various industries. New York and New Jersey were hit the hardest in Phase 1 of COVID-19 from March to April 2020[30].

Zheng and other researchers found out that employee recognition and appreciation were the critical success factors in motivating them and making them feel good. And that's one of the crucial things that are needed in a time of crisis. In Zheng's survey, 44% of the respondents stated that they felt good and relieved when their boss or senior management appreciated them[30]. It motivated them and helped them focus on their tasks. They were elated when their efforts and work were appreciated in team meetings or when the senior management recognized them at group meetings or in front of other colleagues.

A global crisis or pandemic is a time of healing and helping each other. It's the time where we put our differences aside and start appreciating and recognizing people. Leaders and managers must find an opportunity to appreciate and recognize employees and team members to motivate them, alleviate their stress and anxiety, and make them happy. This would lead to higher performance, enhanced team cohesion, a collegial work environment, and an increase in productivity.

Case Study: Appreciation and Recognition on the GMS Project

As mentioned in Part II of this book, Max Dillion (the Business Sponsor of the Grants Management System (GMS) project) used to appreciate and recognize each team member's efforts twice a week during the project status meetings. This practice enhanced the motivation levels, instilled positivity into the team, boosted the team's morale, reduced anxiety and stress of the team members, and made everybody feel good during COVID-19. In addition, Dillon would hold weekly 10-minute one-on-one meetings with the team members to understand and address their concerns.

Tools and Techniques of Appreciation and Recognition

 a. Recognition of team members during weekly staff meetings.
 b. Conducting one-on-one daily or weekly check-ins and trying to understand team members' concern.
 c. Thanking them during one-on-ones and weekly meetings.
 d. Sending them a thank you email.
 e. Video calls using MS Teams, Skype, Zoom, or other software tools.

STRATEGY 2: PROVIDE SUPPORT TO TEAM MEMBERS

This is one of the critical success factors to create a high-performance team, especially during a national or global crisis. As a leader, you must provide individual care to every team member. Every employee and team member is different. Their needs, personalities, and circumstances are different. In some parts of the world, employees and team members expect the leader to resolve their issues or listen to them. You need to conduct weekly or daily (if need be) one-on-ones with each team member until the issues are resolved, or they feel stable. Research studies have shown that employees and team members appreciate the leader who takes the time to listen to them, understand their concerns, and resolve the issues[30].

Based on my research and experience, I have seen that if an employee's issue is not resolved, but you, as a leader, try to help him/her, he/she will be satisfied. Of course, we all want our issues to be resolved, but there would be times when you, as a leader or manager, might not be able to solve them. But, if an employee saw that you at least tried to help him/her, he/she would understand and be satisfied. For example, I remember when one of my employees (call her Lisa) asked me for a salary increase mid-year. After consulting with the HR Department, I found out that I could not give Lisa a mid-year salary increase, but I was authorized to provide an annual bonus at the end of the year. Thus, I explained the HR policy to Lisa and promised her that I would give her the maximum allowable bonus. We agreed, and I did give her the maximum bonus based on her performance. As a Manager and her immediate Supervisor, I approved 50% more than what she was expecting. She was surprised and delighted to receive such a big bonus. Lisa appreciated it very much and became a very loyal employee of the company.

Case Study: Supporting the Team Members

I remember when I worked for Progressive Insurance Company in Cleveland (Ohio) in the late 90s. A dynamic and kind-hearted woman, Janice Clark (a pseudo name), led a team in the IT department. She was one of the most emotionally intelligent women that I have seen in my career. One of the members (Joe Stewart) of her team used to come to work late almost once a week. Stewart was a young and intelligent college graduate. He was a top-performer and had been with the company for a little over a year. Stewart received outstanding evaluations from his peers, customers, supervisor, and senior management. He just had one problem that he would come one-to-two hours late at least once a week in the morning, and sometimes he missed the morning meetings. Janice was extremely happy with Stewart's work, but his late-coming every week was bothering her.

She decided to have a one-on-one meeting with Stewart. Janice explained to him how great of a worker he was, and she really appreciated his hard work, diligence, and quality of his deliverables. Janice also asked him why he was getting late. Stewart was a fresh graduate, and he used to provide financial support to his parents and younger siblings. His Dad had health issues and did not have health insurance, so Stewart used to pay for all the doctors' visits and medication. Thus, Stewart could not afford to buy a new car and his 20-year old car used to break down almost every week. And that's why he was late to work. He was saving money for the down payment, but it would take him another year to save up enough money for a new or used car that was reliable.

Janice asked him how much he needed for the down payment. He said, "$5,000." Janice listened to his entire story and thanked him for his time and for sharing his challenges.

The next morning Janice called Stewart into her office. She asked him if someone would lend her the down payment, would he be able to buy and afford the car payments. He said "yes." Then she asked, how long would it take him to pay back the $7,000? Stewart said, "about two years." Janice took out the checkbook from her purse and wrote him a check for $7,000 as a loan along with a promissory note that he would pay her back in two years. And she did not charge any interest on the loan. Stewart was shocked and had tears in his eyes with joy and happiness. He could not find the words to thank Janice. A couple of days later, Stewart drove into the parking lot with a white Toyota Corolla and showed it to Janice. Stewart was never late to work after he bought the car. Stewart switched departments within the company but kept paying back Janice's loan. The stories about his performance were heard by the CIO as well as the CEO. Stewart was put on the fast-track to the promotion and quickly rose up the ranks. He remained loyal and grateful to Janice.

Janice showed the highest level of emotional intelligence (EQ), Decency quotient (DQ), empathy, and vision by lending Stewart $7,000. All she had to do was "listen" to Stewart and show some courage to help him with his challenges. Janice created a rock star with her empathy, care, generosity, and emotional intelligence. If most of the leaders and managers start to behave and act like Janice, companies worldwide would excel and make their employees happy.

I ran into Stewart about 12 years after this event. He stayed in touch with Janice but moved onto bigger and better places. Stewart was very successful and became the CEO of two companies. He was also appointed on the Board of Directors of some of the US and Middle East companies. His career skyrocketed from the $7,000 loan that Janice gave him when he was a fresh graduate out of college.

Tools and Techniques of Supporting the Team Members

   a. Emotional intelligence, empathy, sensitivity to human beings, and caring for others.
   b. Listening to employees and trying to understand their professional as well as personal challenges and concerns.

c. Helping employees with their emotional issues through empathy and care.

d. Empathetic communication and listening, which is discussed in Chapter 6 of this book.

STRATEGY 3: INVOLVE TEAM MEMBERS IN THE DECISION-MAKING PROCESS

My experience and various research studies show that employees and team members feel happy and delighted when asked for their opinion by their bosses, managers, or colleagues. Employees feel quite thrilled, valued, and appreciated when asked this question, especially during the decision-making process: what is your opinion or your thoughts and insights? When decision-makers ask this question, team members get a sense of belonging in the team, group, and company. They get motivated, thrilled, and enthusiastic because they feel like they add value to the team and the organization, which becomes a source of motivation, inspiration, and high-performance. Appreciation, being valued, and a sense of belonging to the team organization are even more critical during a global crisis like COVID-19 because team members go through exponential stress, anxiety, and uncertainty about the future.

Furthermore, team members appreciate leaders and managers that ask them to discuss issues openly, transparently, and promptly or as soon as they come up. Leaders who involve the employees in the decision-making process are adored more than the leaders who make decisions in isolation or without consulting the team.

You don't have to agree with your employees and team members on every issue and decision. Your job as a leader is to listen to them, seek their input and feedback, and then make a decision in the team and organization's best interest.

As I often state in my lectures and executive training sessions, after listening to all the key team members and stakeholders and seeking their input, it's absolutely fine to decide that is the opposite of the team members' recommendations and feedback. It would be good if your decision is in sync with the team's recommendations, but it does not have to be. Most of the participants of my lectures and courses get surprised when I make this statement. They wonder why it is okay to make a decision that is contrary to the team members' recommendations and feedback. Isn't this conflicting with what we all know about team-building and collective decision-making? The rationale and logic is that most of your team members or employees might not have seen the data, the bigger picture, and the larger context of the issues and challenges that you, as a leader or manager, have seen or experienced. Thus, your decision might be seen as contradictory to the team's recommendations, but you know that it would be good for the team and the organization. You should explain your decision to the team members, and most (if not all) of them would understand and appreciate your candidness. I hope most of your decisions would be in line with the team recommendations, but there might be a situation where you have to go against the team's advice. As long as you have the data, concrete evidence, and the facts to support your decision, it's okay to stick with it. Chances are, when the team members see the data and understand your logic and rationale, they would also agree with your decision.

Case Study: Team Involvement in the Decision-Making Process

I would again use Max Dillon's example from the case study in Part II of this book. Max was very good at engaging the relevant team members in issues' discussions, resolutions, and decision-making processes. He led two weekly project status meetings, generally on Mondays and Wednesdays. Max openly and candidly went around the room (virtual meeting room during COVID-19) and asked each Work Stream Lead to share their issues and concerns along with their inputs on how to resolve them. Then he would open the floor to the rest of the team members and ask the same question.

If a team member raised an issue, it would be discussed along with the possible solutions and logged in the RAID (Risks, Actions, Issues, and Decisions) log immediately after the meeting. The RAID log has been defined in the Project Management Methodology and Tools section of the case study. If follow-up meetings were required, either Max or John would lead those discussions and seek team members' input and suggestions on the resolution. The issue would remain on the RAID log and discussed twice a week until it was resolved and closed.

The transparent and candid approach adopted by Max worked well for the project team. In addition, his approach to involve all the key team members in the decision-making process became one of the critical success factors for the project. Anyone and everybody could voice their opinions, concerns, input, and feedback without the fear of any repercussions.

Tools and Techniques of Team Involvement in the Decision-Making Process

a. Involve all employees and team members in the decision-making process, especially during a crisis or pandemic like COVID-19.
b. Ask all employees and team members this question: what is your opinion and recommendations?
c. Discuss all professional issues openly and urgently or as soon as they come up. Don't delay.
d. Listen to everybody but make your own decisions.

STRATEGY 4: ASSIGN NEW RESPONSIBILITIES TO TEAM MEMBERS DURING A CRISIS

Sometimes we assume that the team members might not want to take additional responsibility, especially during a crisis, because everybody might be overwhelmed with stress and the fear of the unknown. As a leader, you should not make this assumption. Instead, it would help if you looked for team members that might be willing and happy to accept new responsibilities. Some people thrive under pressure because it's part of their personality. On the other hand, some people might not be able to cope with additional stress and responsibilities. But, you can find some team members who are willing to accept the challenge and new responsibilities. They would see it as an opportunity to prove their skills to their boss and senior management.

Some team members would feel empowered and excited about the new responsibilities. They would be eager to take the challenge and be ready to go the extra mile to show their competence and capabilities.

Case Study: Assigning New Responsibilities to Team Members During a Crisis

I used to work for Deloitte, one of the Big four consulting firms, in early 2001 and was leading a project in New York City. Unfortunately, we lost one of our teammates in one of the towers during the 9/11 attack. We immediately found his replacement because the client was nervous and came under a lot of stress due to the 9/11 incident. It was almost impossible to recruit somebody new or pull someone from any other projects due to the ensuing chaos.

We started reviewing my teammates' profiles, especially the ones who were aspiring to be project managers, but they had a year or so to prove themselves. I also asked all the team leaders if they would be interested in taking additional project manager responsibilities. One of them caught my attention, and she (call her Kelly) showed interest as well. Based on her profile, past performance, and client-relationship skills, I trusted her and figured she could successfully deliver the project.

Within 48 hours of the 9/11 incident, I approached Kelly. She was a daring, high-performer, and qualified team leader. Kelly agreed to take on the additional responsibilities of an Acting Project Manager. The client also felt quite comfortable with Kelly, so we gave her the responsibility. I promised her that if she did a good job and successfully delivered the project, I would write a very strong recommendation letter to the senior management to support her case for promotion. Not only that, but I would also ask the client to write a letter to support her promotion as well. Kelly agreed, and she took over the project within 24 hours.

As I expected, Kelly hit the ground running, and she could literally walk on water. She revamped the project schedule, re-assigned some of the team members, and worked very closely with the client and the entire project team. She had a great IQ and emotional intelligence (EQ) skills. Both the client and the project team loved her. Schumer delivered the project one month ahead of schedule, and the client wrote an excellent recommendation letter for her promotion. I also wrote a powerful recommendation letter in support of her promotion. And Schumer got promoted ahead of all of her peers.

The moral of the story is that when you trust and empower employees and give them additional responsibilities, they can excel and deliver amazing and remarkable results.

Tools and Techniques of Assigning New Responsibilities to Team Members during a Crisis

a. Empower and trust your employees and team members.
b. As a leader, look for the hidden talent within your teams and organization.

    c. Reach out to employees and team members and look for ways to provide them career opportunities that can be a win-win for you, them, the project, and the organization.

    d. Ask employees and team members this question: Are they willing to take additional responsibilities?

STRATEGY 5: TEAM-BUILDING SESSIONS AND EXERCISES

I'm sure we have all attended team-building sessions and exercises during the pre-COVID-19 days. Some companies used to organize offsite team-building sessions and retreats for managers, senior managers, and executives. Most of those sessions were enlightening, creative, and thought-provoking in developing effective, efficient, and productive teams.

Executives often ask me: are those team-building sessions, especially offsite retreats, effective? My answer is absolute "yes" as long as they achieve the desired objectives. I have heard some executives complaining about the cost of such events before COVID-19. Some companies spent millions of dollars on these activities. Is it worth spending millions of dollars on your employees? Again, my answer is absolutely "yes."

The most precious asset that a company can own is happy and competent employees. Research has shown that the best competitive advantage for a successful company or business is its employees. And the hardest or almost impossible thing to do is to imitate your competitors' employees' competency and brains. You can pretty much copy everything from your competitors, such as technology, software, infrastructure, strategy, tactics, and others. But, you cannot copy the brains and motivation of your competitors' employees. At least, I have not come across a way to copy or transfer a human brain from one person to another.

This leads to the questions: How do we hold team-building sessions virtually during COVID-19? Can we still keep the same spirit as in-person sessions and make them effective and achieve our objectives? The answers to these questions are provided below.

Having a highly cohesive, intrinsically motivated, and the high-performance team is a competitive advantage that is sustainable and hard to copy. Thus, investing every dollar that a company can afford to spend on its employees and team-building programs is worth it. We say this based on our recently conducted survey of 181 individuals, several research studies, and my personal experience working with Fortune 500 companies across the globe.

Research Study and Survey: Virtual Team-Building Sessions and Effectiveness

Fortunately, technology has improved by leaps and bounds in the last five years. Collaboration and virtual meeting software such as Skype, Zoom, Bluejeans, and MS Teams allow relatively high-quality video and audio calls over the internet. To make it more fun, team members can create their own virtual backgrounds as well. They take you as close to reality as possible. Weekly or monthly team-building sessions using any of the above software can be effective. Some teams have started to have virtual coffee and lunch sessions. Some play video games during lunch hours.

We conducted a survey of 181 employees across various industries in the US from May to October 2020 and asked them the question: Are virtual team-building sessions effective and productive? The results of the survey indicated that 12% of the respondents said they were "very effective"; 42% of the respondents said they were "effective"; 26% said they were "somewhat effective," 11% were "neutral," and 9% said that they were "not effective." A summary of the survey results is shown in Figure 3.1.

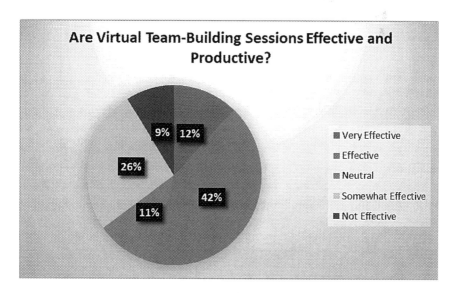

FIGURE 3.1
Survey results of virtual team-building sessions effectiveness.

Tools and Techniques of Virtual Team-Building Sessions

  a. Virtual team-building and collaboration sessions.
  b. Use of software such as Zoom, MS Teams, Skype, Bluejeans, and others.
  c. Weekly or monthly team-building sessions.

STRATEGY 6: INSTILL JOY AND HAPPINESS

Due to COVID-19, the doom and gloom scenarios are everywhere these days, so you must instill joy and happiness into the team as a leader. As the Kearney consulting team said: "In these times especially, joy can be the ultimate driver of team and organizational performance[32]." I agree with them that this is the time to instill joy, hope, and happiness into the team to make them a high-performance team and organization.

The difference between a suboptimum team and a high-performance team can be joy, happiness, hope, and motivation, especially during a global crisis like COVID-19. And that's why leaders, managers, and project managers must find ways to bring joy and happiness to the team. Team members and employees look up to their leaders for inspiration, fun, and happiness.

As Kearney consulting (Nov 2020) said, we are shifting to digital ways of working (DWOW). DWOW is great, but we have to be careful. It's just like technology; it is great when it works. We must adapt to DWOW in a way that facilitates people and makes their lives easier and better.

Most of us have been feeling claustrophobic with lockdowns and other restrictions during COVID-19. Thus, digital ways are great as long as they are used properly, effectively, and efficiently. There has to be a clear distinction between work hours and family time. Whatever schedule we pick, 8:00 a.m. to 5:00 p.m. or whatever arrangements we make with our employer is fine but should not slide into family time.

Case Study: Instilling Joy and Happiness

As mentioned in the GMS case study, Max used to have a monthly team-building session with his staff. Even though they discussed business, Max also tried to make it fun. He went around the virtual table and asked everyone to share at least one fun activity they did outside of work with their family and friends. This changed the mood of the meeting in a very positive way. Once everybody would be in a good mood, they would talk about the challenges and issues they were facing during COVID-19. Max also shared team members' accomplishments during the month, and he acknowledged and appreciated their efforts, which again brought positivity and joy to the team.

Tools and Techniques of Instilling Joy and Happiness

a. Share fun stories about family and friends.
b. Recognize and appreciate team members in staff meetings.
c. Monthly team-building sessions.

STRATEGY 7: ADAPT WITH TENACITY AND CONSISTENCY

One of the critical aspects of building high-performance teams during a crisis or national emergency is that we have to be consistent and tenacious when adapting to new ways of doing things or what we call "the new normal." You and the team must establish the norms and rules of the "virtual game." For example, how will we communicate? What tools will we use? How will all the team members be trained on the tools, i.e., MS Teams, Zoom, and others? What will be the working hours? How often will we meet virtually? Answers to all these questions will establish team norms and help everybody focus consistently, effectively, and creatively.

While we have to be careful with change and adaptation, in general, we don't have much choice during a crisis or national emergency. We have to adapt and change how we do things, no matter how difficult or unpleasant it might be. As the phrase "New Normal" was coined during COVID-19, we all had to learn and adapt according to the "new normal." For example, we all had to wear face masks when going to the shopping malls, offices, grocery stores, or any public place where there was human interaction. We were not allowed to shake hands anymore due to the fear of spreading the virus. Avoid unnecessary road and air travel. This was all part of the new normal during COVID-19, and we all had to adapt to it.

Case Study: Adapting with Tenacity and Consistency

Everyone was in a Halloween costume during the November monthly meeting at our consulting firm. Josh Green, the founder and partner in the firm greeted everybody and went around the virtual room to talk about their Halloween costumes. Some team members had their children in the room for a few minutes before the formal discussion started. This was an excellent way of breaking the ice and making everyone in the room comfortable.

The team discussed the monthly team meetings' charter, norms, and rules. The essential items included the following:

1. The meetings had to start on-time and end on-time. All one-hour meetings would end five minutes before the hour so that people would have time to prepare for the next meeting or take a bio break.
2. All issues would be discussed and recorded. Also, action items would be created.
3. Project managers shared the issues and challenges they faced during COVID-19. Team members shared lessons learned from other projects to help overcome the challenges.
4. Everyone shared their success stories. Celebrations were held to acknowledge, appreciate, and recognize the team members of various projects.
5. It was decided that Zoom would be the standard tool for meetings, and Slack would be used for informal and quick chats. Slack would also be used as a social networking platform amongst the team members.
6. If anybody needed any training on Zoom or Slack, they could contact the HR Department.
7. Consultants were encouraged to work during office hours, and no over-time was allowed unless approved by the client and the firm. Weekends were strictly for the family unless there was an emergency at the client site and the work was approved by one of the firm partners.
8. Quality assurance procedures would be followed on all client engagements. Bi-weekly virtual meetings would be held with the firm's relevant partner to ensure the deliverables' quality and overall project performance.

The rules and guidelines mentioned above helped set the tone for everybody. All consultants adhered to the norms and regulations. It allowed everyone to focus on the clients and set aside time for their families. It also clarified that the firm leadership was serious about the work-life balance. They also respected consultants' family time. Everyone was encouraged to take time off, especially during COVID-19, and spend time with their families.

Tools and Techniques of Adapting with Tenacity and Consistency

- Conduct monthly meetings with some fun activities.
- Create formal rules, norms, and guidelines for meetings and the work-life balance.
- Develop communication protocols.
- Create a team charter, norms, and rules.
- Establish working hours and ensure not to creep into family time.
- Proper training for staff on collaboration tools and software.

STRATEGY 8: EMPLOYEE POTENTIAL, EMPOWERMENT, AND HAPPINESS

Research studies have shown that employee empowerment, happiness, and potential can lead to creativity, motivation, and innovation, which in turn leads to high-performance teams and organizations. They also boost the growth of employees, organizations, and revenues. Accenture recently conducted a detailed and expansive study of 3,200 senior executives and 15,600+ workers across 15 industries and ten countries[33].

Six Dimensions of the Net Better Off Model

As a result of the study, Accenture came up with a "Net Better Off" model for employee and organizational growth that can lead to sustainability, growth, and innovation, especially during a crisis like COVID-19[33]. The Net Better Off model indicates that an employee's potential to deliver at work can be explained through the six dimensions: Emotional and

FIGURE 3.2
Six dimensions of accenture's net better off model.

Source: Adopted from Accenture.

Mental, Relational, Physical, Purposeful, Financial, and Employable. The Accenture research also showed that 64% of an employee's potential was influenced by six dimensions, as shown in Figure 3.2. Employee potential is defined as a person's ability to utilize his/her strengths and skills at work.

Emotional and Mental

Employees' emotional and mental wellbeing is crucial, especially during a crisis like COVID-19. As a leader, you must ensure that your team members and employees stay emotionally and mentally resilient. You should ask questions like: What can the organization and I do for our employees' wellbeing? How can I support all the team members during the crisis and beyond?

Relational

As discussed in various places throughout this book, ensuring that team members stay engaged socially, especially in a virtual team environment, is one of the critical success factors for the team, project, and organization. As a leader, you need to provide an environment so that team members can stay involved in social networking and their voice is heard across the team and the organization. As discussed in this book, you must try to create a culture of inclusivity. All ideas should be entertained and heard before making any key decisions.

Physical

During a crisis, your team might have to work virtually for the foreseeable future. It would be best if you looked into employees' apprehensions about going back to work physically. You need to understand their concerns about physically working in the office post-COVID-19. And, as a leader, you need to address these concerns and apprehensions.

Purposeful

Having a clear purpose for the team and organization can enhance productivity, performance, and efficiency. Leaders must instill a sense of purpose into the team to stay focused on the end goal. Team members must understand the positive impact that their work, task, or project will create for the team, organization, and community. Having a strong sense of purpose among the team members can lead to intrinsic motivation, satisfaction, and high-performance.

Employable

One of the major concerns that employees have is their employability after the crisis is over. Thus, companies must try to alleviate the fear of being unemployed during or after the crisis by retooling and training them on employable skills. Some companies and leaders argue that training is expensive, and they fear that employees might leave the organization soon after they are trained. I have two quotes for these companies and leaders. There is a saying in Nigeria: "If you think education is expensive, try illiteracy." Secondly, I quote the example of a conversation between a

CEO and CFO where the CFO said that he/she did not want to send the employees for training because they might leave after the training. The CEO said, "What if they stay?" Meaning, if they stay and are not trained to do the job, then the organization would have untrained, unproductive, and low-performers, which can lead to loss of revenue, customer service, performance, and efficiency.

Financial

As General Electric's legendry Chairman and CEO Jack Welch said: "Don't reward your employees with just trophies; reward them on the wallet as well." I agree with Welch one hundred percent. It's good to give out certificates and trophies, but the fact is that we all have financial needs. Therefore, you must understand and address employees' financial needs during a crisis and prosperous times. Equitable, fair, and transparent financial rewards are crucial to motivate the workforce and enhance productivity.

Case Study: Employee Potential, Empowerment, and Happiness

I quote a real-life story here, which is related to Progressive Insurance, the company I worked for seven years (1991–1998). As mentioned earlier, it was also on Forbes 2020 list of *The 100 best companies to work for* in the US Progressive had a wonderful, diverse, and inclusive culture. It provided opportunities to everyone based on merit and performance regardless of employees' color, race, gender, religion, and faith.

Progressive Insurance was founded in 1937 (83 years ago) in Mayfield, Ohio. As of 2018, it had annual revenues of $30 billion and 35,000+ employees. It was ranked No. 99 on the Fortune 500 List of Companies in 2019. Initially, Progressive only focused on auto insurance for high-risk drivers as most of the standard insurance companies like State Farm, Allstate, and others stayed out of that market.

I recall the employee and team culture that Peter Lewis (Chairman, President, and CEO of Progressive from 1965–2000) developed over three decades was phenomenal. I had the opportunity to meet and work with Lewis on many occasions during my days at Progressive. I was part of the team that developed the prototype of software to support the 1-800-AutoPro initiative. Whenever a prospective customer called, the system would generate a quote for Progressive's auto insurance policy and showed three quotes from competitors such as State Farm, Allstate, and GEICO. And the interesting thing was that most of the time, Progressive's price came out to be the highest, and the sales team was very transparent and shared all four quotes with the customers. Even the customers were surprised that the sales team was so honest and transparent with them. The concept of 1-800-AutoPro was the brainchild of Lewis. It was a marketing-genius idea. I could not resist the urge to ask Lewis, in 1996, why we disclosed our competitors' prices, especially when Progressive's price was the highest. Lewis smiled and said: "Rizwan, people will always buy from you when they know that you are honest and transparent with them." He was correct. Most of the customers bought Progressive insurance even when its price was slightly higher than the competitors. We conducted a survey and found out why customers still bought the insurance despite the fact it was the most expensive. The No. 1 reason quoted by customers was: "honesty and transparency in sharing all four quotes."

Lewis was right in 1996, and his philosophy was right 24 years later when Progressive became a $30 billion company in 2020. He was right then, and his philosophy still holds: "be honest and transparent with the customers, and they will buy your product or service." Lewis was also a big believer in the power of employees. He believed that happy employees could do wonders for the organization. Progressive invested heavily in employees and sent all the executives, managers, and staff to the team-building sessions. Employees could attend all types of training and education programs during the year. For example, Progressive also reimbursed the tuition fee for evening MBA programs as long as they benefited both the employee and company.

Lewis understood the importance of high-performance teams, diversity, inclusion, and happy employees. He knew that happy employees would lead to happy customers, which would enhance growth and profitability.

According to Aric Jenkins' Fortune article "Meet the CEO of the Insurance Company Growing Faster than Apple," Progressive has become one of the fastest-growing companies in the US, even faster than Apple[34]. Not only that, it has become a role model for other Fortune 500 companies to appoint a female CEO, Tricia Griffith. Griffith was also one of the 24 CEOs on the list of Fortune 500 companies. She started working as an entry-level employee at Progressive over 30 years ago and became the CEO in July 2016. Prior to becoming the CEO, Griffith was also the Chief Human Resources Officer (CHRO), Division President, and Chief Operating Officer at Progressive[34]. She established the first diversity and inclusion program, which has become the backbone of the company.

Progressive also had an annual bonus structure based on individual and team performance. Since it placed immense importance on teamwork, overall team or group's objectives were set, and then the team's performance was evaluated at the end of the year. A weighted formula was devised where most of the weight was given to the team or group's performance, and a smaller weight was assigned to individual performance. The bonus was decided based on a combination of the team's and individual performance. Progressive employees' total compensation, including the base salary, benefits, and annual bonus, were at the top 10% of the market.

If I look back 30 years, under the leadership of Lewis and now under Griffith, Progressive has been following all six dimensions of Accenture's "Net Better Off" model. It cares about the emotional and mental wellbeing of its employees. Progressive has a daycare center and clinic on-site for its employees. Senior executives and managers encourage team members to socialize and arrange team-building sessions, creating a relationship with the company and coworkers. Progressive also ensures employees' physical office space requirements are taken care of in terms of ergonomic chairs, desks, and equipment. It provides a safe, healthy, and secure work environment. Lewis and all other leaders instilled a culture of *Delighting the Customer* at Progressive, and that's why every employee has had a sense of purpose not only to serve but "delight" the customers. As mentioned above, Progressive encourages and pays for employee training and education. Finally, it provides financial security to its employees through a highly competitive salary and bonus structure.

Tools and Techniques of Employee Empowerment and Happiness

- Accenture's "Net Better Off" model.
- Fair, equitable, and transparent financial rewards for employees.
- Inculcate a sense of purpose in the team and organization.
- Safety and security of employees, including emotional and mental health.
- Physical work environment must be safe and according to the needs of the employees.
- Train and retool your employees so that they are employable within and outside the organization.

STRATEGY 9: INCLUSION AND DIVERSITY

One of the critical success factors for leaders worldwide is to ensure inclusion and diversity on the teams. The concept of having inclusion and diversity becomes more pronounced and essential during a crisis like COVID-19. However, some companies, perhaps unintentionally, might recede from the diversity and inclusion practices. They might have more urgent issues to take care of, such as customer support, adoption of new ways of working, consolidation of employee capacity, and the employees' safety and health. As McKinsey said in the article "Diversity Still Matters[35]:"

> "Yet we would argue that companies pulling back on inclusion and diversity now may be placing themselves at a disadvantage: they could not only face a backlash from customers and talent now but also, down the line, fail to better position themselves for growth and renewal[35]."

As human beings, we are all different. We all have different personalities, come from different ethnic backgrounds, and hold different faiths and beliefs. Thus, as a leader, you must reach out and understand the issues and challenges that each member of your team faces. One of the best ways to address this issue is to inculcate a culture of inclusivity and diversity. Reach out to all of your employees, listen to them, and have diversity in your organization. If we review and analyze Fortune Magazine's *100 Best Companies to Work For*, one of the common success factors is the high importance that they all place on diversity and inclusion. They have a highly diversified workforce, and they inculcate a culture of inclusion. Employees have a very strong sense of belonging. Promotions are granted based upon merit and performance and not based on race, color, or religion. And that's what makes these companies the best places to work for. I worked for two of them (Deloitte and Progressive Insurance Company) and personally experienced a highly positive diversity and inclusion culture. Below is a story of how I switched from one of the top 100 best companies (Progressive Insurance) to another (Deloitte). Both of them have a diversified and inclusive culture.

Case Study: Inclusion and Diversity

It was a week of January 1998 when I received a phone call from one of the headhunters. His name was Jeff Steinberg. He was looking for someone with a computer science or MIS degree, Oracle ERP, and project management experience. Oracle was a hot commodity at that time. There were not too many people that knew how to configure an Oracle ERP system at that time. I fulfilled those requirements as I had all the qualifications and the experience he was looking for. Steinberg asked me if I was willing to switch from the industry to management consulting. I told him that I was very happy working for Progressive Insurance company (one of the 100 best companies to work for) and did not have the desire to leave. Steinberg was a great salesman, and he convinced me to go for the interview at least. He arranged my interview with Deloitte Consulting. Quite frankly, I did not know much about Deloitte or the management consulting industry at that time. I figured there was nothing to lose. Plus, I thought it would be good to test my interview skills as I had been working for Progressive for a little over seven years.

I got to Deloitte's Cleveland (Ohio) office at 8:00 a.m. on Friday, January 09, 1998. A very nice receptionist greeted me, and she offered me a cup of coffee. Steinberg recommended taking the day off as sometimes these interviews can last a few hours. I thought to myself; I should be done in a couple of hours. After all, it was just a job interview, so I took it pretty casually. I did wear a nice suit and tie that made me look professional and tidy. A few minutes later, I was introduced to the HR Manager, and he also seemed like a very nice and pleasant person. His name was Jack Hausen. After a few minutes of chat, Hausen shared the interview schedule with me. I was a bit shocked after looking at the schedule. The interviews ran from 8:30 a.m. to 4:30 p.m., including a lunch with the Managing Director (MD) of Deloitte's Cleveland Office. I had never seen and heard of such a hectic interview schedule. Besides the MD, I had interviews with three partners and four senior managers.

I looked at my watch, and it was 4:30 p.m. by the time I was done with all the interviews. I was pretty exhausted. I turned on my cell and had three missed calls from my wife. She did not expect the interview to last more than a couple of hours. As soon as I called her from my car, she said: "Are you okay?" I replied, "Yes, I'm okay," She asked: "Where are you?" I told her that I just got done with the interviews and was on my way home. I told her about the entire interview process, and she was also surprised.

Nevertheless, I was very impressed and thoroughly enjoyed the 8-hour onsite interview process at Deloitte. Everybody acted very professionally. They asked very relevant and thought-provoking questions. On Tuesday, January 13, 1998, in the afternoon, I received a call from Steinberg and said,

"Rizwan, Congratulations! Your interview went very well, and Deloitte is very interested in hiring you." I was happy to hear Jeff's words. However, I still was not sure and convinced that I wanted to leave Progressive. I had been with them for over seven years. I was delighted and enjoyed working for Progressive. I was on the fast-track to promotion due to my performance and knowledge about the latest technologies such as Oracle ERP. I was quite candid with Steinberg and told him about my apprehensions. I also told him that Progressive had a diverse and inclusive culture, which was highly important to me. Being a Pakistani-American, diversity, inclusion, and equal opportunity were crucial for me personally and professionally. Steinberg assured me that Deloitte was a great company to work for, and I wouldn't regret it. And the salary differential was huge. They offered me double the salary that I was making at Progressive. I asked Jeff to give me a few days to think it through and discuss it with my wife.

In the meantime, I conducted the research on Deloitte and discussed the offer with my wife. She recommended going for the offer. Of course, financially, it seemed quite rewarding, but the company culture and the work environment, such as diversity and inclusion, were more important to me than the money. I was very happy with Progressive due to its culture of diversity and inclusion, equal opportunity, meritocracy, and performance-based promotions and bonuses.

After one week of due-diligence and reflection, I accepted Deloitte's offer and joined in February 1998 and never looked back. It was one of the best decisions that I made in my career. I learned so much and made lots of friends while working at Deloitte. I had a wonderful time at Deloitte and assisted many Fortune 500 companies with their business transformations. I loved the culture, diversity, inclusion, and merit-based promotion and performance system at Deloitte. They did not look at the color of your skin, race, religion, gender, or anything of that sort. Partners at Deloitte only reviewed your performance, value-addition to the clients, practice development, knowledge sharing, and contributions to the community. Thus, I was put on a fast-track to a partnership based on my performance. I was ready to go on-deck for presentations to become a partner in the firm, but I decided to join academia and public service and left Deloitte as a Senior Manager in 2003. I had great mentors like Pat Conroy (Vice Chairman and Senior Partner), Jeff Glueck (Senior Partner), and Jeff Davis (Senior Partner). They showed me the ropes and immensely contributed to my success and career at Deloitte and beyond. I have enormous respect and gratitude for them.

Tools and Techniques of Inclusion and Diversity

- Diversity and inclusion is crucial to creating and leading high-performance teams and organizations.
- Merit, transparency, and performance-based promotion, and bonus structure.
- A culture of positivity, collegiality, and fairness.

STRATEGY 10: BUILDING TRUST

We all have heard of some managers and leaders asking this question: How can we trust our employees when they are not in the office and sitting at their desks? This was the situation even way before COVID-19 struck us. Now that we entered the deadly Round 2 of COVID-19 in November 2020, the question has become: How can we rely on our employees while they are working remotely from home? In my mind, both of these questions are valid, and the answer is "trust." Unless there is trust between the leaders and the team members, it would be almost impossible to build a high-performance organization or team. In my experience, I have found that you cannot build an organization or deliver a project without trust. Those of us who have worked on projects, especially complex and large-scale ($50 million and above) and mega ($1.0 billion and above) projects, know that hundreds of variables and decisions are involved in a project. There can be a huge amount of leakage in the procurement process, so having trust amongst the team members is critical. It's almost impossible for a CEO, General Manager, or Project Manager to review every single detail on a large-scale or megaproject unless he/she micromanages everything, which would be a huge constraint for the project. Therefore, a leader must be able to develop trust amongst the team members.

Building trust between the leader and the team and between the team and the organization is crucial for successfully creating and leading a team and company. If employees and team members don't trust the organization, they won't trust the leaders either. And without trust, employee's performance, productivity, and creativity would be hampered.

Jim Ludema and Amber Johnson mentioned in the Forbes online article *Remote Work Is Here To Stay. Three Keys To Building High-Performing Virtual Teams*: There are two types of trust: Institutional and relational trust[36].

As Ludema and Johnson pointed out, both of them are important for leaders, project managers, and organizations[36]. Institutional trust is whether the team trusts the organization and leader. Research studies have shown that virtual teams perform better when they trust the organization[36]. You can build institutional trust through open and transparent communication, equitable treatment, fairness, diversity, and inclusion. In addition, you need to equip your team members with the necessary resources as per their individual needs.

The second key element is relational trust. As Ludema and Johnson described, relational trust is developed amongst the team members through social interactions[36]. During a crisis like COVID-19, we all have to interact through virtual meetings and events socially. Spending a few moments at the start of our meetings and sharing our family stories can provide a human touch to the meetings. Talking about your kids, cats, dogs, and other family-related stories can humanize the conversations during the virtual world that we all are forced to live in, especially during a crisis like COVID-19. These social interactions can help us develop relational trust, which can help us build high-performance teams.

Case Study: Building Trust

According to the GMS case study, when John Stryker (the project manager) joined the GMS project at WSDOT, the project team's morale was relatively low. One of the reasons was trust deficiency amongst the team members. John noticed that team members were non-committal just about everything, and they tried to pass the buck or toss the bear to someone else's court. Some of the team members felt that they might not get the credit for their work. John analyzed the situation. He figured out that the source of the lack of trust was the absence of appreciation and recognition of the team. People were working hard, but they did not seem to get the credit they deserved.

John gave credit to the team members during weekly status meetings, which pleasantly surprised them. At times, he gave the credit for his work to the other team members, which created trust amongst the team members. Every week John would recognize a couple of team members and thank them for their hard work, efforts, and creativity. Resultantly, most (if not all) of the team members started to trust and appreciate John as the project manager. The team began to feel that there was someone who recognized and appreciated their efforts. The result was that the project team started to gel together. And the project team's performance and productivity went up.

In addition, if anyone on the team made any mistakes, John took responsibility for it. This kind of behavior boosted the team's morale and motivation levels. It also helped the team members to trust the project manager, John Stryker. The team felt confident if they made any mistake, they would be backed by the project manager. They all felt appreciated, motivated, and energized.

Tools and Techniques of Building Trust

- Institutional and relational trust-building.
- Recognition and appreciation of the team members.
- Humanize the virtual meetings.
- Social networking and sharing of family stories with the team members.
- Assisting team members during difficult times.

4

Ten Critical Project Management Challenges and Solutions during a Crisis

Project management is one of the key challenges that the public and private sector companies face during any natural disaster, crisis, or pandemic such as COVID-19. Project managers and organizations worldwide faced project management as one of the biggest challenges of 2020 across various industries, including healthcare, IT, construction, manufacturing, financial services, retail, and others. No matter what industry you work in, you have to plan, manage, and execute projects. Thus, project management has become the backbone of the private and public sectors. This leads to a key question: What are the key challenges during a national or global crisis, and how to overcome them? We have tried to answer this question in this chapter, so it must be of interest to every project manager and all organizations that are executing projects around the world. I have outlined the challenges along with recommendations on how to overcome them.

Here is the list of the top ten challenges and solutions that are discussed in the following pages. Challenges are not listed in any specific order or priority as they are equally important depending upon the situation and the nature of the project. Since there is no cookie-cutter approach in project management, especially during a crisis or global emergency, project managers and organizations must use their discretion in prioritizing these challenges for their respective projects.

1. Employee and team management (including virtual teams).
2. Project manager's leadership style and capabilities.
3. The new normal and change management.
4. Risk assessment and management.

DOI: 10.1201/9781003216711-5

5. Procurement and contract management.
6. Stakeholder management.
7. Resource management.
8. Project planning.
9. Cost overruns.
10. Communication.

EMPLOYEE AND TEAM MANAGEMENT

The first and foremost thing to do during a national or global crisis is to ensure your employees' and team members' safety, security, and wellbeing. While delivering a virtual keynote address during COVID-19, someone in the audience asked me: What has been the most critical challenge for companies and project managers during COVID-19? My answer was "managing employees and teams." In my industry, academia, and research experience, I have come to understand that project managers and organizations that take good care of their employees during a crisis are the most successful in satisfying their customers and delivering projects. The additional twist to managing people and teams during a pandemic is managing them virtually as most of the offices are closed. This leads to another question: how do you develop trust among employees and team members while working virtually?

Building trust amongst the project team members can be an immense challenge, especially when there is no in-person interaction. However, there are ways to enhance the interaction virtually using technology and thereby develop trust amongst the team members. Fortunately, there are tools like Zoom, Skype, and others that can mimic personal interaction as close to reality as possible. We highly recommend having video calls with all the team members unless someone prefers audio-only. Don't force or mandate the video call. The last thing you want to do is to cause unnecessary stress and anxiety for the team members by mandating the video call. As Jeff Davis, Senior Partner and Global Chief Commercial at Deloitte Consulting said:

> The pandemic has shifted how we work – but it hasn't erased our very human need for connection. High-performing teams use technologies like Zoom or Teams to foster feelings of live engagement in the work setting.

And those same technologies can also help keep existing social connections strong when combined with experiences like virtual online concerts. Shared experiences, even in the virtual world, can help to power the collective energy or at least help people feel less siloed and alone.

As a leader, you want to encourage the video calls but don't mandate it. A national or global emergency is the time to engage and empathize with the team members and make them feel safe and comfortable. Be flexible and humble, and work with your team. Daily or weekly virtual check-ins with the team during a crisis are crucial to building trust, humanizing interaction, and enhancing communication.

Secondly, I recommend that leaders and project managers should try to understand team members' concerns and address them. Offer empathy to your team members and listen to them. You may not be able to resolve all of their issues, but as a leader, you should listen to them, be flexible, and make yourself available to all team members. Based on my experience in managing global projects, almost 80% of team members would be satisfied if the project manager listens to them and tries to understand their concerns, even if the issues are not resolved. The project manager or leader must show that he/she genuinely cares about the team members.

Early morning or weekly check-ins through video or audio calls can be very helpful. It allows the team to share their concerns so that the project manager can address them during the day or week. For projects with a duration of less than a year, daily and weekly check-ins are recommended. And for projects with durations longer than one year, weekly and monthly check-ins are recommended.

As shown in KPMG's Framework (Reaction, Resilience, Recovery, and New Reality)[37] in Figure 4.1, understanding the team's challenges and concerns and addressing them in a timely and effective manner is crucial in Horizon 0 (KPMG Framework, 2020)[37]. Addressing customers' and suppliers' concerns are equally important. No organization or business can survive without happy employees, customers, and suppliers. Unfortunately, I have seen many organizations treat their suppliers as aliens from a different planet. And that is a very wrong approach. Suppliers are as important as customers, and in some cases, suppliers can make or break you. That's why Boeing pays a lot of attention to its suppliers, and they work very closely with the supplier. Boeing even trains its suppliers because millions of people fly on Boeing planes, and the safety of the passengers is Boeing's number one priority. Boeing cannot take the risk of having suppliers that

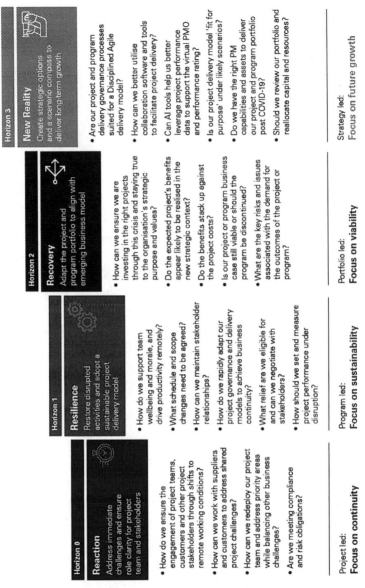

Horizon 0

Reaction
Address immediate challenges and ensure role clarity for project team and stakeholders

- How do we ensure the engagement of project teams, customers and other project stakeholders through shifts to remote working conditions?
- How can we work with suppliers and customers to address shared project challenges?
- How can we redeploy our project team and address priority areas while balancing other business challenges?
- Are we meeting compliance and risk obligations?

Project led:
Focus on continuity

Horizon 1

Resilience
Restore disrupted activities and adopt a sustainable project delivery model

- How do we support team wellbeing and morale, and drive productivity remotely?
- What schedule and scope changes need to be agreed?
- How can we maintain stakeholder relationships?
- How do we rapidly adapt our project governance and delivery models to achieve business continuity?
- What relief are we eligible for and can we negotiate with stakeholders?
- How should we set and measure project performance under disruption?

Program led:
Focus on sustainability

Horizon 2

Recovery
Adapt the project and program portfolio to align with emerging business model

- How can we ensure we are investing in the right projects through this crisis and staying true to the organisation's strategic purpose and values?
- Do the expected project's benefits appear likely to be realised in the new strategic context?
- Do the benefits stack up against the project costs?
- Is our project or program business case still viable or should the program be discontinued?
- What are the key risks and issues associated with the demand for the outcomes of the project or program?

Portfolio led:
Focus on viability

Horizon 3

New Reality
Create strategic options and a scenario compass to deliver long-term growth

- Are our project and program delivery governance processes suited for a Disciplined Agile delivery model?
- How can we better utilise collaboration software and tools to facilitate project delivery?
- Can AI tools help us better leverage project performance data to support the virtual PMO and performance rating?
- Is our project delivery model 'fit for purpose' under likely scenarios?
- Do we have the right PM capabilities and assets to deliver our project and program portfolio post COVID-19?
- Should we review our portfolio and reallocate capital and resources?

Strategy led:
Focus on future growth

FIGURE 4.1
KPMG's reaction, resilience, recovery, and new reality framework.
Source: Adopted from KPMG (2020)[37].

produce bad quality parts. Thus, active engagement with your employees, customers, and suppliers is crucial for a successful company and projects. KPMG also puts a lot of emphasis on supporting the wellbeing and morale of your team during Horizon 1 (KPMG, 2020)[37], as shown in Figure 4.1. Happy teams lead to efficiency, productivity, and high performance.

PROJECT MANAGER'S LEADERSHIP STYLE AND CAPABILITIES

As discussed in Chapter 2, the leader's style and capabilities are critical for a company's success. Similarly, a project manager's leadership traits and capabilities are tantamount to the successful delivery of the project. We have already discussed various styles and competencies of leaders that are also applicable to project managers. The question is: what kind of leadership traits, competencies, and capabilities are required in project managers to deliver projects successfully during a national or global crisis such as COVID-19?

After reviewing various research studies and deriving from my own experience, I believe servant leadership and collaborative leadership style are the most desired and applicable during a national emergency or pandemic. Both servant and collaborative leadership styles allow project managers to serve their employees, customers, and other stakeholders during a pandemic or a national emergency. The essence and focus of both leadership styles are to serve the stakeholders, which can lead to healthy and productive relationships with the employees, customers, suppliers, and the community (in the case of the public sector projects).

Dulewicz and Higgs stated there are 15 leadership capabilities that leaders and project managers need to possess to become successful leaders[29]. Based on our research and experience, the most critical leadership competencies that are required during a pandemic are emotional intelligence (EQ) competencies. Servant and collaborative leadership fall under EQ competencies. And the most important traits to have in a global crisis like COVID-19 are empathy, self-awareness, self-regulation, motivation, and social skills that are also part of Daniel Goleman's emotional intelligence model. Dulewicz and Higgs have further expanded the model with the following competencies[29]:

a. Self-awareness
b. Emotional resilience
c. Intuitiveness
d. Sensitivity
e. Influence
f. Motivation
g. Conscientiousness

Self-awareness

It has been defined by Daniel Goleman and other researchers as the ability to evaluate yourself, understand your own strengths and weakness. Most of us who have been working in the industry for a while have conducted SWOT (strengths, weaknesses, opportunities, and threats) analysis on companies. However, my question is: how many of us have performed the SWOT on ourselves? I asked the same question to 100+ project managers that attended my lecture at the PMI Dallas Chapter in May 2020. And 90% of the attendees answered "no." Do we, as leaders and professionals, know our strengths, weakness, opportunities, and threats? For example, we need to know the areas where we, as leaders and project managers, excel, i.e., analysis, communication, planning, and other skills. We also need to understand our weaknesses. Are we the leaders that can see the bigger picture, or are we only good at micro-level tasks? As a leader or project manager, what are the opportunities for me to thrive? And last but not least is to figure out the threats to your professional career as well as personal life situation. Are you taking too much stress? Are you going through high levels of anxiety and depression? How is your mental health? Do you get worried about the little stuff while ignoring the bigger picture? Answers to all these questions can lead you to conduct a SWOT on yourself. And it will help you chart the best course of action for yourself.

I'm often asked this question by executives and young managers around the world: Should I upgrade my skills by getting a Project Management Professional (PMP), ProSci, or other certifications? Should I pursue a part-time MBA program so that I'm ready for the challenges that might come up during the next 5–10 years? From my personal experience, I can tell you that the best investment that I made in life was getting a Ph.D. and an MBA degree. Of course, earning a Bachelor's degree from the Ohio State University and PMP certification set the foundation for my project management career, but advanced degrees indeed broadened my horizon and took me to places that I never thought I could go to or achieve what I have. I have given lectures in the Middle East, Europe, Asia, and North America. All are based on my experience and academic qualifications. Having the right certifications and degrees definitely helps you to earn the respect and knowledge you need to succeed in your career.

Emotional Resilience

It refers to coping with stress and the ability to adapt during extraneous situations and catastrophic events in life such as getting cancer, death of a loved one in the family, losing a job, and others. Southwick and Vythilingam's research study has shown those people that they can handle minor stressful situations in their daily lives can cope better during a major crisis such as a pandemic or a national emergency[38].

Developing emotional resilience can not only help you in your personal life but also in your professional career. No matter where we go, we cannot avoid stress these days, especially during a global crisis like COVID-19. Thus, it pays off to practice and try to deal with minor stresses in an organized and calm manner. Once we get used to minor stresses in our daily lives, there is a very high chance that we can deal with a major crisis or emergency like COVID-19.

I follow the 80/20 rule. I focus on the big 20% of the problems that would have an 80% impact on my personal life, family, or professional career. The rest either takes care of itself, or I learn to live with the risks and consequences. No matter who we are or how good leaders we are, we will not solve all of the world's problems. It would take an army of emotionally resilient people and more than a lifetime. Therefore, over the years, I have learned to follow the 80/20 rule.

Every project manager is taught that you have to live with some of the risks and execute the projects. You deal with the unknown and known risks as and when they come up. Worrying about a problem, event, or risk would only make our stress and anxiety levels go up, and it wouldn't solve the problem. Understanding the known and unknown risks and being prepared for them would help you cope with the situation when it finally comes up.

Intuitiveness

Researchers have studied human intuition for the past few decades. The basic definition is that a person knows or understands something, but he/she does not have the evidence for it. As William Duggan, the author of *Strategic Intuition: The Creative Spark in Human Achievement* has described three kinds of intuition: basic, expert, and strategic.

The basic intuition is the feeling that you get when you see something or meet someone for the first time. We all have heard of things like, "I met him/her for the first time, and he/she has nice hair." It's a feeling, which could be right or wrong, which we get about somebody or a situation.

For example, I was invited by a Fortune 500 company to one of their Executive Committee meetings as an observer. I noticed that most, if not all, of the executives, were very nice to each other. The topics that they discussed seemed challenging, but there were no disagreements in the room. I got the feeling that there was something either missing or wrong. That was my basic intuition. And once I dug deeper and asked some questions that none of the executives wanted to ask in the meeting, the discussion got too heated. Basically, they all tried to avoid the challenging conversation and waited for someone else to bring up the topic. I'm sure we all have experienced this kind of situation in our professional careers.

The second kind of intuition is called expert intuition. This is something based on your past experience. For example, an emergency room nurse or doctor can spot somebody right away whether they have a heart attack. They have not gone through the protocol yet but based on their past experience and preliminary vital signs of the patient, they indicate that the person has a heart attack.

One of my close friends (Joe), while driving from New York City to Pittsburgh, experienced chest pain on October 2019 and it was a bit chilly. All of a sudden, Joe rolled down his window and started coughing heavily. I asked Joe if he was okay. He said he is okay, but he also said that he wasn't feeling too good. I insisted on getting off at the next exit and finding a hospital. We took the exit and found a nearby hospital. As soon as we walked into the emergency room, we saw a nurse. She looked at Joe and asked him to lay on the bed right away. She examined him and asked him some questions, and then panic set off. She asked me to go outside, and she screamed, *this patient is having a heart attack, everybody.* The entire crew, including the nursing staff and doctors, flew towards Joe and followed the necessary protocol. And the nurse was right. Joe did have a mild heart attack, but she caught it at the right time, and they put a stent into one of his arteries. Not only did Joe survive, but he was able to avoid a massive heart attack due to the "expert intuition" of the nurse.

The third type of intuition is called strategic intuition. It can also be related to the "Eureka" or "Aha" moments that we all feel once in a while. Strategic intuition is the time when you understand a concept, situation, or complex problem that seemed incomprehensible before. This feeling or strategic intuition could come anytime, such as taking a shower, relaxing in a secluded cabin, performing yoga, offering a morning prayer, or doing meditation. As soon as you get a strategic intuition, you immediately have to write down your thoughts on a piece of paper. Otherwise, you might lose the idea or solution.

William Duggan, the author of "Strategic Intuition: The Creative Spark in Human Achievement," said:

> Expert intuition relies on your own experience, while strategic intuition draws on the experience of everyone else in the world as well.

As leaders, we should also take advantage of the strategic intuition, Eureka, and Aha moments and capture our thoughts and ideas on a piece of paper. Based on my experience, I have prepared my best presentations on a McDonald's napkin while having coffee and stopped by a McDonald's on a highway in the middle of nowhere. Now, what I do is jot my ideas on a napkin, take a picture of them, and immediately either email it to me, store it in WhatsApp or Slack.

A few years ago, I was driving to one of the healthcare company's Headquarters in Cleveland, Ohio, which was located in a suburb a few miles away from downtown Cleveland. I was supposed to give a presentation on the business case of a new IT strategy and ERP implementation. While driving, yes, you probably guessed it right, I pulled off and got McDonald's coffee. I also took a bio break and then sat in the dining room and had coffee. I reviewed the presentation and started to get good but divergent thoughts of what I had written down in the presentation. I put my laptop away and started writing on the napkins, yes McDonald's napkins. The ideas and thoughts were so good that I decided to call the client and asked to delay the presentation by one hour because I wanted to revise the presentation. The client agreed, I changed the presentation, and then walked into the company's Board room and presented the business case. The client loved it and immediately signed-off on the multimillion-dollar project. The moral of the story is: Don't let your strategic intuition, Eureka, and Aha moments go wasted.

Sensitivity

I don't know why Emily cares so much about the environment and thinks she has to change the world, said John Foster after finishing the meeting.

If you are one of those sensitive people, you've probably heard these kinds of comments from people like Foster. This leads to the question: What is sensitivity? It is defined as something that you feel for others. If you are a sensitive person, you can feel other people's pain more than the rest of us. You have a natural empathy for everybody around you, including the environment. If you enjoy music, art, nature, then the chances are that you are one of those gifted people that are naturally sensitive to others' feelings and pain.

Human sensitivity is part of emotional intelligence, and some people are gifted and born with sensitivity traits. Others can practice and try to develop those capabilities. Elaine Aron published her book "Highly Sensitive People" in 1996 and brought the concept of sensitivity into the mainstream. As Aron mentioned, there is about 15–20 % of the population has these sensitivity traits. Following are the key traits of sensitivity that Aron and other researchers have pointed out:

  i. Feeling elated by music, art, and nature.
  ii. Being sensitive to pain and other physical feelings.
  iii. Caring about the environment and nature more than others.
  iv. Preferring seclusion over social gatherings.
  v. Sensing noise more than others i.e., clock-ticking, humming sound coming out of equipment, and others.
  vi. Getting shocked or startled easily.
  vii. Experiencing mood swings more than others.

Dr. Thomas Boyce (a pediatrician) founded the "Orchid and Dandelion" theory. His research indicated that almost 80% of children are like dandelions. They can survive virtually in any environment and circumstances. However, there are 20% of children like orchids. They need nurturing and caring, and they are highly sensitive to the environment they grow up in. They are also more numerable to adversity than the dandelion kids. That's why children with orchid traits get affected by their parents' feelings and behaviors faster than the rest of the children, even if they grow up in the same household.

Similarly, there are employees and team members that behave like orchids and dandelions. Most of the employees are like dandelions and can thrive in any environment or adapt to change more quickly than others. On the other hand, some employees are like orchids, so you, as a leader, have to pay special attention to them. Since they are susceptible to what they hear, see, and sense, the leader, has to be sensitive to their needs and address their concerns.

Influence

Persuasion and influence are part and parcel of leadership and team-building. In the HBR article *Harnessing the Science of Persuasion,* Robert Cialdini has explained six principles of persuasion and influence that can be highly effective in leading organizations and high-performance teams[39]. Table 4.1 below shows the summary of the six principles of persuasion

TABLE 4.1

The Six Principles of Persuasion and Influence by Robert Cialdini[39]

Principle	Example	Business Application
Liking:		
People like those like them, who like them.	At Tupperware parties, guests' fondness for their host influences purchase decisions twice as much as regard for the products.	To influence people, win friends, through: *Similarity*: Create *early* bonds with new peers, bosses, and direct reports by informally discovering common interests—you'll establish goodwill and trustworthiness. *Praise* : Charm *and* disarm. Make positive remarks about others—you'll generate more willing compliance.
Reciprocity:		
People repay in kind.	When the Disabled American Veterans enclosed free personalized address labels in donation-request envelopes, response rate doubled.	Give what you want to receive. Lend a staff member to a colleague who needs help; you'll get *his* help later.
Social Proof:		
People follow the lead of similar others.	More New York City residents tried returning a lost wallet after learning that other New Yorkers had tried.	Use peer power to influence horizontally, not vertically, e.g., ask an esteemed "old timer" to support your new initiative if other veterans resist.

(Continued)

TABLE 4.1 (Continued)

Principle	Example	Business Application
Consistency:		
People fulfill written, public, and voluntary commitments.	92% of residents of an apartment complex who signed a petition supporting a new recreation center later donated money to the cause.	Make others' commitments active, public, and voluntary. If you supervise an employee who should submit reports on time, get that understanding in writing (a memo); make the commitment public (note colleagues' agreement with the memo); and link the commitment to the employee's values (the impact of timely reports on team spirit).
Authority:		
People defer to experts who provide shortcuts to decisions requiring specialized information.	A single New York Times expert-opinion news story aired on TV generates a 4% shift in U.S. public opinion.	Don't assume your expertise is self-evident. Instead, establish your expertise *before* doing business with new colleagues or partners; e.g., in conversations before an important meeting, describe how you solved a problem similar to the one on the agenda.
Scarcity:		
People value what's scarce.	Wholesale beef buyers' orders jumped 600% when they alone received information on a possible beef shortage.	Use exclusive information to persuade. Influence and rivet key players' attention by saying, for example:"…Just got this information today. It won't be distributed until next week."

Source: Adopted from Robert Cialdini.[39]

and influence as described by Cialdini[39]: their parents' feelings and behaviors faster than the rest of the children, even if they grow up in the same household.

Motivation

We have already described motivation in Chapter 2 as part of Goleman's model. Here, we focus on the examples of motivation from the Grants Management System (GMS) project's case study in Part II of this book.

Max (the Business Sponsor of GMS) was a great motivator. He had a natural ability to influence and persuade the team to move in his direction. Max could hire talented staff that was intrinsically motivated. He was also good at utilizing extrinsic motivation factors. For example, he would go out of his way to help people to get promoted and get the maximum salary increase. And that's why most of the people were happy to work with Max. Of course, some individuals outside of his group did not get along too well with him, but they were in the minority.

Conscientiousness

There are five personality traits called the Big Five, and conscientiousness is one of them. The other four are extraversion, agreeableness, openness, and neuroticism. Conscientiousness is defined as having the ability to be organized, responsible, diligent, and goal-oriented. Conscientious people also tend to adhere to norms, rules, and procedures. They possess traits such as self-discipline, attention-to-details, reliability, sincerity, goal-oriented, and responsibility. That's why people with conscientious traits make good surgeons and pilots[40]. Another key aspect of conscientious individuals is that they hold more empathy towards others. According to a Chinese research study of 471 nurses, empathy is positively correlated with agreeableness and conscientiousness[40].

The GMS project team members had a high sense of reliability, sincerity, goal-orientation, responsibility, and self-discipline, which helped them to become a high-performance team. Just like conscientious individuals, Max and the rest of the project team members were proactive in decision-making. They did not dwell upon issues and took quick and timely decisions. The team members were goal-oriented. They set a timeline to achieve those goals, such as GMS Pilot Release 1 in June 2020 and GMS Pilot Release 2 in July 2020. This approach kept the entire team focused and helped them to achieve the project milestones successfully.

RISK ASSESSMENT AND MANAGEMENT

When a disaster or pandemic hits, the first thing that comes into leaders and project managers' minds is "risk." They ask or should ask questions like: what are the risks to the people, organization, and project? What are the macro and micro level risks? Who will be affected? What would be the impact on cost, timeline, scope, people, infrastructure, and quality?

Risk assessment, management, and mitigation strategy are the key aspects that most if not all leaders and project managers are trained to do. What makes this more important is the nature of the risks during a national emergency or global crisis. There would be a lot of uncertainty during a global emergency and pandemic. We would have to deal with a lot of unknowns, similar to what we dealt with during COVID-19 and other pandemics.

The question is: what can we do about the unknowns and uncertainty. First, try to understand the situation as much as you can. Assess the damage and losses. Focus on the facts and figures that can be verified. Try to stay away from the hype and propaganda, especially during today's social media overflow. Talk to the people that you trust and discuss the situation with your employees and the team members. Reach out to the people who are in the field and try to gather as much data as possible. Analyze the data, facts, and figures. Verify the data and start making decisions after taking your team into confidence.

One thing you want to avoid during a crisis is solo decision-making, which can exacerbate the situation. Your key employees and team members must be on board with all the decisions that you make. Everybody will not be happy with your decisions. You will not be able to satisfy one hundred percent of the people. You have to focus on the majority of the people and issues. The rest of the problems and people would either understand the situation or would learn to live with it.

Focus, facts, data, prioritization, and decision-making are crucial risk assessment and mitigation strategies. Once you have gathered and verified the critical data and facts, then create a plan and mitigation strategy for each risk. Some of the risks your team will be able to mitigate urgently, some will have to wait, and there will be other risks that you will have to accept and move on. There are tools like the risk register, severity matrix, RAID (Risks, Actions, Issues, and Decisions) log used for the risk assessment and management. Examples of these tools are shown and discussed in the case study of this book.

PROCUREMENT AND CONTRACT MANAGEMENT

Managing the procurement process and contracts with customers, suppliers, and other key stakeholders are crucial and essential, especially during a crisis or pandemic. You want to collaborate with all key stakeholders to avoid lawsuits and ensure that your products and services are delivered to the customers efficiently and timely.

There are certain clauses like force majeure in contracts that either your legal department or attorneys would have to review to ensure that there is an amicable resolution to all the legal issues that might come up during the crisis. But, there are things that you, as a leader or project manager, can do to provide comfort and relief to the supplier and customers. Suppliers are the lifeline of any company, business, or project. Therefore, you must collaborate with them and try to resolve any issues before they go to the legal department or attorneys. Of course, if there is no other way to resolve the issues, then you should exercise your legal rights.

Keep in mind that fighting legal battles can be expensive, time-consuming, stressful, and a resource-hog. Thus, I highly recommend avoiding lawsuits and try to resolve the issues amicably, even if you have to take a little bit of a loss. Taking a minor loss might still be better than the legal battle, especially during pandemic. I advise my clients to conduct pros and cons and cost-and-benefits analysis before trying to file a lawsuit. Research studies show about 80% of the companies try to settle the matter without going to court.

A supply chain is an area that is usually most affected during a national crisis or pandemic. Since companies and businesses in the US heavily rely on products from foreign countries like China, the shipments can be delayed, which can delay the projects and product delivery. Again, you must immediately contact your suppliers and offer help in any way that you can. Don't view the suppliers as aliens from Mars because you are in a crisis together. It would probably hurt your business as much as it would hurt them. I highly recommend you look at your suppliers as business partners that can make you or break you, especially during a situation like COVID-19.

Based on my experience and research, I have found that companies that collaborate with suppliers, show flexibility, and take a realistic and practical approach, come out relatively unscathed during a global crisis. Not only that, some companies come out even stronger than the pre-crisis days because they end up building trust and a stronger relationship with their suppliers. Nobody wants to go out of business during a crisis or pandemic, which is why most companies, businesses, and people understand the hardships that everyone faces both locally and globally and are more willing to collaborate.

STAKEHOLDER MANAGEMENT

Managing stakeholders is a daunting task for project managers globally. I have talked to thousands of project managers around the world, and they all shared this view. One of the key reasons it is such an uphill task is dealing with people and the softer issues. As we say in the management world, it's the softer issues that are the hardest to deal with.

Let's review the key stakeholders on any given project: sponsor, customers (internal and external), team members, suppliers, service providers such as telecom operators, auditors, various departments, lawyers, and others. If you execute projects in the public sector, you would have to deal with the legislatures, politicians, communities, various government departments, and the general public. They all have one thing in common: that's the people. Project managers would have to deal with people from various backgrounds, races, religions, gender, and beliefs. And that's what makes it so challenging to manage the stakeholders. Stakeholder management becomes more challenging when two or more key stakeholders don't get along or have conflicting demands. A real-life case study on stakeholder management is mentioned below.

While observing various projects during COVID-19, our research team found that managing employees and their safety and security were one of the biggest challenges faced by organizations. Similarly, the project managers foresaw managing and taking care of their team members and key stakeholders as the most crucial challenge. Since anxiety, stress, and uncertainty were immensely high among the project team members, this became the most critical aspect that the project manager had to face during COVID-19.

Stakeholder management was one of the topmost challenges that project managers were facing. This was also indicated by the survey of 289 project managers conducted globally by Iryna Viter and her team[41]. She asked the participants of the survey: *What is your main project challenge*

CASE STUDY: STAKEHOLDER MANAGEMENT

In the late 90s, I was a newly promoted project manager of a multimillion-dollar ERP implementation. I had a client where two colleagues (call them Larry and Curly) argued for days on one decision, and that was whether the invoice should be printed on a dot-matrix printer or a laser printer. I asked both of them to talk it over and let me know their decision.

Two weeks went by, and there was no decision, so I decided to convene a meeting with both of them. I asked them to take turns and describe their business requirements to me. Larry wanted to print the invoice on a dot-matrix printer with two carbon copies, which he called the "3-part invoice," and the word invoice should be written in red color. He wanted three copies of the invoice: one for his records, the second for the customer, and the third for the audit records. Then I switched to Curly and asked for his requirements. He did not like the dot matrix printers because it cost more money to maintain them, and they were getting obsolete. Plus, he had to order special paper stock to print the invoice, so he wanted to use the laser printer instead. Then I turned around; I told both of them that I could meet both of their requirements. They were surprised and immediately asked, "how"? I asked them to show me a color laser printer and asked the developers to program it to print them on the color laser printer with the word invoice in red.

The next day I asked both Larry and Curly to meet me in the conference room to test the invoice printing. I asked Larry to click on print and set the number of copies to three, and he did. *Voilà*, there came out three copies of the invoice with the word invoice in red color. Larry was excited, and he started jumping up and down. He said, "Riz, you are not too bad as a consultant. You are not like the other consultants; you can actually do something for me." I thanked Larry and turned towards Curly. He was smiling as well because we printed the invoice on a laser printer instead of the dot matrix. Of course, I fictionalized the names of Larry and Curly, respecting their privacy and identity.

Larry and Curly were small examples of stakeholder management. Sometimes people can argue and fight over little things as the printing of an invoice. That's history now, as we hardly print invoices these days because most of them are issued and paid electronically.

What is your main project challenge in 2020?

VOTES

22%	Project planning	63
30%	Resource management	87
13%	Cost overruns	38
35%	Stakeholder management	101

⬢ Forecast·   289 votes

FIGURE 4.2
Project challenges in 2020. (Iryna Viter, 2020)[41].

Source: Adopted from Iryna Viter[41].

in 2020? Iryna found that 35% of the project managers expected stake-holder management to be the biggest challenge in 2020, especially during COVID-19. This was followed by resource management (20%), project planning (22%), and cost overruns (13%)[41]. Results of Iryna's survey are shown in Figure 4.2.

Risk assessment and management were on the top of the list for project managers around the world. As soon as any natural disaster or pandemics hits, the project managers and sponsors have to conduct the risk assessment and manage them diligently until the project and situation are stabilized.

RESOURCE MANAGEMENT

Project managers know how to manage resources, including financial, human resources, and others. The challenge becomes more pronounced during a global crisis like COVID-19 when there is no precedent. Coronavirus brought a unique set of challenges to companies, businesses, and people across the world. Project managers used to fight for resources even during the pre-COVID-19 era. Now with the pandemic, resource allocation, and management became a more significant challenge than before.

Employees had to abide by social distancing rules and could not come to the office anymore. Most non-essential workers had to work remotely, which presented a unique and unprecedented set of challenges. Various questions popped into the heads of project managers across the globe. How do we collaborate with the team member virtually? How can we trust our employees and team members that are working remotely? How can we ensure quality? How can we synchronize team members and senior management? Answers to these questions are as follows:

As project managers, we are quite familiar with the notion of placing the right people at the right job and at the right time. We also know that it's easier said than done. And most of the time, project managers are not lucky enough to have all three legs of the stool. Either the third leg is missing or broken. The same was true during COVID-19. The resources that project managers planned to allocate were either no longer available or had been assigned to higher priority tasks and projects. Not only did project managers had to deliver projects, but they had to deliver them with lesser resources than pre-COVID-19 days. In addition, strategy and focus changed after the pandemic. Employee furloughs, layoffs, and budget cuts came down due to loss of revenue and profits. Therefore, project managers were asked by the senior management to deliver the same scope with a reduced budget and resources.

The question is, how could project managers address the issue of resource allocation and management during a global crisis or pandemic? The first thing that I recommend is to focus on the end goal. What do you and the sponsor want to achieve from the project? The immediate (30–90 days), short (6–12 months), and medium-terms (1–2 years) goals should be crystal clear. Are there any quick wins that we can achieve in the next 30–90 days?

Success is more important in a crisis because you want to keep the team's morale and motivation level high. And the best way to do that is to achieve some success and boost the team's morale. Success also gives confidence to the team, and it energizes the team members. It would help if you guided the team to focus on immediate and short-term goals. Yes, medium and long-term goals are also important. During a national or global emergency, immediate and short-term objectives are more important to keep the team engaged, motivated, and productive.

You can focus on the immediate and short-term objectives and allocate the resources accordingly. For example, if you are working on an IT project, you can negotiate with the customer to deliver the project in smaller chunks or releases. It's acceptable to the clients most of the time as long as meaningful functionality is delivered in every release.

De-scoping or reduction in scope is also a possibility if you can logically convince the project sponsor and customer. I have used this strategy in the past, and it worked for me. This is something you would have to explore with the senior management and customer. They would most of the time agree, especially in a global emergency, as long as the overall project objectives are met and get meaningful results. You can read the case study in Part II of this book and see how this strategy was applied to the two software pilots successfully, and the customers were happy. As mentioned in the GMS case study in Part II, the project team's morale and motivation level sky-rocketed due to the two pilot releases. It also provided the focus and direction that the team needed to continue working on the project during COVID-19 and finish it by March 31, 2021.

PROJECT PLANNING

A project plan or schedule is used interchangeably. It is one of the essential tools that a project manager can use to deliver projects successfully. As it is often said, the devil is in the details; this also holds true in project management. A detailed project plan along with a contingency plan is required for any successful project. I have seen a lot of organizations and project managers that forget to create a contingency plan. Either they forget about it or don't find it necessary. Based on my project management experience, if a project manager does not have a contingency plan, then he/she does not have a plan.

Some of the basic elements of a project schedule contain lists of tasks, resources (people or departments), task durations, costs, and a calendar (weekends, holidays, and any other off days during the year). The two most commonly used software in the industry are Microsoft Projects (MS) and Primavera. MS Projects is relatively easy to use and is more common in the service industry, i.e., IT, financial services, and others. On the other hand, Primavera is more sophisticated and relatively complex to use. It is commonly used in construction, manufacturing, oil and gas, and other industries. An example of a schedule is listed in the case study of this book.

Now the key challenge is how to create or update the project schedule during the pandemic. It may sound easy, but it is not. The reason is due to the uncertainty that revolves around a crisis or pandemic like COVID-19. It is uncertain what the new priorities are going to be. Will the necessary human and financial resources be available? Will the project team be able to achieve the milestones in a timely manner? In a recent survey that we conducted during COVID-19, I posed this question to the executives: how many of you will miss the project milestones or deadline due to COVID-19? About 90% of them responded, "yes, they will miss the milestones and the project deadline." Then I ask another question: What would be the reasons to miss your milestones or project deadline? The key reasons included:

- Budget cuts.
- Change of priorities by the project sponsor.
- Lack of availability of human resources due to operational issues.

This leads to the question: What can a project manager do to ensure the projects are delivered on-time, within the scope, and according to the budget? First, there is almost an 80–90% chance that the budget would be cut and the timeline would be extended due to a crisis. You need to reassess all three elements: budget, timeline, and scope. Suppose the budget has been cut and human resources are not available according to the original plan. In that case, you need to renegotiate the project scope and timeline with the project sponsor. De-scoping or reducing the project scope is perfectly normal during a national emergency or global crisis. However, you would negotiate the scope with the project sponsor. And based on the revised scope, you would adjust the budget and timeline. And then, you would update the project schedule accordingly.

COST OVERRUNS

Budget or cost overruns are among the most common aspects of project management, especially during a pandemic. Employee furloughs and layoffs can lead to an extension of the timeline, which can cause cost overruns. It is a misconception that a reduction in budget and extension in time will not cause cost overruns. The more we extend the timeline, the more certain that it will lead to project cost overruns. I'm sure you all have heard that time is money. Whenever we spend more time on a project, somebody has got to pay for it.

There is a way to avoid cost overruns, reduce the project scope, and stick to the original timeline. Based on my experience and hundreds of projects that I have reviewed or worked on in the last 30 years, the moment we extend the timeline, there is an 80– 90% probability that cost overruns would occur. My advice is to renegotiate all three iron triangle elements: budget, scope, and timeline. Also, keep in mind that the cost of certain items or materials might go up during a pandemic due to the demand and supply curve, especially if you are executing a construction project. Supply chain networks might be disrupted, which could cause delays and logistical challenges. Therefore, it might drive up the overall cost of the project.

COMMUNICATION

I'm often asked what would be the most important thing during a national or global crisis such as COVID-19? My answer is communication. It is the most crucial element that project managers must focus on. Communication with employees, customers, suppliers, and other key stakeholders is vital for successful project delivery. The first thing a leader must do during a crisis is to revise the communication plan. If you don't have a communication plan, create it. There must be a single point of contact or department for communication. The communication has to be consistent, clear, and concise. I call it the three Cs. If wrong or inconsistent information goes to any of the key stakeholders, it can backfire on the company and the project. That is why there should only be one source of communication.

Below are some of the recommendations on communication during a crisis or national emergency:

Right Communication Channels and Staying in Touch with Employees are Vital

There is a strong possibility that phone lines, internet services, and networks would be affected during a crisis, as it happened during COVID-19. Telecommunication networks and internet services were overloaded due to high call volume and usage. Most of the companies switched to remote work due to lockdowns and stay-at-home orders by most of the States in the US.

As a leader of a company or team, you must pick communication channels that employees can trust. For example, a company's intranet would be a good source assuming people can access the networks during a crisis. If you are a large or publicly traded company, you may want to use media outlets such as CNN, CNBC, or other local news channels to deliver a message to your employees as well as the public. The CEO of American Airlines (Don Carty) used media outlets to disseminate information to employees after the 9/11 attack. The Washington Department of Transportation (WSDOT) leveraged its intranet, emails, and local news channels to distribute the news and information during COVID-19. Washington State Governor Jay Inslee, Secretary of Transportation Roger Millar, and other leaders at the WSDOT did an excellent job of staying in touch with their employees and providing regular updates during COVID-19. They ensured the safety and security of State employees. They also made sure that employees' issues and concerns were addressed in a timely manner during the pandemic.

Since anxiety and uncertainty levels are immensely high during a crisis, employees also want assurance from third-party sources that their companies are being candid and transparent about the information they get about their organizations. It might be a good idea to share information with a third-party blog and have them publish the information about your company. You don't want to use too many communication channels to risk distortion of the news and information. Therefore, you should be selective and choose only credible communication channels that employees can trust.

Focus on the Business is Critical

During a crisis, employees are generally immensely anxious, but they are also enormously willing to help. The best thing to do would be to keep employees focused on the company's core business. Striving to provide the best customer service and focusing on the business is one of the best ways to keep employees engaged and motivated during a crisis. It also helps them to continue their normal work routine and fosters a sense of pride and purpose.

Contingency Plan is Essential

While many companies put together contingency plans, they never have the time to test them or do the mock rehearsals. Most businesses felt varying degrees of impact in the US as well as globally during COVID-19. Some were hit harder than others, such as the hospitality and airline industry. Companies that had robust contingency plans fared better than the rest of the pack. It would help if you had a contingency and business continuity plan in place, and it must be tested quarterly.

Solid Foundation and Quick Decision-Making are Indispensable

Your company's organizational structure and decision matrix must stay current. At the very least, the decision protocols on what, when, and who must be clear: What kind of decisions will be required? When will those decisions be made? Who will make the decisions?

In addition, leaders must be prepared to make decisions quickly. Sometimes you will have to think on your feet and make quick decisions. Thus, as a leader, you must have the ability and confidence to make decisions. Otherwise, it could hurt the business and employees' morale. Employees look up to the leaders and senior management to make quick decisions during a crisis. Your leadership, decision-making, and resilience will be tested during a national emergency such as a pandemic.

Monitoring of WHO and CDC Information During a Pandemic

It is vital to monitor the news and information coming out of the World Health Organization (WHO) and Center for Disease Control (CDC) during a pandemic. It will help you adapt your business plans and strategy accordingly. WHO and CDC did a good job of releasing relevant data and information daily during COVID-19.

Companies that used WHO and CDC data to customize their travel, HR, communication, and contingency plans were better positioned to cope with the COVID-19 crisis. Thus, reliable data and timely updates to the plans are crucial during a pandemic.

THE NEW NORMAL AND POST-COVID-19 STRATEGIES

By now, everyone has heard of the term the *new normal*. What is the new normal? Stress, uncertainty, anxiety, working remotely, and feeling claustrophobic while working from home are all part of the new normal. Lockdown, kids are running around the house while you are trying to have an official virtual meeting, and not connecting with co-workers in-person are also referred to as the new normal. Colleagues are scattered across the US or globally, different time zones, and many other issues. Under the new normal, we all have to learn new ways of doing business. We have to find innovative ways to deliver projects on-time, within budget, as per the scope. This leads to the question: How can we deliver high-quality projects with high stress, anxiety, and uncertainty under the new normal? The answer is described in the next few pages.

First, leaders, project managers, and team members must take a step back and figure out what needs to be done and prioritize all the tasks. As a leader, you need to understand and recognize the challenges in the new normal. Some things that might have sounded unreasonable in pre-COVID-19 days are normal now. For example, working from home and having kids in the background, virtual meetings and collaboration with stakeholders, and managing extra stress and anxiety.

Secondly, as a leader and project manager, you must take care of your team members first. That should be your number one priority. It would be best if you looked after the wellbeing, health, and safety of your employees. Everything else is secondary. No matter how advanced we become in technology and how many gadgets and tools we have at our disposal, it will be the people who will deliver the project at the end of the day. Sure, we now have robots and Artificial Intelligence (AI), but we still have a long way to go before humans are no longer needed, and robots can do everything in companies and projects.

In its article *Workforce Strategies for Post-COVID-19 Recovery,* Deloitte laid out the three guideposts – potential, purpose, and perspective for the "new normal"[42]. They also recommended the five critical actions and strategies for the post-COVID-19 recovery[42], described below and summarized in Figure 4.3.

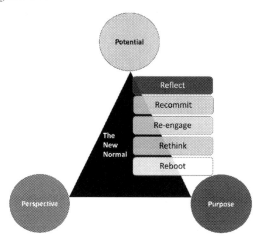

FIGURE 4.3
Deloitte's five critical actions and strategies for post-COVID-19 recovery.

Source: Adopted from Deloitte[42].

1. **Reflect:** Companies need to reflect on what worked during the COVID-19 crisis, what lessons were learned, and what was missed in their response.
2. **Recommit:** Leaders must recommit to the wellbeing, safety, and security of the workforce. They need to understand the physical, psychological, and financial needs of the employees.
3. **Re-engage:** We must re-engage and redeploy our employees to maximize their potential and contribution in the new normal.
4. **Rethink:** Companies and leaders need to rethink work, workforce, and workplaces to utilize the lessons learned from COVID-19 and capitalize the future opportunities.
5. **Reboot:** Leaders need to reboot and re-align HR functions and operations with the high-priority workforce and business needs.

5

Creating an Enabling Environment and IT Infrastructure during a Crisis

COVID-19 has changed the world. It has changed all of us for decades to come. It has transformed how we do business, work as professionals, operate in a team environment, interact with our colleagues, and function as a community, society, or country. As mentioned earlier, it is called the *New Normal*. We all have to adopt new ways of doing business. Working from home in a virtual environment and innovatively managing the work-life balance will be the norm. We must do it to survive and thrive as a leader, project manager, high-performance team, and company. This leads to the question: How can you, as a leader, create an enabling environment to lead a high-performance team and organization that can not only weather the storm like COVID-19 but also be well prepared for the post-pandemic work? We explore the answer to the question in the following section.

According to McKinsey Global Institute's report, *The Future of Work after COVID-19*, 20–25 % of workers in advanced economies like the US could continue to work remotely[43]. They have also pointed out the following three trends, summarized in Figure 5.1 that might persist after the pandemic[43]:

1. **Remote to Work, Travel, and Virtual Meetings**
   This trend might continue due to workers' flexibility, cost savings for companies, and a cleaner environment because fewer vehicles would be on the road.
2. **E-Commerce and Virtual Transactions**
   The use of e-commerce and virtual transactions surged exponentially during COVID-19, and it is expected to go higher in the post-pandemic era. More companies and businesses are expected to move towards digital platforms.

DOI: 10.1201/9781003216711-6

COVID-19 has prompted consumer and business behavior shifts, many of which will persist to varying degrees in the long run.

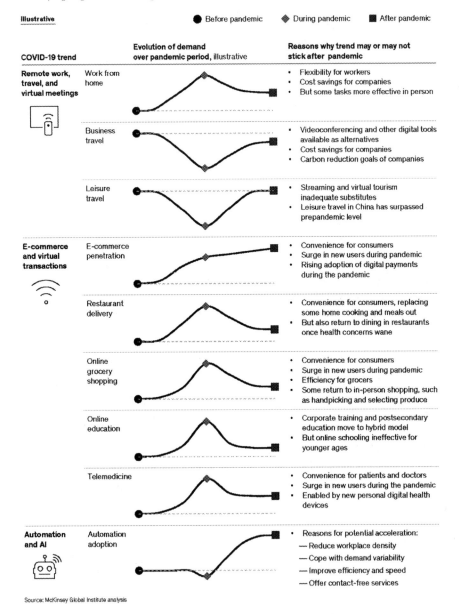

FIGURE 5.1
Three future trends predicted by McKinsey Global Institute.

Source: McKinsey Global Institute[43].

3. **Automation and Artificial Intelligence (AI).**
The pandemic forced many companies to automate their business processes quickly, and some moved towards AI. We expect this trend to move higher due to a reduction in workplace density, efficiency, speed, and the demand for contact-free services.

Based on our experience and research, we believe leaders and organizations that can create an environment with psychological safety and a robust IT infrastructure will be well-positioned to deal with any national or global crisis such as COVID-19. They will be able to build high-performance teams that can overcome the challenges posed during a national or global crisis such as a pandemic. Therefore, in this chapter, we will focus on IT infrastructure requirements, cybersecurity, collaboration software and tools, and how to build psychological safety for virtual environments during a crisis. We believe that these are the most critical elements for any team, organization, society, or country to survive and excel in the foreseeable future. These are the building blocks and foundations for any high-performance team and any organization.

In our daily lives, Western and developed countries are highly dependent on technology. Starting from the heating and cooling systems at our homes to offices and anything in-between, we are dependent on IT even the washers and dryers can be programmed remotely to run automatically at a certain time of the day. All critical industrial sectors of the US economy are dependent on IT, including healthcare, real estate, automobiles, construction, financial services, oil and gas, energy, utilities, schools, colleges, gyms, and anything that you can think of. We all need IT to function as an organization, community, society, or country. That is why the Cybersecurity and Infrastructure Security Agency (CISA) of the US Government have declared IT as one of the 16 critical infrastructure sectors that is crucial for the national security and safety of the United States and its citizens[44].

Another crucial element during a crisis is psychological safety. It is critical for a productive work environment, especially in a virtual setting under the *new normal*. As a leader, the onus is on you to ensure that your employees and team members feel safe and secure while in the office physically or when they work remotely. We discuss psychological safety at length in Chapter 6, but in this chapter, we will discuss it in the context of virtual environments such as team meetings, discussion forums, training, seminars, and others. Psychological safety provides an environment for the employees and team members to talk freely without fear of any punishment, repercussions, and consequences.

Technology is changing very rapidly. Every day there is a new software or tool that is introduced to the market. With the latest technology such as holograms, it would be very much possible in the near future for a speaker or professor sitting in his office in the US to deliver a lecture in UK, Pakistan, India, China, South Africa while audiences can see him. Imperial College London has already tested this technology successfully. However, it may take a few years before home users can utilize it the way we use Skype, Zoom, MS Teams, GoToMeeting, and other software. Fifteen years ago, it was unthinkable that people would be able to make video calls around the world free of cost. You had to spend thousands of dollars on hardware and software to make a video call. And still, sometimes the video call was not as smooth as it is today with the latest software.

The World Economic Forum (WEF) made good recommendations in their article *How digital infrastructure can help us through the COVID-19 crisis.* Below are the key points that were mentioned in the article. All these measures use IT to overcome the challenges of pandemics such as COVID-19[45]:

- While making your IT infrastructure more robust and agile, you should strengthen your digital infrastructure to deal with COVID-19 and surpass any future pandemics and public health crises.
- Artificial intelligence, data analytics, and healthcare systems should be tightly integrated into the public health response to deal with a global crisis or pandemic such as COVID-19.
- Big data, software, and analytical tools can be used to track diseases, citizens' movements, and disease transmission patterns. All these tools, data, and patterns could be used for the prevention of the spread of disease during a pandemic.

FOUR CRITICAL CRISIS MANAGEMENT LESSONS

PricewaterhouseCooper (PWC), in its article *COVID-19: Four essential crisis management lessons,* mentioned four key areas to overcome the challenges during a pandemic[46]. Based on PWC's article and our research and experience, the following four lessons can be highly beneficial for leaders, project managers, and organizations[46]:

Keep Your Employees and Work Environment Safe and Healthy

During a pandemic or crisis, employees and team members look to their leaders for guidance, help, response, and comfort. Therefore, you as a leader of the organization and team must find ways to ensure reliable and timely communication, provide a safe and secure physical and virtual environment, make yourself available to listen and address employees' issues and concerns. You should review and customize your HR and telecommuting policies, procedures, and guidelines according to the challenges posed by the pandemic and crisis. You must be creative in devising the policies and procedures according to the "new normal" because they have to be flexible, agile, and practical. Your employees must feel safe, healthy, and secure while at work physically or virtually.

Focus on Data Accuracy and Reliability

Accurate and reliable data is vital during a pandemic or crisis, especially for planning, communication, risk mitigation, response preparation, and decision-making. According to a 2019 Global Survey conducted by PWC, three-quarters of companies surveyed that had accurate and reliable data fared better in a post-crisis environment than their counterparts. Having reliable and accurate data leads to better scenario planning, crisis response, communication with the stakeholders, risk mitigation strategies, and decision-making.

Build a Robust and Cross-Functional Response Team

Pandemics and a global crisis such as COVID-19 usually impact all areas of the business internally and externally. Therefore, you must create a cross-functional and robust team that has in-depth knowledge of the organization's business and customers. Having a high-performance and cross-functional team would lead to a holistic, effective, productive, and timely response. Ideally, the team should be headed by the CEO for small-to-midsize companies, but it could be headed by a Division or Regional President for large corporations and multinationals. The team must be represented by leaders from HR, IT, finance, customer service, marketing, supply chain, and other key business functions according to the business needs.

Test Your Business Continuity and Crisis Management Plans

Your organization most probably has a business continuity and crisis management plan. If not, you must have one. Otherwise, it might threaten the company or organization's core business as well as survival. For those companies that have a business continuity and crisis management plan, they should test them. Companies that either don't have crisis management plans or don't test them find themselves in hot waters when a crisis hits them. For example, most of the K-12 schools in the US and around the world did not have any contingency and crisis management plans to cope with a crisis such as COVID-19. Schools were not equipped with the proper IT infrastructure and network, teachers were not trained on the necessary online teaching platforms, and students were also not prepared for online learning. That's why schools, teachers, students, and parents struggled for months during COVID-19 because the schools did not have crisis management plans in place, and nobody knew what to do.

During COVID-19, a lot of companies found gaps and flaws in their business continuity plans, so it's always a good idea to test and update them every six months. If a disaster or crisis occurs during the six months of updating and testing your plan, you should be okay as no drastic changes in technology would transpire in six months. Based on your business, if you feel the need, you should update and test your plans quarterly.

IT INFRASTRUCTURE REQUIRED DURING A CRISIS

During pre-pandemic times, before forced shutdowns of whole industries and stay-at-home restrictions, the primary method for dealing with any significant disruption was disaster recovery. Few, if any, could have anticipated the effect a pandemic would have on businesses worldwide. COVID-19 completely upturned the normal work culture. As far as one can see, what will likely determine a company's success or demise will be the level of preparation, or lack thereof, as they encounter the next disaster. This whole scenario leads to the question: What steps can companies take to upgrade their IT Infrastructure? To answer this question, we would take examples from Stephen Wynn's article *How Can IT Infrastructure Help Your Business Prepare for Next Pandemic*[47]? Wynn is the CEO of BOOMTECH and also an IT and cybersecurity expert.

We all know that Companies can and should improve their IT infrastructure to give them an edge in case another disaster comes knocking. The question is: how? Below are some of the critical steps that companies can take to beef up their IT infrastructure and be ready for the next pandemic or crisis.

Remote Productivity

Successful companies used platforms like Microsoft (MS) Teams to stay in touch with their employees. The latest tools and technology allowed employees to work remotely from home. That ensured efficient collaboration among team members, enhanced productivity, and the completion of the tasks. An increase in remote IT infrastructures made it possible for organizations such as healthcare, education, and others to survive and prosper.

Cybersecurity

Due to the enforcement of worldwide lockdowns, work-from-home policies were quickly implemented. However, one major flaw which was left largely unconsidered was that of security. As a result, hackers swarmed to infiltrate private business networks. Therefore, to protect valuable information and their companies' integrity, employers will need to strengthen their cybersecurity systems. Some possible ways of doing so include the use of Virtual Private Networks (VPNs), state of the art antivirus software, constant monitoring of potential threats, encryption of all data transfers, and cybersecurity training. Preventative measures are always better than curative ones. It is best to be prepared for hackers before they even have a chance to attack your computers and systems.

Gartner CFO Survey in 2020 revealed that over 74% of CFOs intend to shift some employees to remote work permanently[48]. The primary reasons behind this change are concerns about another wave of COVID-19 and possible reductions in costs. Employers are hoping to decrease expenses such as office space and unnecessary hardware. The current business environment has no choice but to embrace the world of IT, at the very least, to avoid paying for office spaces that will end up not being used. Moreover, having a larger presence on online platforms will open up doors to the digital economy.

TEN BEST PRACTICES FOR CYBERSECURITY

No matter what type of business we are in, we cannot escape from IT these days. That's why robust cybersecurity and IT infrastructure are essential for virtual teams to function during a crisis. As a leader, you must ensure that team members are well-equipped and have the requisite and secure IT infrastructure to do their work. We have discussed emotional intelligence, decency quotient (DQ), and team-building models in Chapters 2 and 6, but we want to emphasize the need for a strong IT infrastructure for high-performance teams to function. If team members don't have a reliable and efficient network and are unable to connect with each other, it would be enormously challenging, if not impossible, to create a high-performance team.

Cybersecurity is at the heart of everything that we do these days. Most of us use multiple devices to connect to work, i.e., mobile phones, laptops, desktop computers, and others. The more devices we use, the more vulnerable we become. That does not mean you should not use multiple devices. Sure, you can use multiple devices, but you need to connect using a secure network and ensure that your personal, as well as company's data, is secure.

Whether we log into the internet or intranet-based applications, cybersecurity is critical. Securing personal and company data is both crucial and challenging. This is even more critical during a crisis or pandemic. Companies and governments around the world face the challenges of keeping their data safe and secure. The cost of a security breach and data leakage can run into millions of dollars. That's why, as a leader, you must provide a reliable and secure virtual environment to the team. For example, a lot of fake unemployment claims were filed in the US in 2020 during COVID-19. Most of them were due to a security breach and data leakage where employees' social security numbers, date of birth, and other sensitive data fell into the wrong hands. People found out about the fake claims after they received 1099 Forms from the State unemployment agencies, which caused enormous stress and aggravation. Just imagine if one of your teammates had received a notice about a fake from one of the State agencies. It would probably be extremely difficult for him/her to focus on the work while trying to straighten out the mess.

Without getting into too many technical details, we have laid out the ten best practices on cybersecurity, in this chapter, as a general understanding for the readers, so they understand cybersecurity is critical for virtual environments and high-performance teams to operate. Teams cannot function without having a strong, reliable, and efficient IT environment, including cybersecurity.

Cyber threats have become a daily phenomenon, which is why we have decided to list the ten best practices that companies can follow regarding data and cybersecurity. This list has been devised based on my own experience as well as various industry reports published by Gartner[48], University of California Berkley[49], and Norton[50].

Multi-Factor or 2-Factor Authentication

One of the secure ways to login to an application is to use multi-factor or 2-factor authentication. You would log in to an application using an ID and password, but the system would also send you a security code via a registered email or mobile phone that you would need to enter to complete the login.

Use Strong Passwords

This is the most obvious and simple technique but often overlooked. The best practice is to use a minimum of ten characters and a combination of letters, digits, upper case, and lower case letters. There is a website called *betterbuys.com,* where you may test how strong your password is. According to Betterbuys, if you have a simple password with only seven characters like "hijklmn," a hacker could probably crack it in a few seconds. If you make it eight characters, it could take 5 hours to crack. Nine characters would take 5 days, ten characters would take 4 months, and 11 characters would take about 10 years to break. Interestingly, if you make your password 12 characters long, it could take 200 years to break. Again, if you are curious how long it would take to break your password, you may want to test it on Betterbuys.com.

Data Backup

Make sure your personal, as well as company's data, is backed up on a daily, weekly, and monthly basis. You must use redundant means of backup, don't rely on just one source for data backup. For example, I backup personal data on an external drive and storage platforms like Dropbox. I learned this lesson the hard way. A few years ago, I was traveling to Europe on a business trip, and on my way back from France to the US, my laptop was stolen at the Paris airport. Luckily, I had finished the client's work and stored all the data on my external drive. I only lost a couple of days' worth of data. That's when I learned to back up my data daily.

Use of Virtual Private Network (VPN)

Since most of us work from home during a crisis or pandemic such as COVID-19, I highly recommend using a VPN to connect to your company's network and systems. Public and home networks are the most vulnerable and easy target for hackers. Some companies have policies that require employees to use VPN when logging into the system remotely. If you travel outside the US on a business trip, it can increase the security threat, so you should take extra precautions to protect your personal and company data. And that's why using a VPN to connect to the company's system is highly recommended for overseas travel.

Protect the Email Gateway

Most of the cyberattacks happen through emails, where hackers send an email or link. As soon as the recipient opens the email, a virus or malware is executed. It can transmit your data to hackers. That's why you should not open emails and links from unknown sources or senders. I remember getting emails during the Thanksgiving and Christmas holidays with fake sender names like Walmart, Target, and others. Even though the label had a vendor name like Walmart, it was not from the Walmart domain when I looked at the sender's email address. Rather, it was from some unknown domain name. That is why you should pay attention to both the sender's name as well as the email address before opening an unknown email.

Firewall Protection for Work and Home Networks

Most companies install firewalls to protect attacks on websites, intranet, emails, and other systems. You should also install a firewall on your home network, especially if you work from home during a crisis or pandemic such as COVID-19. Your company's IT department should be able to help you with that.

Beware of Phishing and Pop-Ups

The term phishing is just like fishing on a lake or river where hackers would send you the bait via an email or pop-up. If you open the email or click on the pop-up, you would have taken the bait, and it might activate a virus or malware on your laptop, mobile phone, or desktop computer. I have been a victim of phishing and clicked on a pop-up while browsing on my mobile phone. My phone data was wiped out, and I had to reset my phone and re-install all the applications.

Understand Your Company's Policies on Data and System Access

A lot of companies give laptops to their employees with security software and VPN installed on them. They don't want employees to access the systems using their personal laptops due to hackers' threats and loss of confidential data and information. If your company's policy does not allow you to access their network and systems using your personal computer, then you should not. Otherwise, you might be held liable for a breach of your company's policies.

Install Antivirus and Anti-malware Software

It probably sounds intuitive, but a lot of people either forget or are too lazy to install antivirus or anti-malware software on their laptops, desktops, and mobile phone. We think that a virus won't attack us. Let's be realistic and practical. The threat of a virus is real, and it can and probably will happen to us if we don't take the necessary precautions. Therefore, you must install antivirus and anti-malware software on all of your devices.

Keep Latest Software Versions on Your Devices

Most of us make the mistake of not updating our operating system, thinking it's unnecessary or will do it later. Procrastination could cost you dearly in losing your personal or company's data or inadvertently leaking the data and confidential information to hackers. You must update your operating system promptly.

IT INFRASTRUCTURE AND THE DIGITAL ECONOMY

As the pandemic wanes and things begin to reopen, headlines about large chains shutting down are flowing in. Many of these companies focused more on keeping their existing physical spaces afloat and less on creating and promoting an online platform for their clients. However, companies that rose to the task of being present online are now not only surviving but thriving in the digital economy.

In his article, Wynn said, one prominent example of a company jumping on the IT bandwagon is that of Alibaba. As Brian A. Wong, Alibaba executive said, in the World Economic Forum[47]:

> Seventeen years ago, the outbreak of SARS was spreading rapidly across China, and the Alibaba workforce had gone into quarantine. At the time, Alibaba was only four years old, and it was unclear whether the young start-up would survive. Suspending operations would have dealt a devastating blow to the company. But Alibaba employees packed up their desktop computers and telephones, carried piles of documents home, and began to work. The crisis was, in hindsight, a transformative moment for the company[47].

As we can now clearly see, having a robust IT infrastructure allows companies to better stay in touch with their employees and clients in times of turmoil. Building and maintaining high-quality online platforms and offering remote professional services can no longer be considered optional. A strong IT infrastructure and online presence are a necessity for any company wishing to stay alive during a pandemic or its equivalent.

VIRTUAL COLLABORATION SOFTWARE AND TOOLS REQUIRED DURING A CRISIS

The good news is that there are many collaboration software and tools readily available in the market that can facilitate high-performance teams. Most of us are familiar with Zoom, Slack, Go-To-Meetings, and others. It is fairly easy to learn how to use them. Employees and teams can use them with almost a click of a few buttons on their smartphones, laptops, or desktops. Some of these allow you to change your backgrounds, such as customized pictures or landmarks such as the Grand Canyon, Eiffel Tower, or a Ski resort in Switzerland. It makes meetings more fun and lively to see people with nice and interesting backgrounds.

If I look back 15 years, we did not have any of these tools available. We only had video conferencing, which everybody could not afford because the equipment was so expensive. Only the corporations and businesses had the budget to install video conferencing gear. On the other hand, virtual reality technology is becoming the norm, and the cost of connecting with employees has come down enormously. Some large companies and medium-to-small size businesses have been thinking about either eliminating or significantly reducing the physical office space, especially in industries like IT, telecom, financial services, and others.

The concept of a virtual office is here, thanks to COVID-19. Companies and employees have realized that a physical office is no longer a requirement, especially for non-customer facing activities. For example, software developers can sit anywhere in the world and do their work. They don't have to come to the office every day. The new phenomenon or the "new normal" of working remotely during COVID-19 has allowed businesses to cut costs and increase their revenues. Online retailers such as Amazon, Apple, and others have thrived in the pandemic. In his article, *The Next Generation of Office Communication Tech,* Ethan Murray described how companies have been using collaboration tools and virtual meeting software to reduce their on-site footprints by a third[51]. Employees no longer have to commute to work, which has cut down on the environmental pollution as well as employees' travel time to work. Working remotely can be a win-win for businesses, employees, and the environment.

There are many ways to enable the virtual environment using technology that teams can leverage for their daily work. It is essential for teams, especially project teams, to have the ability to connect with other teammates seamlessly. And that's possible through the latest tools and technology. Murray has also discussed some of these tools and techniques. We will reference them in our discussion in the next few sections[51].

Virtual Offices

The concept of virtual office space has been around for a while. About 20 years ago, when I worked for Deloitte Consulting, we did not have a fixed office space. The hoteling concept was introduced, and Deloitte consultants booked their office space like a hotel by dialing a number and reserving it for a specific day and time. With COVID-19, the concept got transformed and eliminated the physical space altogether. Now, all of us can set up a virtual office with voicemail, call forwarding, an Executive assistant working remotely, and a whole lot of other features. And the best part is that your virtual office can stay open 24 × 7. For example, I have a Skype number that works globally, and I can attend to customers' calls from anywhere in the world. The best part is that my customers in the US call a local number, and it does not cost them anything. I even get voicemails through Skype, and I can listen to them anytime. I pay a small monthly subscription fee to Skype, and my virtual office stays open seven days a week.

A virtual office plays a significant role in creating and leading high-performance teams. As a leader, it is relatively easier for you to arrange meetings and talk to the team. People can join remotely and share their ideas. All you need is a mobile phone and internet connection, which are readily available in the US. Thus, teams can perform effectively and efficiently using the virtual office space.

Virtual Focus Groups

If you talk to a Head of Marketing, researcher, or anybody involved in consumer surveys, he/she would tell you how hard it is to conduct focus groups. It used to be a nightmare to schedule them and book an office space. With new technology, we can arrange virtual focus groups and get feedback effectively and efficiently. The good part is that no physical meeting and office space are required. It saves time and cost for businesses as well as employees. Virtual focus groups enhance teams' efficiency and help the leaders create high-performance teams using the feedback from the focus groups.

Technologies like Artificial Intelligence (AI) can be used to interpret and analyze the data that comes out of the virtual focus groups. Since most of the platforms allow you to conduct virtual polls and take notes during virtual meetings, it is relatively easier to collect data and run it through AI software. Again, the latest tools and technology can help leaders building high-performance teams during the "new normal" that we all have discovered through COVID-19.

In addition, companies can use virtual focus groups to gain knowledge of their own companies. For example, the concept of focus groups can be highly effective and useful when company executives are looking to understand the organization's culture. In his article, Murray described an example of a bank that used the concept of virtual groups to improve the status of inclusion and diversity across the organization[51]. It achieved this by interviewing 1,200 employees divided into 20 groups of 60-persons each. Now imagine, 15 years ago, arranging 20 virtual groups with 60 people in each group, it could have been almost impossible to organize so many focus groups in a short time span[51]. Again, these are all ideas for leaders to create high-performance teams in their organizations and make a difference.

Virtual Collaboration

Lastly, due to the pandemic, many employers have had no choice but to halt various initiatives because they could no longer have their employees go to the office and work on projects. With the introduction of virtual offices, however, employers and employees can now continue working on existing and new projects and initiatives.

Many companies have jumped straight into the world of virtual meetings by incorporating instruments like shared whiteboards and co-editing of documents to allow people to work together without the need to be in the same room. Some companies have even made greater leaps using virtual offices than they had during pre-pandemic times. For example, a bank actually launched an online banking business using their virtual office in less time than it had taken them to do the same for another project a year before when people psychically came to work[51]. This was an example of a high-performance that was created during COVID-19 and achieved results better than the pre-pandemic days. The team's success highlights another pertinent point that some of the best teams are created during a crisis, as highlighted in the case study in Part II of this book.

The primary reason for the success of virtual environments could be that using video and audio paired with collaboration instruments brings all the members of the team to the same level playing field. The people who previously did not get a chance to speak up due to louder or overpowering team members can now give their input using their preferred mode of interaction. Moreover, people who couldn't be present for an out-of-town meeting in person are now relieved of the tension of having to fly in to attend the meeting. Therefore, due to an overall increase in all the members' engagement and presence, teams have made greater strides when it comes to brainstorming and performance, which can help create high-performance teams.

Another hidden perk of virtual offices is that the contents of meetings are now already digitized, which saves the time it would have taken to copy work off of a whiteboard or notepad and then transfer to formal reports. Hence, the virtual platforms and meetings have enabled teams to have an open, transparent, and efficient discussion and flow of ideas.

Mixed Reality Realms

We are only at the beginning of what the world of virtual offices will open for us. At this time last year, in 2019, no one could have foreseen that the spread of work-from-home would be this great. Yet almost all major companies are looking for new methods to make virtual environments the norm, becoming the *new normal.*

These changes will surely lead us into a new world of virtual reality where artificial intelligence instruments could be used to make virtual meetings as pleasant as possible, 3D printers could allow teams to test their designs from anywhere in the world. Also, delivery services could use drones for faster home delivery competitively and cost-effectively.

If we look back 15 years, installing video conferencing equipment and high-definition cameras was not only time-consuming but expensive as well. The old technology seems like a pile of rubble sitting in our garage, and we might say the same thing about today's technology. With time, either Skype or Zoom will be replaced by something more effective and efficient, or they might transform themselves into a better and enhanced platform. Having new and better collaboration platforms and technology will enable leaders to make high-performance teams more creative, efficient, and productive.

BUILDING PSYCHOLOGICAL SAFETY FOR A VIRTUAL WORK ENVIRONMENT

Psychological safety has come to light lately and has become more vital during COVID-19. It is defined as an environment where employees and team members can share their ideas, thoughts without the fear of being reprimanded by their bosses or senior management. If employees don't feel psychologically safe, it will kill the creativity, motivation, and productivity of teams, which could obstruct the creation of high-performance teams. Thus, leaders must ensure that employees feel safe and secure while speaking their minds and ideas in virtual meetings, which is the foundation of psychological safety.

The disruption in business activity that the COVID-19 pandemic caused has been immense. Organizations are forced to institute the work-from-home policy for all of their non-essential employees. Non-essential is defined as people who are not required to be on-site to do their jobs, i.e., software developers, financial services staff, and others. Suppose the pandemic's uncertain nature is not bad enough; In that case, people soon will have to face the challenges of psychological safety while working in a virtual environment such as work-from-home. The question is: what can leaders do to create psychological safety for teams in a virtual environment during a crisis? This section analyzes the tools and techniques that can be leveraged to create psychological safety for virtual teams and the environment.

The benefits of conducting face-to-face meetings include examining body language and facial expressions, which might not be too obvious in a virtual environment. However, with high-quality video calls, it is possible to assess body language. In their HBR article *How to Foster Psychological Safety in Virtual Meetings,* Edmonson and Daley described that sometimes all we need to calm our nerves is the subtle nod of agreement of a colleague sitting across from us[52]. With COVID-19, we probably won't be able to sit across the table from our colleagues and teammates. However, we can still use the latest technology, video conferencing, and collaboration to provide psychological safety and achieve our objectives.

Edmonson and Daley, in their HBR article, defined some of the tools and techniques to enhance psychological safety for virtual environments are listed below[52]. A practical example of the use of these tools and techniques is described at the end of this chapter.

   a. Hand-raise
   b. Yes/No
   c. Polls
   d. Chat
   e. Breakout rooms
   f. Video and Audio-only

CASE STUDY: CREATING PSYCHOLOGICAL SAFETY IN A VIRTUAL ENVIRONMENT ON THE GMS PROJECT

Most of these tools and techniques mentioned in this chapter were used by Max Dillon (the Business Sponsor) of the Grants Management System (GMS) project that is described in Part II of this book. Max would kick-off the weekly virtual status meeting and remind everyone to talk freely about risks, issues, and concerns, which provided psychological safety to the GMS team. As soon as Max announced, all team members would feel immensely comfortable and spoke their minds and shared ideas and concerns about the project. The team used to have healthy discussions and debates on the weekly status calls, which indicated that Max successfully provided psychological safety to the team.

Some people used the audio-only, and others utilized the video functionality. Max allowed people to choose any mode they felt the most comfortable with: audio-only or video. Again, this was one of the ways Max provided psychological safety to employees in a virtual environment. He made sure that everyone was comfortable to share their ideas and concerns. Max was interested in people's creativity, ideas, and resolutions to the project team's issues and challenges. He did not care what mode of communication employees chose as long as they were happy and comfortable and contributed towards the project's success.

There were times when discussions got too heated, and Max intervened. He requested the participants to take the discussion offline because there were 40+ people at the status meetings, and he wanted to give everyone a chance to speak. Max would also volunteer to participate and moderate the offline discussions if the team members wanted him to attend. He did not force himself into meetings or discussions. He also used to follow-up with key team members or anyone facing the issues after the status call. He held one-on-one sessions with teammates and ensured that they felt safe and secure to discuss their issues, and provided them the full support. Team members really appreciated Max's support and follow-up. They felt appreciated and motivated by his care and guidance. Resultantly, Max created a high-performance (The Blue Shark) team on the GMS project.

6

The Blue Shark Model of Leading High-Performance Teams

Based on my industry, consulting, and academia experience, we have devised the "Blue Shark Model of Leading High-Performance Teams." As shown in Figure 6.1, the Blue Shark Model has been adopted from Daniel Goleman's emotional intelligence and Bruce Tuckman's team-building model. You might be wondering why we called it "The Blue Shark." The name is similar to the Blue Ocean Strategy[53]. Professors W. Chan Kim and Renee Mauborgne of INSEAD Business School have defined Blue Ocean Strategy as creating new markets for your products and services and stop competing in overcrowded markets and industries called red oceans. They said: *competing in overcrowded industries is no way to sustain high performance. The real opportunity is to create blue oceans of uncontested market space.*[53] Thus, as a leader, you can build a high-performance team using the Blue Shark Model and successfully manage and overcome a crisis.

Examples of the blue ocean strategy include Skype, Wikipedia, and Apple Macintosh computer with a Graphical User Interface (GUI). All these products and services changed the landscape in their industries, increased the size of the pie, and made the competition irrelevant in the short-to-medium term. Since there would be hardly any competition, in the beginning, that's why it's called the blue ocean strategy as opposed to the Red Ocean full of sharks (competition) that would eat your lunch.

Through her research, Audrey Epstein compared the two teams: low-performing (saboteur teams) and high-performing (loyalist teams)[54]. She used the terms "saboteur" and "loyalist," but we will stick with low-performing and high-performing teams. Audrey mentioned in the HBR

DOI: 10.1201/9781003216711-7

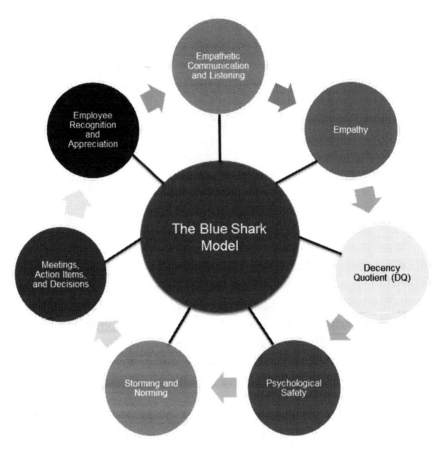

FIGURE 6.1
The blue shark model of leading high-performance teams.

Source: Adopted from Daniel Goleman[1] and Bruce Tuckman's Model[2].

article, compared to low-performing (saboteur) teams, high-performing (loyalist) teams were[54]:

- *292 times more likely to spend time debating, discussing problems, and making decisions.*
- *125 times more likely to address unacceptable team behaviors promptly.*
- *106 times more likely to give each other tough feedback.*
- *40 times less likely to have "undiscussables" that the team can't talk openly about.*

Daniel Pink wrote in his book, *A Whole New Mind: Why Right-Brainers will Rule the Future,* our society has started to acknowledge the new skills such as creativity, empathy, and intuition as opposed to automation, systems, and computers[55]. He stated:

> I say, "Get me some poets as managers." Poets are our original systems thinkers. They contemplate the world in which we live and feel obligated to interpret and give expression to it in a way that makes the reader understand how that world runs. Poets, those unheralded systems thinkers, are our true digital thinkers. It is from their midst that I believe we will draw tomorrow's new business leaders[55].

After reviewing Audrey's results, conducting our research over the years, and based on my industry and academia experience, we have created the Blue Shark Model of building and leading high-performance teams. As mentioned earlier, our model is built on a solid foundation of Goleman's emotional intelligence and Tuckman's team-building model. That's why deploying the Blue Shark Model can help you build and lead a high-performance (The Blue Shark) team and organization that can help you cope with any crisis efficaciously. It can make your company outshine in the industry and deliver projects successfully. The Blue Shark Team can be an uncontested winner in uncharted territory and crises such as a pandemic.

There are seven components of the Blue Shark Model that are shown in Figure 6.1 and elaborated in this chapter:

1. Empathetic Communication and Listening
2. Empathy
3. Decency Quotient (DQ)
4. Psychological Safety
5. Storming and Norming
6. Meetings, Actions Items, and Decision-Making
7. Employee Recognition and Appreciation

EMPATHETIC COMMUNICATION AND LISTENING

If one element that we could overemphasize or re-iterate during a crisis, such as COVID-19, would be empathetic communication and listening. It is also called reflective communication. It would help if you think before you speak. As a leader, you must analyze the impact of your words and action on other people, including your teammates. A sub-element of empathetic communication is empathetic listening. It is also called active listening or reflective listening. It is a way of listening and responding to another person that improves mutual understanding and trust[54]. A leader must listen to his/her employees, colleagues, customers, and other stakeholders very carefully. It means, as a leader, you must pay very close attention to your employees, teammates, and stakeholders and reflect on what they communicate. It would be best if you tried to understand their perspective to react and respond empathetically. That's why we start with empathetic communication and listening in the Blue Shark Team model, as shown in Figure 6.1.

In her article, *The Secret to Organizational Change is Empathy*, Patti Sanchez said: "Studies on organizational change show that leaders across the board agree: if you want to lead a successful transformation, communicating empathetically is critical[54]." It indicates that empathy, organizational change, and empathetic communication are intertwined. Thus, it also shows that *empathetic communication* is one of the critical success factors in leading high-performance teams. Empathetic communication takes into account the following key elements[54]. Table 6.1 shows examples of empathetic and bad communication.

- *What we say or do.*
- *The way we say or do it.*
- *Our impact on other people.*

If there were one piece of advice that I had for you, it would be this. Whenever you need something from a colleague, team member, or anybody and you had to write an email, I recommend starting the email like this:

Hi [name of the person]: I need your help....

You would not believe the impact this small and simple sentence has on people: *I need your help.* I have tried and tested this technique around the globe hundreds of times in my career, and it has worked every time. No matter how difficult or tough a person you encounter, as soon as someone reads this sentence, he/she mallows down. I have tested it around the world in North America, Europe, Middle East, and Asia. This is a universal sentence like the word "love." Everyone wants to be loved and appreciated. Similarly, most people (if not everybody) are willing to help when you ask them.

TABLE 6.1

Examples of Bad Communication Versus Empathetic Communication

Description	Bad Communication	Empathetic Communication
What we say or do	Mark, you said you were going to send me the communication plan. You have not sent it yet. I need it today.	Mark, I need your help. As discussed, can you please send me the communication plan. I would really appreciate if you send it by Thursday 01/28/2021 because I need to send it to my Manager by Friday 01/29/2021.
The way we say or do it	David, do you hate the proposal that I sent you? Since you did not respond in the last 24 hours, you must hate my ideas.	David, hope all is well. I just wanted to follow up on the proposal that I emailed you yesterday. I know you are very busy, but I wanted to get your valuable feedback. I would highly appreciate your response by close of business today, because I need to get back to the client.
Our impact on other people	Lisa, I told you that you could not take a day off anymore. I don't care if someone is sick in your family. We need you at work 8:00 a.m.	Lisa, I noticed that you were off yesterday. Is everything okay with you and the family? Is there anything that I can do to help?

Even people who don't like you or don't want to cooperate with you, as soon as they read this sentence: *I need your help.* They soften up and would try to help or respond positively. Basically, by asking for help, you are lowering your ego and showing humbleness. In addition, you elevate the other person's position by making him/her feel more capable, and it works like a charm. Most people respond positively to humbleness. Thus, you would get a favorable response to your request.

EMPATHY

We have explained Empathy in Chapter 2 as part of Daniel Goleman's model. It is described as listening to each other, understanding peoples' feelings, and putting yourself in other team members' shoes. Jamil Zaki, a Professor of Psychology at Stanford University, mentioned in the HBR article: "In a survey of 150 CEOs, over 80% recognized empathy as a key

CASE STUDY: EMPATHETIC
COMMUNICATION AND LISTENING

It was 10:00 a.m. on November 25, 2020 (right before the Thanksgiving holiday), the weekly status meeting for the GMS project started as usual. John (the Project Manager from the client-side) greeted everybody and noticed that Max (the Business Sponsor) and Jim Holster (the software vendor's Project Manager) had not joined, so he sent them a quick email. Max joined at 10:02 a.m. and apologized for being late because he was in another meeting. Jim sent a message that he was having trouble connecting through MS Teams. Anyway, he was able to join, and the meeting started at 10:05 a.m. There were 20+ team members on the call including, people from WSDOT, consultants, the external quality assurance team, representatives of the IT Division, and others.

The top two items on the agenda were related to Jim. Instead of starting on a positive note, he said, *we have reviewed your request that was sent last week and cannot meet most of your requirements.* Jim was not listening and did not offer any empathy to the client, which are the basic principles of empathetic communication and listening. Just so that the readers have the context, the two changes requested to be made to the software were critical for running the business, and they were both marked as *show-stoppers.* Meaning, the project would not move forward without those two changes. Jim not only said that one of them was not supported by the system, but he also refused to make any modifications or customization to the software, even though the client was willing to pay for the customization. A serious communication breakdown occurred: Jim was not listening, and the client kept repeating the requirements.

Even though John had informed Jim about the agenda and severity of the two issues, Jim was not only ill-prepared for the meeting, but his communication style also lacked empathetic listening. Jim completely ignored John's warnings and put his foot in his mouth. He continued to refuse to make the modifications to the system. This was an example of poor communication, lack of empathy, and bad listening skills on Jim's part.

John tried to intervene to calm down the situation, but Max had already reached the frustration point by then. As soon as he heard

Jim's continuous refusal and noticed that he was adamant, Max took the ultimate position and threatened Jim with the contract's cancellation unless these changes were made to the system.

The entire conversation took place in front of about 20+ team members. It was all due to Jim's inability to listen and comprehend the situation. Not only did he embarrass himself in front of the team members representing the client and other consultants on the project, but he also made the entire meeting so contentious that everybody started to feel embarrassed and shocked. Finally, Nick Flyer (the Technology Work Stream Lead) intervened and tried to calm down the situation. Nick said: *Jim, all we are asking for is an estimate on the timeline and cost to make the changes.* Finally, Jim started to back down and said that he could go back to his team and provide us the estimates on time and cost after the Thanksgiving holidays. John saw an opportunity to diffuse the situation and immediately recapped, thanked Nick and Jim, and moved onto the next agenda item.

What could have been a 30-second conversation was dragged on for 30 minutes due to Jim's poor empathetic communication and listening skills. All he had to do was to listen and request John and Max to take it offline and discuss the issue further. Alternatively, he could have said: "Sure, we would look into your request and get back to you." Instead, he kept saying, *No, these changes cannot be done!* He was not even hearing what the client was asking. Furthermore, Jim did not even realize that it was the day before Thanksgiving, and everybody wanted to take a break, go home, and spend time with their families. Project team members were tired, anxious, and overwhelmed due to COVID-19. They all wanted to have the meeting in a cordial manner and go home happy. Unfortunately, Jim did not grasp the idea of leveraging EQ, empathetic listening, and he chose the wrong time to have an antagonistic conversation. Not only was his style bad, but his timing was also poor.

The moral of the story is; had Jim used empathetic listening, empathy and taken the conversation offline, it would have saved him much time, energy, and embarrassment. After watching both Jim and Max, the entire team's mood got quite somber. The timing of having a heated discussion right before the Thanksgiving holiday was terrible. Jim could have easily requested to postpone the discussion until after the holidays when everyone would have been more relaxed, energetic, and fresh. Sometimes, it's okay to postpone or delay the conversation. As we saw in this case, the timing of a meeting or discussion can also be crucial, along with empathetic communication and listening.

to success[57]." Zaki is also the author of the book: "The War for Kindness: Building Empathy in a Fractured World." In his book, he said: *people adhere to kind and productive norms75*. He also went on to say: *Empathy is contagious: People catch each other's care and altruism[57]*. This phenomenon indicates if you, as a leader, practice empathy, it can replicate throughout the organization and team, which in turn can transform your organization and team as "high-performance." That's why *empathy* is one of the core elements of The Blue Shark Model (Figure 6.1) of creating and leading high-performance teams and organizations.

Understanding your team members' concerns and perspectives is crucial to earning their trust as well as building a bond with them. As Daniel Goleman mentioned[1], it is vital to understand your employees' and team members' feelings, especially during the decision-making process. The empathy level becomes even more crucial in a tumultuous situation, such as the COVID-19 crisis. Some of your decisions can have a profound and long-lasting impact on employees. Thus, as a leader, you must be enormously careful in assessing their impact and seek input from employees and key stakeholders before making those decisions. As Patti Sanchez summed it very meritoriously in her article[56]:

Develop and show Empathy for everyone involved in your corporate transition, and you will lead a team that feels valued, included, and driven to help your initiative succeed[56].

We all have either seen or worked with leaders that use linear, logical, or evidence-based decision-making, but we live in a different time and environment. The world has changed a lot in the last 30 years. Thus, leaders need a different approach and leadership style to manage and lead organizations, teams, and projects. Imi Lo, the author of the book Emotional

Intensity and Sensitivity, said: *For more than 100 years, the sequential, linear, and logical were praised. As we move towards a different economic era, the world's leaders will need to be creators and empathizers*[58]. Imi is right; we need more leaders who can empathize and create harmony within their teams, companies, societies, and countries. That's why we need leaders with emotional intelligence skills such as Empathy.

Post COVID-19 Future of Workplaces and Employees

In its February 2021 report, *The Future of Work After COVID-19,* Mckinsey Global Institute's research findings showed: *workers will need to learn more social and emotional skills, as well as technological skills, in order to move into occupations in higher wage brackets*[43]. A summary of their findings on social and emotional skills is shown in Figure 6.2. It supports our point about the need for leaders to develop emotional intelligence, social, and team-building skills. The McKinsey study also mentions that

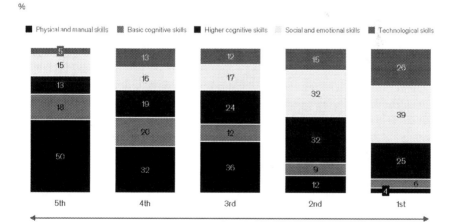

Workers will need to learn more social and emotional skills, as well as technological skills, in order to move into occupations in higher wage brackets.

Time spent using skills in each skill category by wage quintile in the United States¹
%

■ Physical and manual skills   ▨ Basic cognitive skills   ■ Higher cognitive skills   ░ Social and emotional skills   ▨ Technological skills

5th	4th	3rd	2nd	1st
5	13	12	15	26
15	16	17	32	39
13	19	24	32	25
18	20	12	9	6
50	32	36	12	4

Lowest wage quintile   Highest wage quintile

1.   Using O*NET data, more than 2,000 work activities for more than 800 occupations were classified according to the primary skill used.
Source: Employment and Training Administration, US Department of Labor; O*NETOnLine; US Bureau of Labor Statistics; McKinsey Global Institute analysis

FIGURE 6.2
McKinsey's research findings on social and emotional skills.

Source: McKinsey Global Institute[43].

worhkers who want to move into the highest wage quintile would need to spend more time and effort in learning social and emotional skills.

Employees are the most critical asset that any company can have to create a competitive advantage. As Jon Meliones, Chief Medical Director at Duke Children's Hospital (DCH), said:

> "We should listen to our employees. Instead of issuing orders, ask them: what can we (as an organization) do[59]?"

Once you listen to your employees, you will be pleasantly surprised with the suggestions and solutions that employees share with you. That's why legendary CEOs like Andy Grove of Intel, Jack Welch of General Electric (GE), Herb Kelleher of Southwest Airlines, and others listened to their employees and practiced *management by wandering around (MBWA)*. They would wander around various departments, talk to the front-line employees, and listen to them. That's how they would find out about issues, customers' needs, and solutions to many problems.

The premise behind listening to employees and team members is that they are in the trenches on a daily basis, so they understand the issues and customers' requirements. They are in a better position to recommend solutions. Sure, as a leader, you need to leverage your knowledge and expertise and then decide. But, the decision must be based on data, evidence, and employees' feedback. Even if you make a wrong decision, at least you would have the data and team to back you up. Leaders all over the world make bad decisions, but the key is to listen to your employees, learn from your mistakes, and not repeat them.

As we saw in the case study described earlier under the empathetic communication and listening section, Jim Holster did not offer any empathy to the client. He did not even realize the fact that the client was trying to cooperate with him and was seeking his help on the two issues. After noticing his adamant behavior, Max Dillon (the Business Sponsor) also switched his behavior and attitude and gave up on empathy. He took a hard stance and demanded the changes. Otherwise, the contract with Jim's company would be canceled. This was an example where both sides lost the focus and objectivity and showed no empathy for each other, which resulted in a very contentious and embarrassing situation. All Jim and John had to do were to empathize and listen to each other. Unfortunately, we see this kind of behavior in meetings all the time. As a leader, you must stay calm and leverage your emotional intelligence skills, including empathy and self-discipline, to overcome the situation. Practicing empathy and check-ing-in with colleagues daily or weekly can help you develop a bond, col-legiality, and mutual respect, especially during a crisis such as COVID-19.

DECENCY QUOTIENT (DQ)

Leaders and managers make decisions, big or small, almost every day. Their decisions can positively or negatively impact stakeholders, employees, customers, suppliers, shareholders, communities, and others[20]. Therefore, leaders must have what Bill Boulding called "triple-threat leadership capa-bility.[20]" The triple-threat leadership capability includes IQ+EQ+DQ[20]. IQ is the intelligence quotient as commonly known, EQ is the emotional intelligence quotient, and DQ, which is the most crucial for successful and transformational leaders, is the decency quotient.

As defined in Chapter 2, DQ goes beyond EQ. Leaders and managers must have EQ capabilities, but they need to go above and beyond. They must offer immense care and assistance to their employees and team members to help them succeed, which is the essence of DQ. DQ, which includes extra caring and sharing, must become part of an organization and team's DNA and culture to create and lead high-performance teams. A combination of EQ and DQ can create an enabling environment that entails respect for everybody, caring for each other, and valuing everyone's contribution to the team and organization. These ingredients are bound to lead to a productive and efficient work environment, a culture of growth and prosperity, and employee happiness. Research studies have shown that happy employees can lead to better customer service and the growth of the organization. Dr. Ted James, Chief of Breast Surgical Oncology at Harvard Medical School, said:

> In health care, effective teamwork is critical for success, especially during times of crisis. Leaders are called to navigate teams through uncertainty while adapting to new challenges and realities. Achieving high-performance teams requires leaders to manage change effectively, support growth, and promote a culture of excellence.

As Ajay Banga, the CEO of MasterCard, said in his speech at Duke University's Fuqua School of Business[20]:

IQ is really important. EQ is really important. What really matters to me is DQ.[20]

Banga further explained:

If you can bring your decency quotient to work every day, you will make the company a lot of fun for people – and people will enjoy being there and doing the right thing.[20]

DQ is crucial to building a culture of excellence and managing change effectively. Leaders and managers that deploy a combination of IQ+EQ+DQ

CASE STUDY: PRACTICAL APPLICATION OF THE DECENCY QUOTIENT (DQ) ON THE GMS PROJECT

Employees and everyone around you always appreciate extra care, respect, empathy, and attention. Research studies have shown that employees thrive, bond, and perform better in a culture of care, appreciation, and empathy[55]. This was the culture that Max Dillon developed on the GMS project. While he appeared tough and abrupt at times, but he deeply cared about his employees and project team members, including full-time WSDOT employees, consultants, and vendors. Max appeared to be willing to go the extra mile for his staff, consultants, and anyone around him.

One team member (call him Joe) had some medical issues and needed some time off to see his doctor. At times he had to see his doctor during work hours. Max provided extra care and support to Joe. He would call him every day to make sure that he was okay. Max held one-to-one meetings with him daily and provided him whatever assistance he needed. The extra care, decency (DQ), and empathy had a profound impact on Joe. He went the extra mile for the project. Joe even worked off-hours and weekends to get the work done. He became a very loyal and motivated member of the project team. Joe outperformed some other team members, and he also helped Max inculcate decency (DQ) culture and empathy on the project. As Zaki said: *empathy is contagious*[55]. Similarly, we found on the GMS project that DQ is also contagious. As a leader, practices decency and empathy, the entire team can adopt those traits and become a Blue Shark (high-performance) team.

can create and lead high-performance (The Blue Shark) teams, transform organizations, and establish an immense impact.

Today, when we look around and watch the political and business environment in the US, it is quite depressing. If leaders of the public and private sector organizations can bring DQ to their organizations and communities, it could become a uniting force and make all of us happy and better off than the situation we are in right now. By leveraging DQ, companies can unite people and have happier employees that can lead to happiness and tolerance in our communities and societies.

We all need to institutionalize and elevate DQ in our organizations, similar to what we have been doing with IQ and EQ. And, in turn, it would make the world more united and a better place to live and work for all of us.

PSYCHOLOGICAL SAFETY

Another core element of the Blue Shark Team model is psychological safety. It is where the team members talk freely and openly without any fear and consequences. As Laura Delizonna described in the article *High-Performing Teams Need Psychological Safety. Here's How to Create It*, Psychological safety can be described as the belief that you will not be admonished when you do something wrong, and it holds great significance in the way high performing teams operate[60].

Paul Santagata, Head of Industry at Google, smartly put it, *There's no team without trust*[60]. His words came after the insightful results from Google's enormous two-year study on team performance, which showcased that psychological safety is key to extracting the most from your team[60]. The concept of psychological safety is thought to bring with it the freedom for people to let their creativity flow without the fear of being reprimanded.

The importance of psychological safety for employees' functioning in high-stress business environments cannot be stressed enough. Human egos are quite fragile. At the first sign of provocation from a superior official or insubordinate colleague, our brains scramble to process information and treat the situation as a life-or-death threat[60]. Instead of thinking through such a predicament, our brains rush to come up with answers and actions. Sometimes we act without thinking, which can have a devastating impact on individuals, teams, and companies.

A company's success cannot be guaranteed without the positive mental attitude and the trust of its employees. Barbara Fredrickson from the University of North Carolina discovered that staying positive allows us to expand our thinking. The safer and more secure we feel, the more motivated we become[60].

Naturally then, a question arises: How do we foster a sense of security in our workforce? Below are the six steps that we can take to answer this question and provide psychological safety to employees as well as teams.

Act as an Ally, Not an Enemy

As Laura Delizonna says in her article, *We humans hate losing even more than we love winning*[60]. When we feel we are about to be put down, we can quickly adapt to mitigate our losses. This leads us down the wrong path and we, more often than not, start to disengage. To avoid such an outcome, we must assess the situation and reflect and ask ourselves this question: *What is the best way we can reach an equally beneficial conclusion*[60]? When we start to approach problems in such a way, we stave off the life-or-death reactions that occur when conflicts arise. And it helps us not only to diffuse the situation but also come up with a win-win solution that would be acceptable to everybody on the team.

We Are All Human

Before digging too deep into disputes, we should take a step back and recognize what outcome everyone on the team or organization would desire. Behind the shielded outer shell, everyone craves for almost the exact same things: *appreciation, respect, and harmony*. We all want to feel respected and valued[60]. It is only natural! Santagata put the phrase *Just Like Me* to good use with his team[60]. When we consider that the other person has ideas, a family, and wishes for peace and happiness, *just like me,* we start to build trust and a positive environment for everyone[60]. This kind of thinking and behavior are referred to as empathy in Daniel Goleman's model on emotional intelligence[1].

Always Think One Step Ahead

We should always try to think about the reactions our messages would elicit and then think about the counterpoints to each of those reactions. For instance, we may need all the facts to get our point across during a negotiation to prevent self-justifying behavior. Santagata asks the question, *If I position my point in this manner, what are the possible objections, and how would I respond to those counterarguments*[60]? He then goes on to say, *Looking at the discussion from this third-party perspective exposes weaknesses in my positions and encourages me to rethink my argument*[60]. We need to make sure our message is heard and acknowledged and not misinterpreted as unjustified criticism.

When you think ahead and anticipate questions from team members and stakeholders, it helps you think through the answers to the potential questions and prepare for discussions and reactions from the audience. Just remember, there will always be at least one person in the meeting or audience who will disagree with you or criticize your ideas. If you prepare yourself ahead of time, you won't be surprised and professionally handle it. You cannot anticipate everything, but try to do as much as possible before the meeting or presentation and prepare accordingly.

Explore Instead of Assigning Blame

When you engage in conversation with a team member, and it comes off as though they are being blamed, you lose their trust. In his research at the University of Washington, John Gottman showed that blame often led to elevated levels of conflict, and in turn, disengagement from team members[60]. To counter this, we must look to attain all the facts first. Instead of outrightly highlighting troubling behavior, point it out as an observation. Ask them what they think might be causing it, and then ask them what they think might be the solution. In this way, you appear supportive and trustworthy, and the issue is brought to the team member's attention without indulging in a conflict.

Asking questions and taking advice from team members can diffuse any potential conflicts. It would also put the opponents of your ideas at ease because you gave them the opportunity and space to engage with you. Some team members want to be heard. They don't necessarily expect you to implement their ideas, but they want their voice to be heard by the leader. Listening and asking questions can do wonders in teams. People feel valued, respected, and appreciated when their leader or boss asks for their opinion or advice. Exploring or brainstorming new ideas with teammates can provide the necessary environment and psychological safety to foster innovation, productivity, and high-performance on teams.

Feedback Is Crucial

Whenever you are done negotiating with a team member, always ask for feedback on how you delivered your message and what they think you could have done to improve. By doing so, you can highlight the main points in communication that can immensely help the team down the road. More importantly, this garners trust. It lets your team know you care about how they are being addressed. For example, these were the words of a senior manager at Google after Santagata gave him some tough feedback, *This could have felt like a punch in the stomach, but you presented reasonable evidence, and that made me want to hear more. You were also eager to discuss the challenges I had, which led to solutions*[60]. Whenever you want to give constructive feedback to someone, be sure to have evidence and let the data speak for itself. Avoid assumptions and heresy because that is the worst form of giving feedback.

Data, facts, and evidence can go a long way when you are ready to give constructive feedback to a colleague, subordinate, or stakeholder. Most of the people would accept facts and figures during a constructive feedback discussion. For example, showing data and quoting specific examples during mid-year or annual performance reviews of employees can make difficult conversations much smoother than without any data or evidence. Similarly, if a team member made a mistake or did not complete a task as per the requirements, you should document the instance, date, timing, and specifics. It will allow you to have a constructive discussion with him/her at an appropriate time, such as a one-on-one meeting. And don't delay the constructive feedback for too long. Don't wait for three or four months. During my professional career, I would document any abnormal behavior or suboptimum performance by any of the employees or team members. I would discuss it in a weekly or monthly one-to-one meeting. I would provide and seek feedback after the discussion. This approach helps both the leader and the teammate, building trust, credibility, and collegiality.

Know How the Team Feels

It is a best practice to know how your team is feeling at any given point in time. Checking up on the team members periodically, such as weekly, monthly, and quarterly, can keep them engaged and productive. You can take the team's pulse by asking direct questions, or it can be done by conducting frequent surveys. Ensuring your team feels safe psychologically is imperative for the flow of out-of-the-box thinking and ideas, which can lead to innovation and breakthroughs. The more safe and secure the team members feel, the more they engage and produce better results.

On the GMS project, the Organizational Change Management (OCM) Team used to conduct a quarterly survey called *The CULTURE Survey*. The acronym stood for: Control (C), Understanding (U), Leadership (L), Trust (T), Unafraid (U), Responsive (R), and Execution (E). There were seven variables that measured the team's overall morale, satisfaction, leadership, and performance. It also sought suggestions on how to improve the team's performance as well as the IT system that was being implemented. The participants of the survey included both the internal and external team members and key stakeholders. Survey Monkey was used to create and administer the survey. A snapshot of the survey results is placed in Annexure-A.

The Culture Survey provided all team members an opportunity to respond anonymously. It also allowed the project leadership to identify improvement areas and take action promptly. If you are a project manager, business sponsor, or leading a project, I highly recommend conducting a similar survey quarterly. It would show you how the team feels and the kind of improvements required to make your team a high-performance (The Blue Shark) team and deliver the projects successfully.

STORMING AND NORMING

Since Taylor's model on forming, storming, norming, and performing has already been explained in Chapter 2, we will not spend too much time here. Instead, we will focus on the practical application of the model and discuss a case study.

We emphasize the storming and norming stages; since most teams are either inherited or formed by upper management, you may not have much choice in their selection. This in itself poses a challenge to the smooth functioning of the team. If you can pass through the storming stage relatively unscathed and get to the norming stage, you can most definitely move on to performing without much trouble.

Most of the organizations and projects don't fail in the forming part. They fail to get past the *storming stage*, which is the most crucial stage. As a leader, you want to pass through the storming stage as quickly and unscathed as possible. Storming is the stage where most personal and professional conflicts develop and escalate to a level where the entire team gets stressed out, and productivity goes down. It could happen because only two people could not get along and dragged down the entire team and project. You might think about how only one or two people make the team or project fail. Based on my experience of managing projects for over 30 years, I can tell you that I have seen hundreds of projects fail due to one or two team members' condescending behavior, abrasive personality, lousy attitude, and pessimism. As a leader, you must quickly identify those individuals on the team and either remove them or diffuse them so that they cannot spread negativity and pessimism across the team. Some examples of how to counter this kind of people are shown in this chapter, as well as the GMS case study (Part II).

Once you get past the storming stage, then norming is relatively easy. And once the team gets into the norming stage, all you need to do, as a leader, is to enable the team with a bit of coaching, and they will sail through the performing stage. Remember, the most challenging is the storming stage, which requires extra time, effort, and energy.

MEETINGS, ACTION ITEMS, AND DECISION-MAKING

Meetings must be organized and action-oriented. Team members can lose interest and motivation when meetings are not organized, and decisions are not made. Yes, we all hate long meetings without any real objectives and action items. And yes, meetings waste a lot of time, but the reality is that meetings are not going away. If anything, we have to hold more meetings during COVID-19 even though the meetings are virtual these days. The fact is that we cannot escape from them.

Use of Empathy during Meetings

Meetings don't have to be boring and without objectives. As Annie Mckee wrote in her article, *Leaders Can Leverage Empathy to Conduct Great Meetings*, there is no reason why we cannot and should not make meetings more fun and productive[62]. The fact is that meetings are where most of the collaboration, creativity, and innovation still happens, so why not make them more fun.

CASE STUDY: A STORMING PHASE OF THE GMS PROJECT

Linda Whiteheart (the OCM Lead) and John Stryker (the Project Manager) of the GMS project went through the *storming* phase right at the onset of when John joined the project. He started with the GMS project on March 03, 2020, and Linda sent John a rather scathing email on March 19, 2020. He was surprised to see the tone of Linda's email, especially when John had been on the project for hardly two weeks. And Linda was a highly qualified and well-respected person, so John was perplexed. And all of this was happening when COVID-19 had hit in March–April 2020. People were depressed, anxiety levels were high, almost 30 million jobs had been lost in the US, and the entire nation was under immense stress due to the pandemic. COVID-19 had become a global crisis.

Below are some of the key points of Linda's email.

John – *Monday's generally work and it is a good idea to capture what is upcoming and where we are together.*

Specifics I am looking for on these calls/meetings:

- *You listening for understanding of what is on our list of to do's?*
- *You helping with planning NOW for near future items for Workstream leads.*
- *You making sure to track needed action for you, us, the team, the project.*

John was a seasoned professional and project manager. He had worked in the industry for almost 30 years and knew communication protocols very well. After reading Linda's email, especially the accusatory tone using the word "you, you, and you," he figured out the challenge and uphill battle that he would encounter with Linda. It was interesting to note that this kind of communication was coming from the OCM Lead, who was supposed to be the bridge-builder on the team. Scathing emails from Linda to John continued until April 17, 2020. John decided to meet with Linda and apply Tuckman's model and enter the *storming* phase of team-building.

Here's what John wrote in his email to Linda on Friday, April 17, 2020, 8:42 a.m. He also copied Max Dillon (the Business Sponsor) of the GMS project.

> Linda, I respect you a lot as a colleague and experienced professional, but please see your email below from March 19th.
>
> Does this email sound respectful to you? Should an OCM Lead talk like this using the word "You," "You," "You"? Does this email even sound professional?
>
> Please let me remind you, RESPECT is MUTUAL, NOT a ONE-WAY street. And it's
>
> EARNED, not dictated.
>
> Let's discuss this while Max is on the line with us

John had realized that he had to get through the *storming* phase with Linda pretty quickly to execute and deliver the project successfully. That's why he decided to meet with Linda so they both could go through the storming and norming stages of team-building. John knew that the longer he waited, the harder it would get. And if he had waited for too long, it might be too late to rescue the project. John knew he needed the OCM Lead (Linda) to succeed.

After reading John's response and realizing that he had copied Max, Linda got flustered. She cancelled the meeting on Friday, April 17, 2020, and took the afternoon off. Linda wanted to digest the questions that John had posed in his email. John took a bold step to respond to Linda as he was a consultant and she was a full-time WSDOT employee with 30+ years of service. Linda could have gotten John removed from the project as he was a new-bee on the project and John took the risk because he knew it would be right for the project. He realized that he had to quickly go through the "storming" stage to take the project forward. John knew that Linda was knowledgeable and experienced and felt confident that he would negotiate an amicable solution with her. John believed in respect and negotiation.

Linda reflected over the weekend and joined the meeting with John and Max on Monday, April 20, 2020. Max started the meeting and gave a motivational pep talk to both Linda and John. Max was an excellent motivational speaker and mediator. After he was done, Max passed the mic to Linda. It appeared like Linda had mellowed down. Here's what she said:

> John, first, I apologize for what I said and did. We could have treated each other better than we did. I would like to start over and work with you.

After hearing Linda's apology, John accepted her olive branch and here's what he said:

> Linda, I'm also sorry if I said anything that hurt your feelings. I have the utmost respect for you as a colleague and experienced resource on the GMS Project team.

They both smiled and gave each other a virtual hug on the video call and worked happily after that. Ever since that meeting, John never received any scathing emails from Linda. They both agreed to have weekly one-to-one meetings and candidly discussed issues with each other. And they became friends and developed a good working relationship that helped the project. Linda did an excellent job of leading and managing change on the project.

This was a good example of getting past the *storming* stage of team-building. Both Linda and John showed magnanimity to each other and became highly productive members of the GMS project team. They agreed to respect each other's roles, cooperate, and iron out their differences during their weekly one-on-one meetings. It also seemed like both Linda and John had read Daniel Shapiro's book, *Negotiating the Nonnegotiable: How to Resolve Your Emotionally Charged Conflicts,* where Shapiro advised people to avoid the *vertigo* problem in conflicts. Vertigo is "when you get so emotionally consumed in a conflict that you can't see beyond it," according to Shapiro[61]. Thus, Linda and John did not let *vertigo* take them over and resolved their differences amicably.

The moral of the story is that all teams have to go through the four *(forming, storming, norming, and performing)* stages of team-building. The toughest is the *storming* stage. The sooner you go through the storming stage, the better it is. On the other hand, the longer you wait, the harder it gets. Sometimes one team member (generally the project manager or a team lead) has to take the lead. On the GMS project, John took the initiative and decided to have the storming session with Linda, which paid off as he was able to build a high-performance (The Blue Shark) team with Max and Linda's assistance. Resultantly, the project was delivered successfully: on-time, within the approved budget, and according to the scope.

Sure, we all know the basics: set the right agenda, invite the right people, and be better prepared. Annie has suggested using emotional intelligence competencies to make meetings more productive, collaborative, and fun. Empathy and self-management of emotions are components of emotional intelligence that can be used to conduct great meetings[62].

Why should we use empathy for meetings? Empathy lets you read people; it enables you to assess people's emotions: Who is upset? Who is resisting? Who are the trouble makers, and so on? Empathy will let you see and read how people react to your ideas. Some people would always agree with you and defer to your ideas. It might feel good to hear people agreeing with you and admiring your views. But, this is where your self-regulation would come into play. It would help if you control your emotions and not fall prey to people who may manipulate you by admiring you every step of the way. They might fool you with false praise, so beware of their hidden agenda and motives. Flattery and persuasion skills are probably as ancient as humanity. As Robert Cialdini, a Professor of Psychology said in the article "Harnessing the science of persuasion[39]:"

> *Sometimes, the praise doesn't even have to be merited. Researchers at the University of North Carolina writing in the Journal of Experimental Social Psychology found that men felt the greatest regard for an individual who flattered them unstintingly even if the comments were untrue[32].*

Therefore, don't fall into the trap of flattery and cloud your judgment and decision-making. Similarly, if you get upset too fast during meetings just because someone disagreed with you, it can be detrimental for you and the team morale. Team members might not share ideas because they might be afraid of upsetting you. And if they stop sharing their ideas, it would kill creativity and innovation. On the other hand, if you, as a leader, exhibit positive emotions and show that you are receptive to all kinds of ideas and welcome constructive feedback, team members would be encouraged and mirror that behavior.

Don't forget emotions are part of life. It's human nature to show emotions. We have to manage our emotions positively so that it fosters collaboration, innovation, and productivity. When people are encouraged to have divergent views and ideas, it makes them feel good. And when people feel good, they become happy and positive, making meetings and teams more fun and productive. As Annie notes in the article, there is a *strong neurological link between feeling and cognition. We think more clearly and more creatively when our feelings are largely positive*[62]. This indicates that positive feelings can generate creativity, which can lead to more productive meetings.

Various research studies indicate that emotions are infectious, so you should manage and exhibit emotions carefully. It does not mean that you should only show positive emotions and never display negative emotions. You, as a leader, should adapt and show emotions based upon the situation. There might be times when you want to show displeasure because the situation warrants that kind of behavior. As long as you can manage and control your emotions, you can set a positive tone and enabling environment for meetings.

Another aspect to watch out for in meetings is to make them focused. We might think that we can multitask, but most of us are not good at it. As Daniel Goleman said in his book *Focus,* we are not nearly as good at multitasking as we think we are[63]. Therefore, you should focus on the topics discussed in the meeting instead of keeping checking messages on your cell phone. If team members see you on the phone and not paying attention, they will start to exhibit the same behavior, and soon the meeting would become a waste of time for the entire team.

Action-Items

Meetings without concrete action items and decision-making can lead to boredom and waste of time. If team members see no action items coming out of meetings and decisions being deferred, it would be a clear sign of inefficiency and low productivity. Therefore, as a leader, you must ensure that appropriate action items are created during meetings and decisions are made on time. Otherwise, team members will lose interest in meetings.

Max Dillon deployed empathy and emotions management very well at the GMS project meetings. He was very good at showing both positive and negative emotions at the meeting. Most of the time, he showed positive emotions, and people walked away with positive feelings and a sense of happiness about their work. Max appreciated and recognized people during large meetings, which motivated them, and they became more productive. Also, he made sure there were action items generated out of every meeting. Max was a quick decision-maker. Most of the time, he made business decisions during the meeting, which was one of the GMS project's critical success factors.

It seemed like Max had read Harvard articles on emotional intelligence and how to run meetings effectively. He conducted the meetings in a very positive, efficient, and effective manner. Sure, there were times when Max showed his displeasure during the meetings with specific issues and outcomes, but he focused more on the positive aspects and root causes of problems. He attacked the issues and not the people. He always showed empathy towards project team members and would go the extra mile for his team.

Decision-Making

Don't separate yourself from your team during a crisis like COVID-19. As Liz Kislik mentioned in the article, *Leaders, are you feeling the burden of pandemic-related decisions?* leaders that share in their team members' pain are more respected, and they feel confident in making tough-decisions[64]. Many companies had to suffer financial losses during the pandemic and ask employees to go on furloughs or take pay cuts. When leaders make these tough decisions, they must take the responsibility to share them with the employees personally. Delegating the news of these decisions to direct reports or lower-level staff can be demoralizing, disrespectful, and demotivating for the team[64]. It also lacks empathy that is badly required during a crisis. For example, one company CEO came to the videoconferencing call and explained why furloughs and pay cuts were necessary, and it was to save jobs in the company. He further shared that he was also taking a pay cut, and he answered employees' questions. In the end, employees felt positive, and the morale was high even though the CEO shared the bad news with them.

EMPLOYEE RECOGNITION AND APPRECIATION

As a leader, you should focus on recognition and appreciation. Research studies have shown that appreciation and recognition are one of the greatest motivating factors for teams and employees[31]. This is more relevant during a national crisis, emergency, or pandemic when anxiety and stress levels are high. Research studies have shown that recognition and appreciation can lead to high-performance, employee-engagement, loyalty, and trust. Not everyone looks for monetary rewards, but everybody looks for appreciation. As US President Teddy Roosevelt said: *People don't care how much you know until they know how much you care.*

There is a difference between recognition and appreciation[31]. When someone does a good job, he/she is recognized by the senior manager, and in turn, he/she might get a promotion, bonus, or a raise. Sometimes you get a *thank you* or a *job well done* note from the boss. All these are examples of recognition. You get recognized after you have done something good for the team or the organization. Recognition can be highly motivating and exciting for the team members as it gives them a sense of accomplishment. There are four key characteristics of recognition:

i. It is conditional because it is based upon an employee or team member's performance.
ii. It is based on what had been done in the past, which means what someone had already executed.
iii. It is scarce because there is a limited amount of recognition. For example, you cannot give everyone a bonus or an equal amount of bonus because it is based on performance.
iv. It comes from senior management.

On the other hand, appreciation is something that we all crave for. Whether you are a junior employee, manager, or US President, we all long for appreciation, according to Mike Robins[31]. As Oprah Winfrey said in her commencement speech at Harvard[31]:

I have to say that the most critical lesson I learned in 25 years talking every single day to people was that there's a common denominator in our human experience....The common denominator that I found in every single interview is we want to be validated. We want to be understood. I've done over 35,000 interviews in my career. And as soon as that camera shuts off, everyone always turns to me and inevitably, in their own way, asks this question: "Was that OK?" I heard it from President Bush. I heard it from President Obama. I've heard it from heroes and from housewives. I've heard it from victims and perpetrators of crimes. I even heard it from Beyoncé in all of her Beyoncé-ness.... [We] all want to know one thing: "Was that OK?" "Did you hear me?" "Do you see me?" "Did what I say mean anything to you[31]?"

CASE STUDY: GMS TEAM RECOGNITION
AND APPRECIATION

During weekly meetings on the GMS project, Max publicly recognized every team member who did a good job. This was one of Max's leadership traits that he often used words like: "thank you, great job, and well done." For example, one of the Pilot Applications of GMS was going to be released on July 23, 2020, but some preparations needed to be done on the July 4 holiday weekend. One of the team members (Sharon Boyle), required for the preparation, was on vacation during that week, including the long weekend. However, she realized the importance and urgency of the "Go-Live of the Pilot Release." She logged-in remotely for a few hours during her vacation and made sure everything was ready for the Production Server.

After the holidays, when Max found out that Sharon worked during her vacation, he asked everybody to applaud for Sharon (virtually, due to COVID-19) during the weekly status meeting. Almost 40 team members attended the meeting. Sharon was delighted and motivated to see Max and the rest of the team's recognition and appreciation. She continued to be a super-star on the project and went the extra mile to complete the tasks on-time. Max appreciated Sharon's efforts so much that he recommended her for promotion as well.

What Oprah talked about was appreciation in her speech. She was saying that everyone looks for appreciation. When we show appreciation to our colleagues, team members, employees, suppliers, customers, managers, and business partners, it can lead to trust, leading to motivation and high-performance[31].

Part II

Case Study
The Blue Shark Team at WSDOT during COVID-19

Part II of this book comprises Chapters 7–14. These eight chapters describe the story of an IT project successfully implemented at the Washington State Department of Transportation (WSDOT) during COVID-19 by creating a Blue Shark (high-performance) team.

Also, it shows the readers how to implement the Blue Shark, Goleman, and Tuckman's model to lead high-performance teams and deliver projects successfully worldwide, especially during a crisis such as COVID-19.

The total cost of the project was about $4.0 million. It took 28 months, from February 2019 to June 2021, to complete with 40+ resources, including part-time employees. The author of this book collected the data and observed the project team for 15 months, from March 2020 to June 2021.

DOI: 10.1201/9781003216711-8

7

The Blue Shark Team at WSDOT

A national or global crisis can be harsh on most people and businesses, but some good things and lessons also erupt out of a crisis. The most recent example was Amazon; on February 02, 2021, it declared record revenues of $125.56 billion for the fourth quarter of 2020. COVID-19 contributed significantly to Amazon's income as the coronavirus infections and deaths soared, unfortunately, in October–December 2020. Most people did their Christmas shopping online due to the pandemic.

As Daniel Coyle mentioned in his book "The culture code," "A surprising fact about cultures: many were forged in moments of crisis[65]." Similarly, the Blue Shark (a high-performance) team was created on the Grants Management System (GMS) project in the middle of COVID-19. This case study is a story of a real-life project that went from failure to success during the pandemic. The lessons learned can be applied to any crisis and across industries, including healthcare, IT, telecommunication, construction, manufacturing, financial services, oil and gas, consulting, public sector, and others.

The story is about an IT project successfully implemented during COVID-19 by creating a Blue Shark (high-performance) team. The total cost of the project was about $4.0 million. It took 28 months, from February 2019 to June 2021, to complete with 40+ resources, including part-time employees. The author of this book collected the data and observed the project team for 16 months, from March 2020 to June 2021. The project team members, vendors, and consulting companies' names and identities have been disguised and fictionalized to respect and protect their privacy.

The Public Transportation Division (PTD) of the Washington Department of Transportation (WSDOT) decided to implement Grants Management System (GMS) to manage the Federal and State grants distributed across the State of Washington. The grantees or sub-recipients

DOI: 10.1201/9781003216711-9

of these grants included local governments, transit authorities, non-profit organizations, tribes, and others. The project was re-launched in February 2019 after a failed attempt.

Almost a year had passed for the project, and Jeff and Max were not convinced that the vendor would implement the system on-time, within budget, and according to the scope. They could not see a clear path and direction coming from the vendor. Thus, Jeff and Max felt the need to enhance project management capabilities and decided to bring a strong project manager. They wanted a project manager who could have strong IT, project management, leadership, and team-building skills. Green Tree Consulting was hired to manage the overall project, guide WSDOT through the entire project management lifecycle, and follow *PMBOK* guidelines of the Project Management Institute (PMI).

It was 8:00 a.m. on February 06, 2020, the Executive Sponsor (Jeff Beaumont) and Business Sponsor (Max Dillon) of the GMS project reviewed the External Quality Assurance (QA) Team's Monthly Status Report and noticed that 7 out of the 11 key performance indicators (KPIs) had turned yellow, and they seemed to be heading towards red, which could be a disaster for the project. Thus, Max and Jeff concluded that they needed a strong project manager to help them turn-around the project. A copy of the summary of the External QA Team's Monthly report is placed in Annexure-B.

Since Green Tree Consulting had the project management responsibilities for the project, the decision was made to call Josh Green, Founder and Partner, at Green Tree. Max had given Josh an ultimatum to find a qualified and strong project manager within 30 days. Josh agreed and found John Stryker, who joined the project on March 03, 2020. John joined the project in the middle of chaos because the quality indicators looked bad, according to the External Quality Assurance team's report (Annexure B). The project appeared to be in a stand-still position on March 03, 2020, when John joined. In March 2020, two significant events occurred: WHO declared coronavirus (COVID-19) a pandemic, and Washington State issued stay-at-home orders. It appeared like John had the work cut out for him.

Green Tree Consulting was based in Olympia, Washington. It was a small boutique consulting firm specializing in project management, learning and development, and organizational change management (OCM). Most of their clients were in the public sector in Washington State, including the Washington Department of Transportation (WSDOT), Health and Human Services (HHS) Department, and others. They were hired for the overall project management role on the GMS project.

Purple Heart Consultants was a small consulting firm focusing on testing and software quality assurance (SQA). Their role on the GMS project was to test the software and ensure it was free of bugs. Also, Qualitatum Group was appointed as External Quality Assurance Consultants, which the State of Washington mandated. Their role was to identify risks, monitor the project's overall health, and generate a project monitoring report for the senior management at WSDOT every month. They were also part of the Executive Steering Committee of the project.

Both Green Tree Consulting and WSDOT Management realized that the project manager had to have strong leadership and team-building skills and project management experience. Therefore, John Stryker was hired as a Project Manager.

PROJECT BACKGROUND, SCOPE, AND OBJECTIVES

The Grants Management System (GMS) project's objectives were to acquire a commercial off the shelf (COTS), vendor-hosted, web-based solution that enabled WSDOT's Public Transportation Division (PTD) to streamline business processes and replace their legacy system with a centralized grants management system.

WSDOT was responsible for managing state and federal grant funds distributed to public transportation providers across Washington State. About 25 staff members were involved in managing approximately 200 sub-recipient grants, representing over $210 million of the combined Federal Transit Administration (FTA) and State grant funding on a biennial basis (2-year period).

Prior to the GMS implementation, WSDOT managed and distributed the grants with various tools, such as excel spreadsheets, electronic and paper documents, and a database that was implemented with an MS Access user interface and a SQL Server backend. The database was custom built for WSDOT using external software development resources and required significant WSDOT staff resources and external assistance to keep it working.

A grants management Request for Proposal (RFP) was first released in April 2018. The RFP was subsequently canceled with the intent to edit prohibitive requirements and re-issue. The RFP was rereleased in early February 2019. An Apparent Successful Proposer (ASP) was announced in June 2019, and a contract was signed with Star Technology in September 2019.

A dedicated project team was created to execute the project. The organization chart is placed in Annexure C. The team comprised about 40 members, including WSDOT Subject Matter Experts (SMEs), consultants, the External Quality Assurance team, and the vendor resources.

As per the Investment Plan (IP) approved by the Office of the Chief Information Officer (OCIO) of Washington State, the initial total project budget was approved for $3.77 million in August 2019 with a project closure date of June 30, 2021. The first revision to the IP with a budget of $3.45 million (a downward revision) was approved in August 2020 due to the utilization of internal resources as opposed to the consultants. The OCIO approved the second revision to the IP with a $3.99 million budget on November 10, 2020. The second revision was necessary due to COVID-19, state-wide employee furloughs, and lessons learned from the software's two pilot releases. The budget was revised to $3.99 million, and the final go-live schedule was extended from December 31, 2020 to March 31, 2021, with a project closure of June 30, 2021, as initially planned. A copy of the budget revisions, along with the reasons, is shown in Table 7.1.

The GMS project was implemented in two phases:

- Phase 1:
  - Pilot Release 1 – Regional Mobility Grant (RMG) Application in June 2020.
  - Pilot Release 2 – Consolidated Grants Application in July 2020.
- Phase 2: Full Deployment and Stabilization of the ten modules of RMG and Consolidated Grants by March 31, 2021, with a Project Closeout on June 30, 2021.

As part of good governance, transparency, and quality assurance, Washington State had decided to build a project oversight mechanism for all projects. This translated into hiring consultants for key areas in addition to the software vendor. Green Tree Consulting was appointed for the overall project management, Purple Heart Consultants was appointed for the testing and Software Quality Assurance (SQA), and Qualitatum Group was appointed as External Quality Assurance (QA)

TABLE 7.1

GMS Project Original and Revised Budget

Description	Original (8/12/2019)	Revised on 8/3/2020	Revised on 10/12/2020
Total Project Cost:	$3,779,357	$3,459,472	$3,999,542
Five-Year Maintenace Cost:	$732,110	$841,045	No Change ($841,045)
	—	—	—
Reasons for Revision:	—	—	—
Reasons for Revision	N/A	1. Total budget was reduced from $3,779,357 to $3,459,472 by replacing Orgnizational Change Management consultant with an in-house (WSDOT) resource(s). 2. The 5-year maintenance costs have increased slightly by $117,935 from $732,110 to $841,045 due to the web hosting costs of the two servers (test and production) as opposed to the one server as originally envisioned.	1. COVID-19 caused unprecedent work conditions for WSDOT employee as well as consulting resources that required adjustments in the Project Schedule. 2. Due to WSDOT Employee Furloughs, the Agency personnel had to reschedule and extend System Validation, Integration Testing, User Acceptance Testing (UAT), and Training sessions. Therefore, it required the Project Schedule to be extended from 12/31/2020 to 03/31/2021. 3. Lessons learned from the two Pilot Applications of Regional Mobility Grants (RMG) and Consolidated Grant along with the ground realities mandated re-calibration of the Project Schedule. 4. The Total Budget was enhanced from $3,459,472 to $3,999,542 due to extension of WSDOT as well as consulting resources from 12/31/2020 to 03/31/2021. The GMS Project is 100% funded by FTA. 5. In light of the facts mentioned above, the GMS Project Team along with the Vendor created a more realistic and achievable Project Schedule with a Final Go-Live of 03/31/2021 and Project Closure of 06/30/2021.

Source: GMS project archives.

Consultants. In addition, there was an oversight from the Office of the Chief Information Officer (OCIO). These steps were taken to safeguard public funds and ensure the successful delivery of the project. The project organization chart is placed in Annexure C.

Project Scope

The scope for the GMS project was as follows:

Organizational

The organizational scope included over 300 system users, including WSDOT employees, sub-recipients (grantees), and the Attorney General's office. The initial implementation would be for Regional Mobility Grants Application Pilot, followed by Consolidated Grants Application Pilot, then a complete go-live of the remaining ten modules.

Functional

The new Grants Management System (GMS) will process Regional Mobility Grants (RMG) and Consolidated Grants with ten modules. It will:

- Manage each grant program's entire lifecycle, including programming or funds, application, evaluation, and award.
- Support management of sub-recipient grants and third-party contracts, expenditures, schedules, and resources. This included invoicing and financial management.
- Support sub-recipient oversight activities (e.g., site visits). It included all aspects of compliance, project change management, and project performance and closeout.
- Provide Inventory date required to support asset management processes.
- Support WSDOT's contract management and reporting processes related to the grants. It included contract-boilerplates' management and approval by the Attorney General, drafting, execution, and management of agreements between WSDOT and Grantees, as well as project reporting.
- Provide application (canned) and ad-hoc reporting.

- RMG and Consolidated Grants Applications, along with the ten modules, will be implemented. Below is the list of the modules:
  1. Application Review
  2. Grants Tracking
  3. Awards
  4. Contracts
  5. Claims/Invoice Processing
  6. Contract Amendments
  7. Status Reports
  8. Site Visits
  9. Compliance
  10. Closeout

The following elements were planned within the system to support other functions performed within the division:

- A comprehensive mailing list for the Public Transportation Division.
- Inventory Tracking and Management.
- Summary of the public transportation.

Technical

- The solution will be hosted by the vendor on a cloud.
- The conversion of data between legacy systems and the new solution will be performed by the vendor.
- Data validation will be conducted by the WSDOT Subject Matter Experts.

Out of Scope

The following elements were excluded from the proposed project scope:

- Reports produced in other State budget and financial systems such as Transportation Executive Information System (TEIS) and Transportation Reporting and Accounting Information System (TRAINS) were not part of the GMS scope. GMS would remain a source to produce specific expenditure reports required to support the state budget process.

- Reports required within the Federal Transit Award and Management System (TrAMS) such as Federal Funding Accountability and Transparency Act (FFATA), Milestones Progress Report (MPR), and Federal Financial Reports (FFRs) were not part of the GMS scope. GMS will remain a source to produce particular Federal Transit Administration (FTA) reports such as Program of Projects (POP) and Program Sheet (Prog) to support FTA's application and award process.
- Procurement and Contracting of third-party products and services handled by other WSDOT divisions such as the contracting office and consulting services are not part of the GMS scope.

Future Enhancements

- Data interfaces between the new solution and legacy applications.
- Use of third-party data analysis tools for the Data Team.

Project Goals, Objectives, and Performance Measures

The project's goals, objectives, and performance measures are defined in Table 7.2.

Assumptions

The project had the following assumptions:

- The entire scope of the project would be implemented.
- The solution would implement core business requirements in phases (as opposed to a single go-live).
- The solution would be a configurable Commercial off-the-shelf (COTS) system.
- The solution would minimize customization.
- WSDOT resources would be available during critical project activities (as per the project resource utilization matrix), such as design and functionality validation.
- WSDOT would not host the solution (no on-site hosting). The solution will be hosted by the vendor.

TABLE 7.2

Goals, Objectives, and Performance Measures

Golas and Objectives	Performance Measures and Benefits
Objective 1: Simplify invoice process and improve data accuracy	**1:** A single system to process invoices with default ability to submit data without any fatal flaws. **2:** 50% reduction in staff time spent on invoice processing – Reduction from receipt of invoice-to-date to date-submitted to Accounting and Financial Services (AFS).
Objective 2: Reduce overall grant application processing time	**1:** PTD: 50% reduction in time to prep and submit and review an application; **2:** 50% reduction in time to prep and submit an application; **3:** 75% reduction in time spent preparing the federal program of projects, budgets, and the labor spreadsheet.
Objective 3: Automate awarding funds process	**1:** 75% reduction of time in report compilation; **2:** 100% of all Grant information is auditable and in compliance with State and FTA rules; **3:** 100% elimination of errors (data entry) when building reports and invoicing.
Objective 4: Improve and streamline site visit process	**Measure:** Provide efficiency and effectiveness. Improve communications and streamline documentation entry and accuracy.
Objective 5: Improve overall auditability, accuracy and compliance in reports and reduce staff hours in report compilation	**1:** 75% reduction of time in report compilation; **2:** 100% of all Grant information is auditable and in compliance with State and FTA rules; **3:** 100% elimination of errors (data entry) when building reports and invoicing.
Objective 6: Reduced customer effort for grant applications, reporting, and invoicing.	**Measure:** Project Team, Community Liaisons, and Business Services Team (BST) working through measures to present to the Business Sponsor for approval.
Objective 7: Reduce overall time spent preparing and reviewing contracts	**Measure:** 80% reduction in staff and customer time.
Objective 8: Provide inventory management capabilities	**Measure:** 75% reduction in time spent tracking and management of assets.

Source: GMS project archives.

- All users of the solution would have access to an electronic web-based device (e.g., computer).
- There will be a period of extensive customer support from the vendor (called Hypercare) at the final Go-Live.

Constraints

The project had the following constraints.

1. WSDOT resources were constrained because the Subject Matter Experts (SMEs) workload might add some time constraints to their day-to-day operations.
2. The schedule was constrained for the following reasons:
   a. Regional Mobility Grants Application Module must be in production by June 2020.
   b. Consolidated Grants Application Module must be in production by July 2020.
   c. The solution must be implemented by 12/31/2020, which was revised to 03/31/2021 due to the COVID-19 pandemic.
3. Funding was constrained to a fixed amount with very little room to change.

Source: All the information and data provided in this chapter have been adopted from the GMS project archives.

8

Key Challenges Facing the GMS Project

Things seemed okay on the surface, but, in reality, the Grants Management System (GMS) project was not moving forward. John Stryker (the new project manager) noticed quite a few challenges that needed to be addressed urgently for the project's success. According to the External QA Monthly Reports (Annexure B), the project started in February 2019, but some of the quality indicators turned red in September 2019. Three out of the eleven quality indicators were red: the overall project health and environment, project integration management, and risk management. An additional three were yellow: time management, cost management, and procurement management. Only 5 out of the 11 indicators were green in September 2019, which sounded the alarm bells in Business Sponsor and WSDOT Management's ears.

In November 2019, slight improvements were made, which turned the red indicators to yellow, but the quality indicators should have been green at that stage of the project. The WSDOT management was not satisfied with the overall project performance, so they decided to look for a new project manager. In December 2019, the Business Sponsor had asked Green Tree Consulting to replace the project manager and bring somebody more experienced with leadership, team-building, and project management skills.

After about two months of search, Green Tree found John Stryker, and he joined the project on March 03, 2020. Max Dillon (the Business Sponsor) introduced John to all the team members during his first day on the job. Fortunately, John started before the lockdown and COVID-19 restrictions, so he met most of the team members' in-person.

John realized that he had to hit the ground running to rescue the project and save it from further delays. Everything was under the microscope; everybody watched as the project was getting delayed, and the quality

DOI: 10.1201/9781003216711-10

indicators were not looking good, or at least they were not at a point where they should have been. His assessment after completing the first week on the project was as follows:

1. Due to a communication gap, there was a significant disconnect between the project team and the vendor designing and implementing the software.
2. Trust deficit between the project team and vendor was also one of the critical challenges. There were grievances on both sides of the fence (the project team and vendor), which should have been addressed. Some team members felt that they were not getting the requisite support and time from the vendor. And the vendor also felt disrespected by the team. Things were really bad, causing tears on both sides.
3. Since this was the second attempt to implement GMS, slowing down the project seemed to be the team's strategy.
4. Critical project management elements were missing. For example, the project management plan required updates, the vendor management plan was missing, and monthly risk review meetings needed to be scheduled. Also, the project schedule had significant gaps due to a lack of feedback from the vendor.
5. Even though project team members' roles and responsibilities were defined as shown in Annexure-D, there were still gray areas that caused confusion and uncertainty for the team members, especially the Work Stream Leads.
6. Misunderstanding and absence of clarity on roles and responsibilities created confusion among the team members. For example, in January 2020, Max, with the intent to fill the gap created on the project management side, made a comment to Mark Stromberg (the Business Analyst): *Mark, you are doing a good job; continue the good work for us until we find a replacement of the project manager.* Mark interpreted the comment that he was the interim project manager, although there was no official announcement and Larry Purpleheart was still there. In March 2020, John Stryker took over as the new project manager, but it took some time to clear the confusion regarding who the real project manager was.
7. Larry Purpleheart was the official Project Manager before John Stryker took over on March 03, 2020. He was considered to be the nicest and most friendly person on the project. Larry got along very well with everybody on the team. Larry's strength was that he was

very pleasant. He was polite and gracious, so he did not challenge anyone on the team even when tasks were getting delayed. Some people took advantage of Larry's softer personality. He was a thorough gentleman, highly qualified, and non-confrontational person. Due to confusion and lack of clarity on the roles and responsibilities, Larry chose to save his relationship with the team members over pushing them to complete their tasks.

8. Max Dillon was a good, firm, and quick decision-maker. Unfortunately, he was fed insufficient data, causing some decisions to be ineffective, which led to delays in the project. Despite Max's efforts to take swift actions to save the project, the project seemed to stand-still due to a lack of effective project management on the vendor side.

9. The project required the spirit of team-work, empathy, motivation, and collegiality. Max was trying very hard to motivate the team. However, the absence of a clear path and paucity of effective project management strategy (from the vendor and consultants side) prevented real progress on the project, causing anxiety and stress among the team members.

10. The issues documented in the RAID (Risks, Actions, Issues, and Decisions) log needed to be reviewed and addressed promptly.

While John was trying to decipher all the project's challenges, the World Health Organization (WHO) declared the coronavirus (COVID-19) as a pandemic on March 11, 2020. The WHO announcement came nine days after John joined the project. At that time, nobody knew that COVID-19 would change the world order, and the project management landscape would change for months and years to come.

During the interview in late February 2020, the WSDOT management had stipulated that the project manager (John Stryker) had to be on-site Monday–Friday, and required him to move from Dallas, Texas to Olympia, Washington. Therefore, John packed up and moved to Olympia on March 01 and joined the project on March 03, 2020. On March 11, eight days after John joined the project, WHO declared COVID-19 as a pandemic. On March 23, 20 days after John joined the project, the State of Washington issued the "Stay at Home" order to protect everybody from the COVID-19 virus. Thus, John observed nothing but challenges.

The entire country was shut down during April 2020, after the stay-at-home and the lockdown orders. John could have stayed in Dallas and worked remotely and did not have to go through the hassle of relocation. Unfortunately, flights got canceled in March and April 2020, and everybody was scared of traveling. He could not fly back even if he wanted to, so John got stuck in Olympia for months without any family. Sometimes that is how project managers have to work, away from family and friends. Perhaps all of us can understand, with varying degrees, the anxiety and stress levels experienced during the pandemic. But to be completely alone without the comfort of home or any family members around is something few of us experienced during COVID-19. John did not have much choice but to chin up, adapt in a matter of hours and days, and steer the GMS ship in the right direction as a project manager.

9

Who's Who on the Project

There were over 40 team members on the project, so it would be too long to talk about every single one of them. However, the readers need to know the key team members, their experience, role on the project, background, and the team dynamics. A copy of the organization chart is placed in Annexure C.

As you read through the case study, you will notice issues and behaviors common in project teams and organizations worldwide. Therefore, the case study shows you how these issues were addressed and resolved while managing and delivering the project successfully during a global crisis caused by COVID-19.

EXECUTIVE SPONSOR

Jeff Beaumont was the Executive Sponsor of the project. He was also a member of the Executive Steering Committee that had the oversight of the project. Jeff was a Director at WSDOT and had been there for almost 30 years. He provided an overall direction and advice to the Business Sponsor and project management team. Jeff held four Master's degrees and was a quick decision-maker. He had excellent leadership, team-building, and management skills.

BUSINESS SPONSOR

Max Dillon was the Business Sponsor of the project. He was a full-time employee at WSDOT and was responsible for the project's overall delivery and implementation. Max was also the project manager's (John Stryker's)

DOI: 10.1201/9781003216711-11

counter-part on the client-side. He successfully managed funding and delivery of transit, rail, ferries, and highway construction projects for the last 20+ years. Max held a Master's degree in civil engineering. He had been working at WSDOT for over 20 years. Therefore, he understood the PTD and WSDOT business processes very well. Max was a quick and firm decision-maker. Since GMS was his first IT project, he quickly overcame the learning curve to manage it. The WSDOT management felt that Max was the right person to lead the GMS project due to his management, leadership, decision-making, and team-building skills. Max had the natural ability to motivate people and resolve conflicts.

OVERSIGHT CONSULTANT FROM THE OFFICE OF CHIEF INFORMATION OFFICER (OCIO)

Chris Niceheart was the oversight consultant from the OCIO of Washington State. He was a very knowledgeable, talented, and competent person. Chris had over 30 years of experience and provided excellent guidance to the project management team. He was a member of the Executive Steering Committee and shared his expertise and advice with the Business Sponsor and Project Management in the monthly meetings. His role was to monitor quality, risks, and critical project indicators: scope, budget, and timelines. Since Chris monitored multiple projects across the State, he shared lessons learned from the other projects with the project management team, which helped immensely for the project's success.

PROJECT MANAGER

John Stryker had 30+ years of experience in the industry, consulting, and academia. He had managed multimillion-dollar IT projects at Fortune 500 companies as well as the public sector. John brought not only strong project management but team-building and leadership skills. He had a PhD in Project Management, an MBA, and was a Certified Project Management Professional (PMP) from the Project Management Institute (PMI).

ORGANIZATIONAL CHANGE MANAGEMENT (OCM) WORK STREAM LEAD

Linda Whiteheart was a full-time employee at WSDOT. She had an overall experience of 30+ years, so she was appointed as the project's OCM lead. Her role was to ensure smooth communication across the team, consultants, and stakeholders. She managed the overall change and transformation that took place due to the software implementation. Her job was to ensure that GMS was accepted by internal and external stakeholders and end-users of the system. She was a qualified and ProSci Certified change management expert. Her colleagues across WSDOT highly respected Linda. She had been with WSDOT for many years and had a vast network across the organization, which helped the project.

BUSINESS ANALYSIS (BA) WORK STREAM LEAD

Mark Stromberg was a consultant from Purple Heart Consultants hired by WSDOT to perform the project's business analysis. He joined the project during the requirements gathering phase along with WSDOT employees and the vendor. Mark remained on the project for a little over two years. He conducted the fit-gap analysis of GMS and created the As-Is and To-Be maps. Once the requirements gathering phase was complete, Mark spearheaded the software design and functionality validation along with the WSDOT subject matter experts (SMEs). He had 30+ years of experience with ERP systems, accounting software, and business analysis. Mark was also a Certified Public Accountant (CPA), which made him very meticulous just about everything. Most of the time, he saw things as black or white. He was an intelligent and qualified person to do his job as a Business Analyst.

TESTING WORK STREAM LEAD

Bill Hofstede was a consultant from Purple Heart Consultants and was responsible for the Software Quality Assurance and Testing of the new system (GMS). He was a very analytical person and could have also been an excellent legal expert or lawyer for the project. He led the SQA and Testing team. Bill was a qualified SQA expert and did an excellent job of leading the team.

OCM CONSULTANT

Helen Swift was an OCM consultant from Green Tree Consulting. Her role was to assist Linda with critical tasks such as designing the surveys, creating training materials, and overall change management. Helen was ProSci Certified and had 30+ years of experience under her belt. She had helped multiple clients successfully with organizational change management over the years. Helen was a highly respected member of the project team.

DATA MIGRATION (DM) WORK STREAM LEAD

Larry Purpleheart became the Data Migration Lead after John Stryker took over as a project manager. Larry was the nicest person on the team. He got along very well with everybody on the team. Larry was the kind of person who did not want to confront anybody and wanted to have a cordial relationship with everyone on the team. Since Larry was technically very strong, highly knowledgeable about WSDOT data, and got along very well with everybody on the team, Max Dillon decided to keep him as the Data Migration Lead. He reported to John on a day-to-day basis.

TECHNICAL INFRASTRUCTURE WORK STREAM LEAD

The Technology Work Stream was headed by Nick Flyer, an ex-army and a Certified Systems Architect with 30+ years of experience. Nick was a pretty straight-forward guy. He did his job and tried not to get into organizational politics. Nick followed up on action items diligently, closed the issues promptly, and got the job done. He was a polite and humble person.

TRAINING WORK STREAM LEAD

Linda was the Training Work Stream Lead until July 30, 2020. The OCM activities required Linda's undivided attention, and she was overworked due to her WSDOT responsibilities. Therefore, Max Dillon decided to replace Linda with Ashley Hemings as the Training Lead. Ashley was a very analytical person, had a strong accounting background, and was highly organized. She had 30+ years of experience. Ashley was a logical person and got along very well with Max, John, and the project team members. Ashley worked very closely with the vendor and quickly streamlined the Weekly Training Schedule. The vendor also liked Ashley, and they got along very well. This was a pleasant surprise and a good and timely decision made by Max, according to the vendor (Star Technology).

EXECUTIVE STEERING COMMITTEE (ESC)

The ESC was comprised of the Executive Sponsor, Business Sponsor, a representative of the Finance and Accounting Services Division at WSDOT, a representative of Washington State's OCIO, IT Director at WSDOT, and a representative of the External Quality Assurance Team. It played a crucial role in providing project oversight, policy guidelines, and advice to the project management team, including the Business Sponsor and Project Manager. They monitored the risks, quality, and project progress (scope, budget, and timeline) monthly. Further details on the roles and responsibilities of the ESC are provided in Annexure D.

EXTERNAL QUALITY ASSURANCE TEAM

As part of the good governance and transparency, the State of Washington had mandated that all projects have external quality assurance consultants to monitor and evaluate the projects and risks. Therefore, Qualitatum Consultants was appointed by WSDOT as the external quality assurance firm. Their mandate was to monitor project risks and quality. They also evaluated the project progress weekly and monthly and provided feedback to the project management team and the senior management at WSDOT. Besides, they provided feedback to the Executive Steering Committee every month.

Qualitatum created an independent monthly project status report and shared it with the project team and the senior management at WSDOT. It was an extensive report and covered all key areas that were relevant to the project. A snapshot of the monthly status report summary is shown in Annexure B.

THE STAR TECHNOLOGY TEAM (VENDOR)

Star Technology was selected as the software vendor and implementation partner. The Public Transportation Division of WSDOT signed the software (Grants Management System) implementation agreement with Star. Star had a solid technical team, including Jim Holster, Kim Butler, Nancy Higgins, and Tariq Aslam. Jim and Tariq looked after the technical side, such as behind the scene coding. Jim was also the project manager from the Star side. Kim and Nancy were responsible for software design and training as well as functionality validation. They also held weekly training and Q&A sessions with the Subject Matter Experts (SMEs) and consultants.

The Star team was quite strong on the technical side, and they had good software (Grants Management System) that met WSDOT's business requirements. Their customer service and response to technical issues were also commendable. Star's project management capacity was suboptimal, but it was compensated by Green Tree's and John Stryker's project management capabilities.

SOFTWARE QUALITY ASSURANCE (SQA) AND TESTING TEAM

The State of Washington required to appoint an independent SQA and Testing team. Therefore, Purple Heart Consultants were appointed for the SQA and Testing role. The testing team included Bill Hofstede and Joe Stemon. Their mandate was to test the software functionality, report any bugs found in the system, identify any technical risks, and ensure that all technical issues were addressed according to WSDOT's business requirements. Purple Heart used Spira Test software to test the system functionality and created very detailed log files with the test results. They also created a weekly status report shared with the project team and senior management at WSDOT.

10

Organizational Challenges and Team Dynamics

Shortly after joining the project, John had realized that he had jumped into a red ocean full of sharks, but it was too late for him to reverse course. He had already relocated from Dallas, and COVID-19 had locked down the country by the end of April 2020. There was no turning back for him at that point. John took this project as a challenge and decided to turn the red ocean to blue and create a blue shark team out of what he inherited.

John decided to implement Dan Goleman's emotional intelligence model and Bruce Tuckman's team-building model while executing the project. Either he would fall on his face by implementing these models, or it would become one of the most successful projects during COVID-19. Since John was both a professor and project manager, he decided to accept this as a challenge. He took a big risk because it would make him a failed professor and project manager if he had failed. And his reputation of 30 years would probably go down the drain. On the other hand, if he had successfully implemented Goleman and Tuckman's models and delivered the project successfully, he would have created a success story during a global crisis and COVID-19. The case study would be of interest to leaders, academics, and project managers around the world.

On March 04, 2020, John's first order of business was to have one-to-one meetings with all the Work Stream Leads. Initially, some meetings got quite heated because the project manager and the team members had to go through forming, storming, norming, and performing stages. John kept reiterating the words like *focus* and *no show-stoppers*, which seemed alien to some of the team members at that time. There were times when one-on-one sessions got very heated, but John kept listening to the team members. The key was that he kept the communication channels open.

DOI: 10.1201/9781003216711-12

During one-on-one sessions, both sides talked openly and agreed to provide constructive feedback without consequences. Initially, it made the team members very uncomfortable because they had not gone through these kinds of sessions with any project manager. With time they understood the significance of these sessions and synchronized with each other.

During those meetings, John also received constructive feedback from the team members. He kept listening and adapting his style along the way. One of the team members said:

> John, you are too loud, and you interrupt people. This is the west coast; we let people finish their sentences before we speak.

John kept his patience and thanked the team members for the feedback. He digested and reflected on the feedback that he received during the first two weeks on the project. He immediately adapted his style. He would wait till the end to talk in the meetings and give other team members a chance to speak. He was extra careful and made sure that he did not cut anybody off in the middle. He toned down his voice and made it less authoritarian.

After a few weeks of adapting his style, he received feedback from the Business Sponsor. Team members were quite happy with John's immediate adaptation of style and acknowledged that the project manager listened to them and took constructive feedback very well. John's adaptation of style also triggered open and healthy communication with the work stream leads and other team members. Slowly the team members started to recognize John as a good listener, executor of the project, and decision-maker. One team member commented on John's management style and said: *He is polite but firm. He knows what he is doing.* It was good to receive positive feedback, but John's challenges had just begun, as described in the following pages.

A STORMING SESSION WITH MARK STROMBERG

In one of the one-to-one meetings, Mark and John started to yell at each other. John quickly realized the intensity of the situation and saw an opportunity to apply Tuckman's team-building model. He immediately switched himself into a complete listening mode. He allowed Mark to yell and scream for almost 15 minutes without interruption and gave him the opportunity to let it off his chest. At one point, Mark said, *John, you don't know what you are doing, you are pissing people off. You are encroaching upon people's domain.* John kept listening, and after 15 minutes, when Mark stopped, he spoke. John had realized that he had entered the "storming" phase with Mark, and this was an opportunity to quickly go through that phase, which was essential for building a high-performance team.

John asked Mark to take a deep breath and asked him to walk through the issues slowly and one at a time. It was audio-only in March 2020, and it went on for almost two hours. John laid out the process, and they both agreed to listen to each other and come up with a plan and solution. It appeared that Mark and John were able to avoid the *vertigo* phenomenon described by Daniel Shapiro[61]. Vertigo is when two parties get so consumed in a conflict where they cannot see beyond the problem[61].

After two hours of heated debate and evading vertigo, Mark and John defined the domain and boundaries for each other on the project. They:

a. Agreed to resolve their differences during one-on-one meetings.
b. Decided to stay calm and not yell at each other, no matter how tough the issues were.
c. Agreed that they would take the constructive feedback as an opportunity to improve and strengthen their relationship.
d. Concurred that Mark would not send any emails at 4:00 a.m. without discussing them with John the phone first.

John also requested Mark to trust him and follow his advice for two weeks. If Mark did not like the results after two weeks, he could go back to his way of doing things. Mark agreed and followed John's advice and direction for two weeks, and he was pleasantly surprised with the results that are described below:

- The list of Mark's tasks had gone down. John had taken responsibility for some of the tasks that worried Mark.
- John started to support and appreciate Mark and his professional opinion in the meetings. He gave Mark credit for the great work he was doing.
- After two weeks of experimentation, the trust level between John and Mark soared, and Mark thanked John for creating the space and environment to talk candidly and manage his workload and stress.
- It took Mark and John four weeks to get through the forming, storming, and norming stages of the team-building model.

- They went from yelling and screaming at each other to being good friends. John also deployed some of the critical components *(empathy, motivation, self-discipline, and social skills)* of Goleman's emotional intelligence model to strengthen his relationship with Mark.
- Mark's stress level had gone down after two weeks of working with John and following his advice.
- The result was that Mark and John became friends, and they fully supported and trusted each other during the entire project.

THE "YOU" PHENOMENON

It was 9:30 a.m. on a Thursday in April 2020, and the Weekly Training and Design Meeting with the vendor had started, and it was supposed to last until 10:30 a.m. Kim Butler and Nancy Higgins from Star Technology led those meetings and provided the SMEs and consultants an opportunity to ask questions. Five minutes into the meeting Alfred Hanson (one of the SMEs) started talking. Alfred was a nice, young, fresh-out-of-college, and polite person. Here's what he said to Kim in front of the 12+ team members, including the External QA Team:

> "Kim, you said you had uploaded the templates to the Test System. I checked, and most of them are wrong. I spent a lot of time developing these templates, and you did not upload them correctly. I'm trying to understand why you did not upload them correctly. Why are you not double-checking them after you upload them? I spent a lot of time creating those templates, and they are wrong in GMS."

Kim realized the intensity of the situation, and she responded:

> "I'm sorry, Alfred, you feel that way. But, I was hoping to get your feedback so that I could make any changes you wanted us to make."

For some reason, Alfred would not let go and said:

> "No, Kim, I don't understand why you could not format the text properly."

At that point, John intervened and asked Alfred to move forward and not dwell on this issue. Kim also assured Alfred that she would make all the changes he wanted, and the meeting continued. John could relate to the "you" phenomenon because he went through a similar episode with Linda early in the project, described in Chapter 6.

Shortly after the meeting, John and Max received an email from the Star Technology CEO citing Kim and Alfred's incident. Star asked both John and Max to counsel Alfred to address the issue and avoid this kind of situation in the future.

Earlier on the project, the "you" phenomenon was quite rampant in the team. Most of the team members used the word "you" in a way that sounded accusatory. For example, let's analyze what happened in the communication between Kim and Alfred. Although Alfred was right about some of the things in the contract templates, the way he said, it sounded accusatory. Instead of using the word "you," if he had said, *Kim, Star Technology said that they updated the Test system, but I noticed Star did not do it.*, it would have made the entire conversation a lot easier. All Alfred had to do was replace the word "you" with "Star Technology," and things would have gone much smoother. Besides, Alfred did not have to dwell on the issue. One example was enough, and he should have moved on, especially when 12+ team members were attending the meeting.

Business Communication 101 says: use the word "you" when you want to praise somebody. For example, Dan, you have done a great job. If you're going to provide constructive feedback, try to use a passive voice. An example would be, the contract templates were not uploaded correctly. There is no need to mention any names. Also, sometimes we forget that vendors and consultants are also human beings. They could also make a mistake, and we should forgive each other, especially when somebody apologizes publicly.

PROJECT TEAM'S RELATIONSHIP WITH THE VENDOR

When John took over as project manager, he heard many complaints from some of the team members against the vendor (Star Technology). Their view was that Star did not provide the requisite support and knowledge to the project team. They practically despised Star and had nothing to say except negative comments. After listening to the project team member, John scheduled a virtual meeting with the Star team and heard their concerns. They were generally okay with the project team members, but they also complained against two-to-three people.

Since John was the project manager, he did not want to take a position because that could further exacerbate the situation. John knew that the project manager must become a buffer between all stakeholders through his experience, especially when the relationship was contentious among some of the team members. He decided to investigate and started a fact-finding mission. After talking to various team members and holding multiple meetings with Star, John found out that Star and their team were quite supportive, responsive, and efficient in addressing project team members' issues and concerns.

Also, he decided to have a weekly check-in meeting with Star on Thursdays. The objective was to provide an opportunity for Star to discuss issues candidly and find solutions collectively. John and the Star team got off to a very good start and built an excellent relationship and rapport with each other in a very short period. Star had a solid technical and customer support team but needed capacity-building in project management.

THE OCEAN WAVES

One of the few things that John did during his first 30 days on the project was that he made sure there was only one point-of-contact with the vendor (Star). He decided to become the sole point of contact between the project team and Star. He asked all team members to channel all communication through him. There was an enormous reaction like the ocean waves from some of the team members. They perceived it to be putting limits on their authority and communication with the vendor. John politely stuck to his decision and asked them to follow his decision for 30 days, and then he would re-visit it. One of the team members said to John:

> Who are you to stop us from communicating with the vendor (Star Technology)? We don't need your permission.

John just smiled and thanked the team members for being candid, but he still stuck to his decision. This was the time when the team was going through the *Storming* stage of the Tuckman model. John was not around at the "forming" stage of the project, so he did not have any control over selecting the team members. As a project manager, he was handed over a team and asked to make it work and deliver the project on-time, within the budget, and according to the scope.

This was one of the examples where a project manager has to take flak from some of the team members but still stick to his/her decision. John knew what he was doing, and he believed in himself. He had a broader agenda and vision of creating a high-performance team that some of the team members could not envision at that time. Above all, he had the full support of Max Dillon (the Business Sponsor).

The reasons John took this decision were as follows:

a. He wanted to separate the noise from reality when it came to the vendor's support and service delivery. John heard a lot of complaints against the vendor from 3 out of the 40 team members when he joined the project, so he wanted to get the facts straight.

b. The vendor got confused when they heard from three or four different members on the same issue. And there seemed to be a different version of the issue(s) that was presented to the vendor. It wasted a lot of time and energy on both sides: the client and the vendor.

c. John wanted to streamline the communication between the project team and the vendor. He also wanted the communication to be effective, productive, efficient, and timely.

By volunteering to be the single point-of-contact, John was able to:

i. Find out that the complaints against the vendor were about 90% more noise than reality. It was more like a drama created by two or three individuals on the team.

ii. Develop an excellent working relationship with the vendor.

iii. Build a bridge between the project team and vendor.

iv. Streamline and organize the communication between the vendor and the team.

v. Resolve technical issues in an efficient, effective, and productive manner.

vi. Make all stakeholders more accountable and responsive.

After about three weeks of having one-on-one meetings with the vendor, John invited Jody Foster (a permanent WSDOT employee and one of the designated System Administrators) to his meetings with the vendor. As part of the bridge-building between the vendor and the project team members, he introduced Jody to the vendor and made her a permanent member of his meetings with the vendor. Jody also liked the idea and was happy because she got to hear and learn about the technical issues as well as the overall functionality of the system. In addition, the knowledge and understanding that she gained through the one-on-one meetings with the vendor prepped her to support GMS as a Systems Administrator. Jody was also supposed to run the Help Desk after the system Go-Live, so she was really excited and appreciated John's approach and initiative.

About four weeks after Jody had been attending the vendor's meetings, John asked Jody if she would be comfortable being the single-point-of-contact between the project team and the vendor. Jody was pleasantly surprised, but she liked the idea and agreed to do it. As soon as Jody agreed, John made the announcement. All team members were happy with the news except a couple because they thought they should have been the point-of-contact. And now they would have to go through Jody.

Two out of the forty team members seemed unhappy with John's decision, but John kept moving forward with it. He knew he could not make everyone happy. John made Jody the single point-of-contact for all communication with the vendor, especially on the design and technical issues during the week. Max (the Business Sponsor) also liked and appreciated the decision.

John and Jody agreed on Standard Operating Procedures (SOPs) on communication with the vendor, and Jody did an excellent job of sticking to the SOPs. No matter what, she would not deviate from the SOPs in the weeks and months to come. Here are the SOPs that were decided:

- Jody would create a log file of all the issues that would come up during design and functionality sessions that were typically held on Monday–Wednesday.
- She would send the log file to the vendor daily with a copy to John, Mark, and the relevant SMEs that raised the issues.
- She would consolidate all the pending and open issues and send the consolidated file to the vendor at the Close Of Business (COB) Wednesday. John and Jody would follow up with the vendor on the Thursday Q&A session.
- This weekly process continued till the end of the project.

All those SOPs worked out very well for the client and the vendor. Other positive aspects of making Jody the point-of-contact are as follows:

- The transition from consultants and vendors to the client (WSDOT) started sooner (April 2020) than later.
- Jody started to get familiar and trained on how she would be dealing with 12 months down the road when the consultants and vendor would be transitioned out.
- The Help Desk team, including Jody, felt very comfortable with this approach. They were being trained while the system was being designed and implemented.
- Jody did an excellent job of logging the issues, follow-ups, and communication with the vendor, which ultimately helped the team and the project.

11

Change Management, EQ, and DQ

Linda Whiteheart led the OCM team. She spearheaded all change management activities on the GMS project. Linda was excellent in managing the change, but her plate was more than full because she had additional responsibilities besides the GMS project. She had the customers' and stakeholders' pulse, so she did a good job of assisting Max and John. Linda was supported by Helen Swift, a consultant from Green Tree Consulting. Whenever Linda needed an extra hand, Helen jumped in and put the OCM activities on track.

Helen had an immensely high intellect (IQ), emotional intelligence (EQ), and decency capabilities (DQ). She carried herself very well and took the entire team along and helped Linda, Max, and John create a culture of excellence through a combination of IQ+EQ+DQ, as defined by Bill Boulding in the HBR article (Boulding, HBR). She was polite but firm and got the tasks done. Max, Helen, and John believed in and practiced what Goleman said: "Emotional Intelligence: Why it can matter more than IQ." (Goleman, 2005). Linda and Helen became a great team and did an incredible of managing change across WSDOT.

Fortunately, Max had realized in March 2020 that Linda had too much on her plate. Thus, he decided to increase Helen's role and involvement in the project. And the decision paid off because Helen was an excellent and experienced resource. Not only did she help Linda to manage the critical tasks and activities, but she also executed some of them and got them completed in an efficient and timely manner. In addition, Helen coached Linda on conducting team-building and change management activities.

There were several challenges and issues that Max and John faced during the course of the project, including heated debates with the team members who were more vocal than others. Some of the events are highlighted below to give the readers an idea about the challenges that John faced, especially during his initial 30 days in March 2020, which I call the "honeymoon" period of John's tenure at the GMS project.

A Project Manager is like a parent having multiple children. As parents, you love all children, so you cannot take sides or discriminate with one against the other. Therefore, John decided to listen to all the team members. And with Linda and Helen's help, he came up with a strategy and planned to support the project team.

MOVING FROM THE BALCONY TO THE DANCE FLOOR

Often, leaders stay away from the action (dance floor) and watch the employees and teams from the balcony. It's good to get into the trenches and see what the front line employees face. Similarly, it's highly beneficial for project managers to know every team member and stakeholders on the project.

John observed that one of his predecessors' downsides (Larry) was that he stayed away from the action. For example, Larry did not participate in the system functionality validation sessions with the SMEs. He let the Business Analyst work with the team and potentially missed out on the critical issues during those sessions. He did not attend the Design and Training sessions conducted by the vendor (Star Technology). Again, that was a missed opportunity as well. The design and training sessions allowed the Project Manager to understand the team's issues and challenges. John made sure that he attended all meetings, events, and training sessions. He did not miss any opportunity to interact with the team, vendor, and other stakeholders, which paid off. He understood the pressure points of the team. John was always current on all the issues on the project and took immediate action wherever necessary.

As a leader, you need to figure out when to stay on the balcony and move to the dance floor. This is also called the art and science of managing people. It involves judgment, EQ, and DQ. Mastering these skills helps you build a relationship with the team members, which helps to create a high-performance team. Both John and Max understood these concepts quite well, and they deployed EQ and DQ to stay current on the project issues, build trust with the team members, and motivate the team.

Max also attended all the weekly meetings. In addition, he held one-on-one meetings with key team members to get a pulse of the team and project. He was always on top of things. Since Max was a quick-decision maker, whenever he saw an issue, he took action. He was proactive in assessing the project risks, understanding the issues, and managing change. John and Max played as a tag-team and complimented each other. They talked daily and exchanged notes, and kept each other apprised of what happened on the project at any given point. They knew when to get involved and when to pull away from the action, let the team debate and decide on the issues. This approach worked well and helped to manage change.

HERDING THE CATS

As Linda would say: "Leading a high-performance team is like herding the cats." High-potential individuals and members of high-performances teams can act in eccentric ways, so you have to bring them to a common platform. Generally, the team members who possess a high IQ would require a leader(s) with high EQ and DQ abilities to focus on the tasks and project. That's what Linda, Max, Helen, and John did on the GMS project.

The GMS team consisted of high IQ individuals that preferred to act autonomously, which led them to deviate from the project plan. Sometimes they did not focus on the relevant project tasks and activities. They digressed and got sidetracked unintentionally. Thus, Linda and Max leveraged their emotional intelligence (EQ) and decency (DQ) capabilities to convince them to focus on the project. This was all part of the change management.

John built a reputation of using two words quite often: *focus* and *no show-stoppers*. Team members joked around and mentioned these two words every time they saw or talked to John. Slowly, but surely these words became *catchphrases* on the project, and everybody embraced them. Linda also reminded John that these were his first few words when he joined the project. While people laughed about them, in reality, the team made great progress after focusing on the tasks that were on the critical path. They also made sure that there were *no show-stoppers* on the project. Even when show-stopper issues came up, the relevant team members, along with Max and John, got together and resolved those issues.

SLICING AND SHARING THE PIE

One of the challenges was that team members' domains and responsibilities were not clearly defined. Roles and responsibilities (Annexure D) were defined for each position on the project, but they lacked clarity. It was not clear which team members would do what tasks on a day-to-day basis. Therefore, Max and John got together and elaborated on key team members' responsibilities and boundaries, especially the Work Stream Leads. They added the granularity to Work Stream Leads' job description that was required to do their work daily.

Once Max and John were done clarifying the roles and responsibilities, which they called the slicing of the pie, they got to the next level of information sharing. They ensured that the Work Stream Leads and other team members shared the critical information essential for change management. Linda and Helen were kept in the loop as they were part of the OCM team.

Max empowered the Work Stream Leads to make decisions and execute their tasks as they deemed appropriate. However, they reported any risks, issues, and show-stoppers within 24 hours to Max and John for immediate action and decision-making. In addition, all risks, issues, and decisions were logged in the RAID log, so they were visible to all team members and stakeholders, including the External QA Team.

COMMUNICATION CHANNELS AND FEEDBACK

The OCM team, under Linda's leadership, created multiple communication channels and feedback loops. They devised a robust communication and training plan, conducted culture and pulse surveys, organized virtual roadshows, held meetings with customers, and organized Change Champions Meetings quarterly. Linda and Helen were instrumental in creating these plans and executing them. In addition, weekly project status and one-on-one meetings with team members and stakeholders were immensely fruitful in managing the change that was caused by the implementation of GMS.

Linda and Helen always sought feedback from the team members, customers, and stakeholders. They passed the comments and feedback on to Max and John, who listened to the team's and stakeholders' concerns and addressed them promptly. Communication and information sharing was crucial in GMS' project's success and change management.

The OCM team executed the communication plan that ensured open and transparent communication: upward, downward, and laterally. Both Linda and Helen steered the ship in the right direction from an OCM perspective, and timely executed the change management activities.

THE 4:00 A.M. EMAILS

Mark had a habit of firing off emails at 4 a.m. that annoyed some people on the team. Even though he had good intentions, sending emails at 4 o'clock in the morning and providing constructive feedback early in the day was probably was a bit unsophisticated. During a one-on-one meeting, John requested Mark to use *empathy* and try to see how the other side felt after seeing constructive emails at 4 a.m. or as soon as they logged into the system in the morning. John politely suggested to discuss the issue on the phone and not send emails unless it was mutually agreed and absolutely necessary. If the issue was resolved on the phone, there was no need for the email unless Mark felt the need to document the resolution or decision. Since Mark and John had developed a good working relationship, they both respected and listened to each other. Mark happily accepted and implemented John's suggestions.

Mark also ensured John that he would not send any emails without discussing them with John first. After a couple of weeks, Mark came to John and thanked him for his suggestion of not sending emails without discussing on the phone. Not only did it cut down on the number of emails, but it also reduced the stress on Mark and other team members. Resultantly, both John and Mark understood each other's work style. Mark also started to empathize, which led to a high level of trust among the team members. John followed-up and followed-through on whatever was discussed in the one-on-one meetings, which built his credibility with Mark and the rest of the project team. A combination of empathy, trust, politeness, and credibility was one of the secrets of creating a high-performance (The Blue Shark) team on the GMS project.

USE OF TECHNOLOGY DURING A CRISIS

Due to COVID-19, all meetings were switched to a virtual-mode. The GMS project team became a heavy user of the technology and virtual meeting platforms. Both Max and John used to turn-on the videos whenever possible and when people felt comfortable with the video. But, they did not make them mandatory as some people might feel more comfortable with the audio, especially during COVID-19 when people are stuck at home and sitting in casual attire. Max and John knew that their job was to make team members comfortable to talk freely, share ideas, and be more productive.

THE GELLING OF THE BLUE SHARK TEAM AT GMS

Daily and weekly communication sessions broke down the silos and provided team members an opportunity to share their grievances. After airing their differences, the team members started to show empathy for each other, which was one of the key pillars of emotional intelligence as per Daniel Goleman's model. Psychological safety and empathy led to trust-building, which led to motivation and a high-performance team. As defined in Chapters 2 and 6, empathy is when a team member listens to his/her colleague and tries to understand his/her perspective. It's like putting yourself in other's shoes and trying to feel what he/she feels.

KEY TURNING POINTS ON THE PROJECT

There were a number of turning points that led to the creation of the Blue Shark (high-performance) team and project success. Following events and decisions played a crucial rule in the implementation of Goleman and Tuckman's model, change management, and transformation on the GMS project:

1. Max (the Business Sponsor) and Jeff Beaumont (the Executive Sponsor) made a good decision in March 2020 to bring in a strong Project Manager with experience in emotional intelligence (EQ), team-building, leadership, and project management skills.

2. In March 2020, Max also appointed a part-time OCM consultant (Helen Swift) from Green Tree Consulting to assist Linda because she was overworked. Helen did a great job of executing the OCM tasks and steering change management activities in the right direction. Helen proved to be an excellent resource for change management. She also assisted both Max and John in motivating the team. Helen helped to resolve conflicts amongst the team members. She had immense knowledge and experience with change management, so everybody, including Linda, respected her. She enjoyed expert power on the project. Linda, Helen, Max, and John were the *quadruple-success* factors. They possessed IQ, EQ, and DQ skills, which were necessary and vital for creating the Blue Shark team and project success.

3. John's two-hour "storming" session with Mark (the Business Analyst) during the second week of March 2020 initiated the storming stage of team-building. John and Mark had a heated discussion. They did their level-set with each other, defined the domain and boundaries for themselves, and established a communication protocol under which they both operated for the rest of the project. After the "storming" stage, they became good friends and supported each other, which helped the project.

4. The "storming" session between John and Linda in April 2020 paved the way for their friendship and excellent working relationship. John's decision of meeting with Linda on her scathing emails and Max's role as a mediator played a critical role in setting the tone and course for the rest of the project. Had John not met Linda and set the tone early on, there was a strong possibility that Linda would have John removed from the project, which would have either delayed or failed the project again. It appeared like Linda wanted Mark to be the Project Manager as he was ready to take over from Larry. Max provided full support to John, which sent a message to the project team that John was to stay on the project until it was delivered successfully.

5. Max and John devised a project implementation strategy in March 2020 and decided to roll out the project in two phases and smaller pilots. Max had a clear vision as to what he wanted, and John helped him to achieve it. The GMS team achieved the low-hanging fruit by rolling out the Regional Mobility Grants Application Pilot in June 2020 and Consolidated Grants Application Pilot in July 2020. It helped cut down the noise and pessimism and gave an immense motivational boost to the project team. People, including Senior

Management of WSDOT and customers, could not believe that parts of the GMS were live, and the customers started to use the system in August 2020. These were unbelievable moments for the project team, WSDOT, and the customer. All of this happened when COVID-19 was at its first peak in July 2020.

6. Max made a good decision in July 2020 to replace Linda with Ashley as the Training Work Stream Lead effective August 01, 2020. It allowed Linda to focus on change management activities, and Ashley did a great job of streamlining the training sessions and developing a cordial relationship with Star Technology.

7. Appointing Larry (the former Project Manager) as the Data Work Stream Lead was another excellent decision that Max took. Retaining Larry on the project and leveraging his technical abilities paid off as he did a good job of data migration from the legacy to the new system. Also, Larry possessed the project history as he had been working on it for over a year when John took over from him. It was nice to have him around so that John could reach out to Larry whenever he needed him.

8. Shortly after the lockdown in Washington State in March 2020, Max decided to leverage the latest technology and virtual meeting platforms. Max mandated the entire team to switch to a single virtual meeting platform (MS Teams) for all audio and video calls and team meetings. It was an excellent decision by Max, and it paid off. Not only did it allow efficient and reliable communication amongst the team member, but it also brought them to a common platform that enabled the entire team and stakeholders to collaborate in a smooth, organized, and effective manner. In addition, switching to MS Teams saved money on the State's phone bills because the project team did not have to use conference call bridge numbers and regular telephone lines, which got choked during the early days of COVID-19.

9. Having a robust IT and communication infrastructure was vital during a crisis. Quickly adapting to technology and virtual platforms played a significant role in managing change during the pandemic. The fact that the entire project team was able to work remotely without a hitch was remarkable. The credit goes to the WSDOT's IT Division for developing and maintain such a good IT and digital infrastructure.

10. A combination of IQ+EQ+DQ, storming sessions with the team members, timely and quick decision-making by Max, efficient and reliable communication, strong OCM support, and breaking the project into phases and smaller chunks were crucial for the project's success during COVID-19.

12

Project Management Methodology, Tools, Techniques, and Processes

PROJECT MANAGEMENT METHODOLOGY

The GMS project team followed Project Management Institute's *PMBOK* methodology along with WSDOT's standards and guidelines throughout the project management life cycle. Key phases of the project management life cycle are shown in Figure 12.1. And the key activities performed during various phases of the project management life cycle are shown in Table 12.1.

While adhering to the *PMBOK*®, WSDOT guidelines, and due to the project's criticality, the GMS project was organized in a series of specific Project Stages as defined in Table 12.2. A stage divided the project deliverables, milestones, and activities into manageable groups. This enabled effective management of the work and allowed decision gates at the end of each phase. It also ensured that the business objectives outlined for the project were met within the constraints and at the quality expectations of the customer.

TOOLS AND TECHNIQUES

Several tools and techniques were used to monitor risks and issues on the project. Some of the key tools that were immensely helpful for the project are described in the following pages.

SharePoint Portal

A SharePoint portal was created for the project that also became the documents repository. A snapshot of the GMS SharePoint portal is placed in Annexure E.

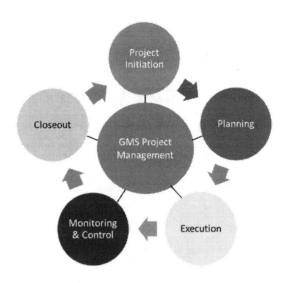

FIGURE 12.1
GMS project management -methodology.

Note: *PMBOK*˚ is a registered trademark of the Project Management Institute (PMI)

Source: Adopted from PMBOK˚ Guide.

Risks, Actions, Issues, and Decisions (RAID) Log

The project team used a RAID (Risks, Issues, Actions, and Decisions) log to track key project issues, risks, and decisions from inception through resolution. The project team reviewed the RAID log weekly to track status and updates. Each RAID log item was assigned to one, and only one, specific project team member. A screenshot of the RAID log is placed in Annexure F.

RAID Item Types

For every RAID log item, the item type must be specified. The definition of each item type is described in Table 12.3.

Risk Items

Identification and Categorization

Risks were identified throughout the project. During monthly risk review meetings with the Work Stream Leads, risks, and issues were discussed, assessed, and either logged or updated. In addition, if a risk was identified

TABLE 12.1

Project Management Phases of GMS

	Project Management Phases for the GMS Project (PMBOK®)				
	Project Initiation	Planning	Execution	Monitoring & Control	Project Closeout
Project Integration Management	Develop GMS Project Charter	Develop Project Management Plan (PMP) for GMS	Manage the GMS Project and Workstreams	1. Monitor and control the GMS project. 2. Manage the change the control process.	1. Close the GMS project. 2. Document lesson learnt
Project Scope Management	–	1. Collect requirements 2. Define project scope	–	Validate and control GMS project scope	–
Project Schedule Management	–	Develop the project schedule with tasks, activities, resources, and timeline	–	Control and update schedule	–
Project Cost & Budget Management	–	Determine project costs and budget	–	Control costs and budget	–
Project Quality Management	–	Development of Quality Management Plan by the Quality Assurance Group/ Consultants as per WSDOT's guidelines	Manage quality through a thrid party QA Group / Consultants as per WSDOT's guidelines	Control quality in collaboration with the Quality Assurance Group/Consultants	–
Resource Management	–	Manage activities and resources through the project schedule	Manage the project team	Manage resources	–

(Continued)

TABLE 12.1 (Continued)

Project Management Phases for the GMS Project (PMBOK®)

	Project Initiation	Planning	Execution	Monitoring & Control	Project Closeout
Communication Management	–	Create a communication plan and mechanism through the SharePoint portal and weekly status meetings	Manage communication among key stakeholders	Monitor communication. Ensure key stakeholders are receiving the project information in a timely manner	–
Risk Management	–	Identify and manage risks through the Quality Assurance Group/ Consultants	Manage risks in collaboration with key stakeholders and the Qaulity Assurance Group/ Consultants	Monitor risks along with Quality Assurance Group / Consultants	–
Procurement Management	–	Assist in procurement management	Assist in procurement for the GMS project	Assist in monitoring and controlling the procurements	–
Stakeholder Management	Identify key stakeholders of the GMS project	Plan key stakeholder engagement and weekly status meetings	Engage key stakeholders in discussions and weekly status meetings	Monitor stakeholder enagaement	–

Note: PMBOK® is a registered trademark of PMI.
Source: GMS Project Archives.

TABLE 12.2

GMS Project Stages and Activities

Sr. No.	GMS Project Stage	Key Activities
1	**Initiation**	This stage consists of the key activities to begin the project, including creation of a project charter, vision and mission, goals and objectives, defining the requirements, and creating the project scope. Key stakeholders and workstreams are also identified at this stage.
2	**Planning**	Project schedule is developed, including the project activities, tasks, timelines, milestones, deliverables, resources, and workstreams. Work breakdown structure (WBS) and Organizational Breakdown Structure (OBS) are also developed at this stage.
3	**Monitoring and Control and Project Governance**	Agency readiness is assessed and project governance structure is created. Monitoring and control procedures and activities are defined, which will continue through the project closeout.
4	**Procurement**	This stage entails procuring the GMS solution vendor, contracting with the vendor for implementation services, and organizing the project activities.
5	**Organizational Change Management (OCM)**	The organizational change management activities are initiated during this stage of the project, and will continue through project closeout.
6	**Execution**	Following are the sub-stages that have been defined to expedite the Go-Live of the GMS project:
	A) Design Development	This stage includes developing the detailed functional and technical design documents. This also includes evaluating the vendor solution against the agency business requirements to identify any gaps. The outcome of design will be the complete scope of work to configure the solution, implement interfaces and data conversion.
	B) Configuration	This stage includes establishing the baseline environments, completing configuration of the design, and conducting review sessions. Additionally, work to prepare existing (legacy) systems to send and receive data with the new solution is completed.
	C) Testing	This stage includes testing the solution configuration by the vendor (Unit), by the project core team across multiple platforms (SIT), and then by project users and key stakeholders (UAT).

(Continued)

TABLE 12.2 (Continued)

Sr. No.	GMS Project Stage	Key Activities
	D) Training	End-user training is conducted to validate the configuration and ensure that the Agency personnel are prepared to being using the system.
	E) Cutover	Cutover activities are performed to switch the users from the legacy to the new GMS. Also, it is ensured that the system is production-ready.
	F) Deployment / GMS Go-Live	New GMS will be deployed and the users will start using the system.
	G) Support	This stage consists of those activities to ensure the transition to operations and the end users are well supported. Key performance indicators are used to assess the health of the implementation and identify areas of support.
7	Project Closeout	Once the transition to operations is complete, lessons learned are documented and the project is closed.

Source: GMS Project Archives.

in day-to-day project execution, it was logged and either assessed immediately or at the next monthly risk review meeting.

RAID items logged as risks were categorized and ranked for both impact and probability. The ranking was recorded on the RAID log item. The PMI Probability and Impact matrix (Figure 12.2) was used to identify the probability and impact of a risk.

TABLE 12.3

RAID Log Item Definitions

Item Type	Definition
Risk	An uncertain event or condition that, if it occurs, has a positive or negative effect on a project's objectives. A risk is something that has <u>not</u> happened yet and isn't guaranteed to happen.
Action Item	Detailed tasks or activities that must be completed may or may not have a one-to-one relationship with a task on the project schedule. They are assigned to a specific resource and due by a specific date.
Issue	Something which jeopardizes the project and which must be addressed. When a risk occurs it becomes an issue.
Decision	An item that requires approval to implement. A decision will require an assessment, a recommendation for a specific course of action, and a review prior to approval.

Source: GMS Project Archives.

		Impact				
		Trivial	**Minor**	**Moderate**	**Major**	**Extreme**
Probability	Rare	Low	Low	Low	Medium	Medium
	Unlikely	Low	Low	Medium	Medium	Medium
	Moderate	Low	Medium	Medium	Medium	High
	Likely	Medium	Medium	Medium	High	High
	Very Likely	Medium	Medium	High	High	High

Note: *PMBOK*® is a registered trademark of the Project Management Institute (PMI)

FIGURE 12.2
PMI probability and impact matrix (*PMBOK*˙).

Note: *PMBOK*˙ is a registered trademark of the Project Management Institute (PMI).

Action Items

Action items could be added to the RAID log by any team member, ensuring that the fields listed below were filled in.

Issue Items

An issue could be an item that impacted the project negatively if not addressed. Either it would be addressed immediately, or a meeting would be held to discuss the issue and find a resolution.

Decision Items

Decisions captured recommendations, approval, communication, and outcomes of project decisions.

PROCESSES

Project Work Streams

The GMS project was organized into various Work Streams (Figure 12.3) to produce deliverables and achieve the milestones. The Work Streams allowed the project activities and tasks to be organized to ensure effective execution and alignment with the business processes. Each Work Stream would be assigned a lead to produce the project deliverables.

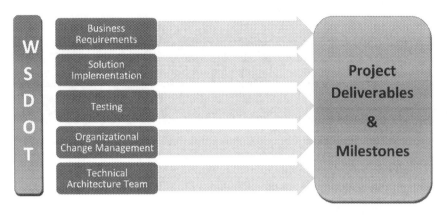

FIGURE 12.3
GMS project work streams.

Source: GMS project archives.

Project Work Streams and their key responsivities are described below:

- Business Requirements
  - Identifying, documenting and validating the business requirements.
  - Supporting the development of the solution design documents.
  - Ensuring the design, configuration, test cases, and delivered solution met the business requirements.

- Solution Implementation (vendor)
  - Utilized the business requirements to develop the functional and technical design.
  - Configured the solution to meet the design specifications.
  - Established the solution environments (e.g., development, QA, training, and production).
  - Provided hosting, backup, and support for the environments.
  - Provided knowledge transfer to and for PTD and WSDOT's configuration specialists.

- Testing
  - Responsible for developing and executing the test plans to ensure the configured solution met the PTD and WSDOT's specific requirements.
  - Organizational Change Management (OCM).

- Planning and execution of activities to ensure a successful transition from the legacy system to GMS.
- Ensuring end-user, customers, and key stakeholders' acceptance of GMS.
- Training of internal users, customers, and external stakeholders.
- Execution of change management activities, including surveys, newsletter, workshops, and scheduling of change champions meetings.

- Technical architecture (network, security, data, and reporting)

  - Ensuring that the technical infrastructure would support the new solution.
  - Working closely with the vendor to integrate the new technology into the existing environment.
  - Ensuring business processes replaced by the new system were accounted for and remediated, if necessary, to minimize the impact.
  - Coordinated work with external agencies as necessary to support access to enterprise data, the integration architecture, and reporting.

Roles and Responsibilities

Detailed responsibilities for each role on the project is placed at Annexure D.

Project Decision-Making

The GMS Business Sponsor was responsible for day-to-day project decision-making. Decisions were documented in the RAID log. Any decision related to project scope, schedule, budget, or other resources were referred to the Executive Steering Committee. Table 12.4 illustrates the decision-making roles and escalation process.

Definitions of Decision Involvement	Definition of Impact Terms
C = Consult	Minor = changes that do not affect scope, schedule, budget, or business processes
REC = Recommend	Moderate = changes that affect business processes; affect the scope or schedule with no financial impact; or multiple minor changes.
A = Approve	Significant = changes that affect the scope, schedule, and/or budget; or multiple moderate changes
I = Inform	

Source: GMS project archives.

TABLE 12.4

Decision-Making Roles and Escalation Process

Business Decision Teams	Subject Matter Experts (SMEs)			Decision Review Team			Executive Decision Team	
Decision-related to a specification or requirement that:	Subject Matter Experts (SMEs)	IT/Technical SMEs	GMS Team	Project Manager	Functional Manager	Business Sponsor	Project Executive Sponsor	Grants Steering Committee
a. Does not change current business activity within a business process; same functionality, only one configuration option; no change to the schedule	C	C	C	REC	A	I	I	I
b. Does not change a current business activity within a process; same functionality; multiple configuration options; no change to schedule	C	C	C	REC	A	I	I	I
c. Changes a current business activity within a business process; has a minor impact; affects a single functional area or multiple functional areas; change to the schedule	C	C	REC	REC	REC	A	I	I

d.	Changes a current business activity within a business process; has a moderate impact; affects a single functional area or multiple functional areas; with team consensus; no financial impact	C	C	REC	REC	REC	REC	A	I	I
e.	Changes a current business activity within a business process; has significant impact; has a financial impact	C	C	REC	REC	REC	REC	REC	A	I
f.	Requires additional customization to the COTS solution; has a financial impact	C	C	REC	REC	REC	REC	REC	REC	A
g.	Is outside of the current scope; requires a change request; has a financial impact	C	C	REC	REC	REC	REC	REC	REC	A

Source: GMS project archives.

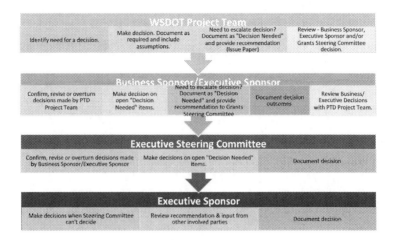

FIGURE 12.4
GMS decision-making process.

Source: GMS project archives.

Project Team Decision Process

The project team followed the decision-making process as shown in Figure 12.4.

Conflict Resolution Path

As we all know, conflicts arise on projects. Therefore, a conflict resolution path (Figure 12.5) was defined to know what to do whenever a dispute arose.

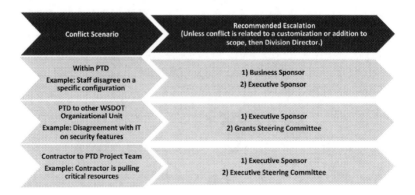

FIGURE 12.5
GMS conflict resolution path.

Source: GMS project archives.

TABLE 12.5

RAID Log Item Entry Process

Step	Name	Person Responsible	Action
1	Entry	Any project team member	Items are entered as they arise by project team members. If a team member believes a previously resolved RAID item needs to be re-opened, they will contact the PM team to reopen and reassign the item.
2	Review & Updates	Project Management Team	The PM team will review all items with a status of "Active" to make sure that it is a valid item and that it has been filled out correctly. The PM team may ask the requester to fill out additional detail or to suggest an assignee.
3	Communication	Project Management Team	A list of Overdue and Upcoming items will be emailed on a weekly basis, highlighting who each item is assigned to, and asking for status updates. In addition, the status will be tracked on the tactical scheduled and reviewed during daily huddles. A report will be run and published weekly with all closed items. It is the expectation that the team reviews this to ensure that no items have been closed prematurely and that they have the information they need to continue their dependent tasks.
4	Resolution	Assigned To	Once complete, the task will be marked "Inactive" and the item will be updated with the appropriate amount of detail and closed.

Source: GMS project archives.

RAID Workflow and Review Process

Table 12.5 describes the lifecycle of a RAID item and the process of logging an item into the RAID log.

13

Project Governance, Monitoring, Control, and Evaluation

Various tools and mechanisms used for governance, monitoring, control, and evaluation of the project were quite effective for successfully delivering the Grants Management System (GMS) project.

PROJECT GOVERNANCE

Grants Management made up a large body of work that was performed by the Public Transportation Division (PTD) of Washington State Department of Transportation (WSDOT). PTD established several cross-functional teams to address various issues associated with managing subrecipient grants. A specific GMS Project Team was established to identify all grant management processes and functionality needed for a GMS. In addition to the project team, an Executive Steering Committee was established that oversaw the project's activities. It was charged with decision-making on recommendations of the project team and Business Sponsor.

Successful outcomes of the GMS project was critically important to reduce the administrative burden of grants management while increasing WSDOT's ability to provide accurate and timely reports to the Federal Transit Administration, WSDOT Executives, and the State Legislatures.

Governance for the GMS project comprised an Executive Sponsor, Business Sponsor, External Quality Assurance Team, Oversight from the Office of the Chief Information Officer (OCIO), and the Executive Steering Committee. The project governance structure is shown in Figure 13.1.

A detailed Project Organization Chart is placed in Annexure C.

DOI: 10.1201/9781003216711-15

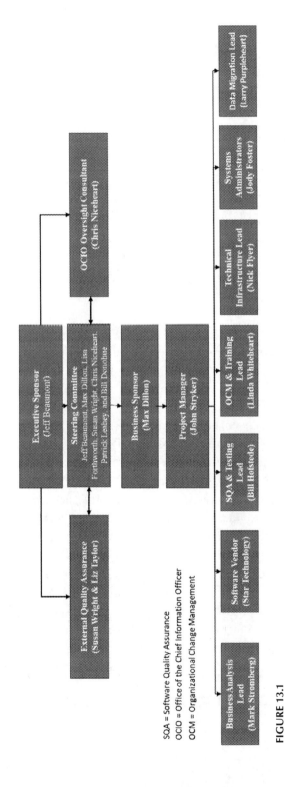

SQA = Software Quality Assurance
OCIO = Office of the Chief Information Officer
OCM = Organizational Change Management

FIGURE 13.1
GMS project governance structure.

Executive Steering Committee (ESC)

The ESC acted like a watchdog for the project and met monthly to assess risks, monitor, and evaluate project progress. The composition of the ESC was as follows:

1. Executive Sponsor
2. Business Sponsor
3. Director of Accounting and Financial Services
4. IT Director at WSDOT
5. Director WSDOT Audit Office
6. A representative of the External Quality Assurance Team
7. A representative of Washington State OCIO.

Oversight by the OCIO of Washington State

The Washington State mandated oversight by the Office of the Chief Information Officer (OCIO) for all IT projects executed by different agencies. Therefore, the GMS project fell under the OCIO watch. A representative of the OCIO was also a member of the Executive Steering Committee (ESC). The OCIO representative attended the monthly ESC meetings and provided feedback on the overall project progress.

The OCIO also had specific monthly reporting requirements in terms of the project budget, actual project-to-date costs, timeline, scope, and risk assessment. The three (scope, timelines, and cost) elements of the iron triangle, as often referred to in the project management methodology, were reported to the OCIO dashboard along with the project risks and mitigation strategy. The assessment of budget, scope, and timeline was also shown as green, yellow, or red to get a quick pulse of the project by the senior management of WSDOT.

The OCIO oversight was a good governance mechanism to safeguard public money and ensure project success. It also provided an additional opportunity to monitor and evaluate the project monthly by an independent Washington State agency.

Roles and Responsibilities

This was a simple but potent tool. Responsibilities were defined for each of the roles on the project. A copy of the roles and responsibilities is placed at Annexure D. It might seem quite intuitive, but many project managers forget to do this, and it leads to chaos on the project. For every task on the project schedule, there should only be one person listed as "responsible," and there can be multiple people listed as "support." Having two or more people responsible for a task is a recipe for disaster. Therefore, Max (the Business Sponsor) ensured that only one person was responsible for each task on the project.

PROJECT MONITORING, CONTROL, AND EVALUATION

The GMS project was monitored, controlled, and evaluated weekly and monthly through various tools and techniques described in the following pages.

External Quality Assurance (QA) Team

As mentioned earlier, the External QA Team was responsible for monitoring project risks, quality, and critical issues weekly and monthly. They created a monthly status report (Annexure B) for the senior management of WSDOT as well as the Steering Committee. They were also a member of the Executive Steering Committee. In addition, the External QA Team attended all weekly status, design, and training meetings conducted by the vendor.

Change Control Process and the Board

A Change Control Board (CCB) was established for the project. Key members of the CCB, along with the roles and responsibilities, are shown in Table 13.1.

The CCB was established as governance, monitoring, and control mechanism for the project. They monitored the project's budget, scope changes, and timeline. All changes had to go through the CCB and ESC for review and approval.

The CCB met as and when necessary at the request of the Business Sponsor or the Project Manager. They met when there were any changes to the project budget, scope, and timeline.

TABLE 13.1

Change Control Board (CCB) Roles and Responsibilities

Role	Name(s)	Responsibilities
PTD Management Team	Jeff Beaumont, Max Dillon, and Alan Swift	The PTD Management team will serve as the Change Control Board (CCB) and retains the highest level of authority.
Executive Sponsor	Jeff Beaumont	The Executive Sponsor has the authority to modify, approve, deny, or override requested changes.
Steering Committee	Jeff Beaumont, Max Dillon, Lisa Forthworth, Susan Wright, Chris Niceheart, Patrick Leahey, and Bill Donohue	The Steering Committee is an oversight and advisory body. The Executive Sponsor may choose to consult with the management team or GMS Steering Committee as appropriate.
Business Sponsor	Max Dillon	The Business Sponsor has the authority to modify, approve, or deny changes within certain thresholds and criteria. The Business Sponsor may choose to consult with the Executive Sponsor, the management team, or GMS Steering Committee as appropriate.
Evaluator	Various WDOT and external evalutors	The Evaluator is an expert assigned by the Business Sponsor. The Evaluator is assigned to analyze the impact of a proposed change and/or facilitate the analysis.
Requester/Stakeholder	GMS Team Members and Stakeholders	The Requester can be any project stakeholder. The Requester submits the new Change Request (CR) via the WSDOT GMS SharePoint site.
Project Manager	John Stryker	The Project Manager is responsible for facilitating the Change Control process. He/She will track all the activities while the change request(s) is being reviewed, coordinated, and verified to ensure that the change request is implemented correctly.

Source: GMS Project Archives.

Change Control Process

It was possible that changes to the current scope, schedule, or cost of the GMS project could become necessary for various reasons, such as the COVID-19 emergency. In that event, the GMS Business Sponsor and Project Manager, in collaboration with the project team and project governance, would use the following procedures to identify, analyze, approve, and control changes to scope, schedule, and or budget.

A scope change is referred to as any modification or new requirement deviating from the baseline established in the Statement of Work, scope, schedule, budget, or any approved baselines managed by the project team.

Change control referred to a series of procedures by which all project changes were assessed and approved. All potential changes were compared against the project baseline in terms of functionality, schedule, cost, upgrade capability, maintainability, and resources. Possible scope changes would be analyzed, tracked, and managed using the RAID log (Annexure F) as described in the Risk Management section.

The process for managing change requests for the GMS project is as follows. The flow chart of the change request approval process is also placed in Annexure G.

- The change control process began with the identification of a change that might impact scope, schedule, cost, or other resources. Often, awareness of such changes came through the resolution of project issues. Issues might spawn a need for a change as part of the issue resolution.
- Potential changes were recorded in the Change Control Register maintained on the project's SharePoint site. New changes were identified and recorded in the log. Team members would record a short description and reason for the change, the potential impact of the change (scope, cost/budget, and time), and the date identified.
- The GMS Project Manager and Project Team reviewed new change requests during the weekly status calls. The team tried to resolve the issues in the meeting. However, any issues requiring more time were taken offline. The Business Sponsor also attended those meetings.

- The Business Sponsor would assign the remaining new change requests (if any) to the appropriate project staff for analysis. The project staff would analyze the reasons for the requested change, the impact on scope, schedule, cost, or other resources, alternatives to satisfying the reasons for the change, and prepare a discussion/decision paper if warranted. The paper would include the analysis, recommendations, and a due date for the completion of the solution.
- The GMS Business Sponsor would review completed discussion/decision papers and determine if further review or action was required using the following criteria:
- A change that affected the scope, schedule, cost, or other resources would be elevated to the GMS Executive Steering Committee for their review and approval.
- The Executive Steering Committee reviewed the outstanding discussion/decision papers. The change in scope, estimated cost, schedule, and resource impact would be examined. The Executive Steering Committee would dispose of any discussion/decision papers that required immediate action, and the RAID log (Annexure F) would be updated accordingly.
- Final action might be one of the following:
- Approved changes would be entered into the RAID log and assigned to the appropriate team member for further action. The RAID log would be maintained throughout the lifecycle of the change.
- Deferred changes would be placed on hold status in the RAID log. They would be periodically reviewed to determine if sufficient time, resources, and budget were available to complete the changes prior to testing and implementation.
- Rejected change requests would be placed on closed status in the RAID log, along with an explanation for the rejection.
- In case the steering committee could not reach an agreement by consensus, the Executive Sponsor would make the final decision.

Go-Live Readiness Scorecard

The Go-Live Readiness Scorecard (scorecard) was put in place to ensure that the system was ready, bugs-free, and there were no significant risks to the project by going live with the new system. The scorecard was endorsed by the External QA team and OCIO. The key objectives to have the score-card in place 45 days prior to the Final Go-Live was to conduct a risk assessment and ensure all business policies and processes had been put in place to support the new system. A sample of the Go-Live Readiness Scorecard for the Regional Mobility Grants (RMG) Application Pilot release is placed in Annexure H.

A presentation was made to the OCIO about 45 days (in February 2021) prior to the Final Go-Live of March 31, 2021. The Project Manager presented the scorecard to the OCIO and the ESC. Both the OCIO and ESC were satisfied with the risk assessment and mitigation strategy and approved the Final System Go-Live of March 31, 2021.

Project Schedule

The project was divided into two phases, and a detailed project schedule was created for each of them. A snapshot of the project schedule is placed in Annexure I. The project schedule was reviewed line-by-line in the weekly All-Hands-on-Deck meeting attended by all team members, the vendor, and the External QA Team. All open issues listed in the RAID log (Annexure F) were also discussed in the meeting.

Weekly, Monthly, and Quarterly Standing Meetings during the COVID-19 Crisis

Effective weekly, monthly, and quarterly meetings were the hallmark of the GMS project success. Max (the Business Sponsor) and John (the Project Manager) led the meetings in a way that the agenda was clear, and all the core team members were given an opportunity to discuss issues along with the resolution. The objectives and mechanics of each meeting are discussed below.

Executive Steering Committee Monthly Meeting

The ESC mandate was to monitor and control the project costs, budget, timeline, scope, and risks. The ESC members also provided advice to the Business Sponsor and Project Manager every month on the project's execution. They assisted the project management team in removing any bottleneck that might have come up during the project.

Weekly Vendor-Led Design and Training Sessions

The vendor held weekly software design and Questions & Answers (Q&A) sessions for the Work Stream Leads, consultants, Subject Matter Experts, External QA team, and other relevant project team members. These sessions helped the SMEs to validate the software design and functionality. And they also helped the Testing and SQA team to understand the system design and test the functionality.

Monday Morning OCM-BA-Project Manager Check-In

Every Monday at 8:00 a.m.–9:00 a.m., the OCM Lead (Linda), Business Analysis Lead (Mark), OCM Consultant (Helen Swift), and the Project Manager (John Stryker) met to discuss any outstanding issues and devised an action plan for the week. Effective August 01, 2021, Ashley joined the meeting after she took over from Linda and became the Training Lead.

The meeting helped to improve communication between the OCM, BA, Training Work Stream Lead, and the Project Manager. The objectives of the meeting were as follows:

a. Have open communication between the OCM, BA, Training Lead, and the Project Manager to discuss broader issues that would impact key internal and external stakeholders across the spectrum.
b. Ensure proper updates and messages were delivered to the project team, customers, and external stakeholders, i.e., transit agencies and authorities that were sub-recipients of the grants from the Federal and State Governments.
c. Review and discuss the weekly training and software design validation sessions' agenda and schedule. The vendor conducted the actual training and design sessions, but Linda (later on, Ashley) used to coordinate them.
d. Review and discuss issues that came up during weekly software design and functionality validation sessions.
e. Discuss any other issues or risks to the project and schedule.

The weekly check-in meetings were helpful as they kept key Work Stream Leads informed about broader aspects of the project. It also helped to discuss the issues in a smaller group.

Monday Morning Weekly Status Meeting

Every Monday from 10:00 a.m. to 11:00 a.m., a project status meeting was held. The attendees were all core team members (about 20 of them) except the vendor. The vendor was excluded because WSDOT team members felt the need to talk openly and freely without any fear of creating any ill-will with the vendor.

The meeting's objective was to have an open discussion on any pending and critical issues from the prior week so that an action plan could be devised to find a solution during the week. Also, smaller sub-teams of 2–3 members were created to follow up on the action items and issues and resolve them quickly. Max appointed a sub-team leader and gave him/her complete autonomy on how he/she wanted to conduct the meetings. John and Max made themselves available if the sub-team lead wanted them to attend the meetings.

John led the meeting along with Max (Business Sponsor). John went around and asked each Work Stream Lead to discuss any issues, concerns, or risks and asked for their feedback. Once the Work Stream Leads were finished, John opened the floor to all team members to discuss any issues.

Initially, the meeting took almost a full hour. But, as the project team got more focused, organized, and action-oriented, the meetings went much faster and smoother and became highly productive. By October of 2020, some meetings lasted for only 15 minutes because the project team had started to work like a "well-oiled" machine. At that time, the project team had become a high-performance team and had successfully entered the "performing" stage of Tuckman's model.

OCM-Project Manager Weekly Check-In

In April 2020, Linda and John decided to have a one-on-one meeting every Wednesday from 8:30 a.m. to 9:00 a.m. to discuss all issues. The objectives of this meeting were to:

a. Allow both Linda and John to discuss issues and devise a strategy to resolve them.
b. Meet via the video call during COVID-19 and make it as personable as possible. It was quite helpful when you could see the person as opposed to talking on the phone. The video made it more cordial when you could look at each other through a live video.

c. Identify any issue(s) or decisions that needed to be escalated to Max as he was the Business Sponsor and ultimate decision-maker on the project.

d. Continue to build a friendly and professional relationship with each other.

The meetings helped to strengthen the working relationship between Linda and John. Overall, Linda was an amiable and kind-hearted person. After a few meetings, both understood each other's personalities, strengths, and weaknesses, and they gave each other the space they needed to work as productive members of the project team. They both leveraged key elements (self-awareness, self-discipline, and empathy) of Daniel Goleman's emotional intelligence model and strengthened their relationship, which ultimately benefited the project and WSDOT.

Wednesday Morning Weekly All Hands-on-Deck Meeting

This was an all-hands-on-deck meeting every Wednesday from 10:00 a.m. to 11:00 a.m. Almost 40 people attended it. Everybody, including the External QA Team as well as the vendor, joined the meeting. The objectives were to discuss critical issues, deadlines, milestones, deliverables, and risks to the project. John and Max jointly led the meeting with a complete focus on issues, risks, resolution, and action items. Business decisions were taken and recorded in the RAID log (Annexure F).

John kicked-off the meeting by reviewing open issues in the RAID log (Annexure F). He went over the list issue-by-issue. All issues were discussed, and action items were generated and documented. Again, sub-teams of 2–3 people were created, if necessary, to follow up and find solutions to open issues.

If any risks to the project were identified, John noted them and personally followed upon them. External QA Team also provided their risk assessment and feedback to the team. John also led all the monthly risk review and assessment sessions and involved the relevant team member whenever necessary.

The second item on the main agenda was to review the Project Schedule line-by-line. All tasks that were coming due in the next 30 days were reviewed and discussed. Each Work Stream Lead covered his/her area on the project schedule and gave an update. If anybody were to miss the deadline, it was immediately identified, discussed, and action items were created to ensure the task's timely completion. The project schedule became the Bible for the GMS project. John would update the project schedule weekly and sometimes twice a week, depending upon the task and the action items. Both the RAID log and the project schedule were kept on the SharePoint Portal of WSDOT's intranet. All team members had access to the SharePoint Portal.

Just like Monday morning meetings, these meetings used to last for about an hour. But, as the team got more organized and focused, the meetings ended in 20–30 minutes. The meetings got immensely productive and action-oriented as the trust and motivation levels were elevated.

Weekly Wednesday Afternoon Meeting on Data Migration

Data conversion and migration are critical for IT projects. Converting legacy data can be a very laborious and time-consuming job, but it is an extremely critical element of the project. Therefore, a separate Work Stream was created for data migration, which was led by Larry Purpleheart. Larry was extremely technical and had lots of experience with data conversions on his previous projects. Also, he understood WSDOT's legacy system very well, so he was the perfect person to lead the data migration. Larry used to present the data migration progress and identify any issues and bottlenecks that needed to be removed by the Business Sponsor or Project Manager. Relevant SMEs and stakeholders also joined the meeting.

Weekly Thursday Morning Q&A Session with the Vendor

Due to COVID-19, the vendor could not be on-site, so communication and interaction with the vendor was a challenge that needed to be overcome for a successful software implementation. In addition to email interaction as well as training and design sessions on Tuesdays, John was able to negotiate a 30-minute Q&A session between the WSDOT subject matter experts and the vendor to resolve any issues that used to come up during the week. The Q&A session on Thursdays played a crucial role in moving forward the system design and functionality validation. Emails were great, but sometimes it was much easier, faster, and better to talk on the phone or video. It could help clarify the issues and enable all parties to develop a solution expeditiously. Live communication with the vendor during COVID-19 was one of the lessons learned for the GMS project.

Monthly Risk Review Meetings

Risk review meetings were conducted every month, especially during COVID-19. The Project Manager led them. Participants of the meetings included all Work Stream Leads and the External QA Team. The objectives of the risk review meetings were:

a. Brainstorm and identify risks to the schedule and overall project in terms of budget, timeline, and scope.
b. Continuously assess the impact of COVID-19 on the project's overall health and come up with a mitigation strategy promptly.
c. Identify the "show-stoppers" and find a solution expeditiously.
d. Assess the risks that might come up down the road, devise a mitigation strategy, and inform the senior management quickly.
e. Create action items for any imminent risk(s) or threats to the project and schedule. John's responsibility was to follow up on the action items and ensure that they were resolved in a timely manner.

The meeting minutes were uploaded to the SharePoint Portal and were accessible by all team members.

Monthly Project Manager-External QA Team Meeting

Since the External QA team was responsible for the project's risk assessment and quality assurance, they had a monthly formal meeting with the Project Manager and the Work Stream Leads. They wanted to ensure that the Project Manager knew all the critical risks and issues on the project and a proper follow-up and resolution path was adopted. These meetings were quite useful in terms of proactively managing the risks and critical issues.

Quarterly Change Champions Meeting

The OCM team organized a quarterly Change Champions Meeting and invited all project team members, internal and external stakeholders, customers, sub-recipients, and management. The purpose of this meeting was to create awareness about GMS amongst PTD and WSDPT employees. It also allowed the stakeholders and customers to ask questions about the project as well as GMS functionality.

RAID Log

A snapshot of the RAID log is shown in Annexure E, a very effective tool used by the GMS Project Team. The RAID log was created on the SharePoint Portal accessible by all team members through the WSDOT intranet. John reviewed the RAID log with all the team members in the weekly meetings on Wednesdays. The External QA Team was also present on the Wednesday call to conduct the review and assessment.

The issues and resolutions, along with business decisions and their rationale, were logged in the RAID log. The External QA Team also reviewed these decisions from a risk assessment perspective.

Monthly Newsletter

The OCM team published a monthly newsletter. The objective of the newsletter was to highlight project progress, milestones, and deliverables. And it was also a way to inform all PTD staff members on the overall project performance, features, and timeline. A snapshot of the Monthly Newsletter is placed at Annexure J.

Quarterly Culture and Pulse Surveys

We have already discussed the culture survey in Chapter 6. The OCM team conducted another survey that included external stakeholders and customers of WSDOT. The customers included sub-recipients or grantees that received the grants from the federal and State Governments. They were also the end-users of the Grants Management System. A snapshot of the survey results is placed in Annexure A.

Quality Management

A Quality Management Plan was developed to define the acceptable level of quality determined by the business. It described how the project would ensure high levels of quality in its deliverables and work processes. The plan was posted on the SharePoint Portal. Also, the External QA Team ensured the quality of the project deliverables and overall project.

Vendor Management Plan

As a best practice, a Vendor Management Plan was created to monitor and evaluate the vendor's progress and quality of the deliverables. A Deliverables Form was created as part of the Vendor Management Plan. This form was tied to the vendor's payments. The vendor was paid after the Deliverables Form was signed-off by the Subject Matter Experts, relevant Work Stream Leads, the Project Manager, and the Business Sponsor.

PROJECT CLOSEOUT

The purpose of the project closeout was to:

- Ensure that the project met its goals and objectives.
- Document lessons learned.
- Identify best practices to be applied to future projects across Washington State.
- Ensure that a proper transition to operation plan was in place.

POST IMPLEMENTATION REPORT

The Post Implementation Report was an assessment and review of the project and final solution. The Project Manager worked with the Business Sponsor to complete a report after GMS was deployed and the project was completed. The report provided:

- A summarized timeline of events,
- Final budget,
- Key deliverables,
- The degree of project success,
- The extent to which the project objectives were met,
- Benefits realized,
- Any significant challenges or barriers faced by the project team,
- Key lessons learned, and
- Recommendations for future projects.

ADMINISTRATIVE CLOSEOUT

These were the tasks that needed to be completed before the project could be closed, such as developing a transition to operations plan, archiving project artifacts, payment of invoices, etc. The Project Manager worked with the project team to create a checklist of activities that needed to be completed and by whom to close the project.

FUTURE ENHANCEMENTS LOG

While John asked the project team to focus on critical business processes and system functionality, he did not want to lose sight of the "nice-to-have" features that the end-users wished to have in the system. An "Enhancements Log" was created, maintained, and updated every week. It was used during the weekly software design and validation sessions. The SMEs made sure that the software had all the crucial functionality when they went live, but they also documented nice-to-have features that needed to be addressed in future releases of the system.

PROJECT PERFORMANCE, CRITICAL EVENTS, TIMELINE, AND MILESTONES

The project went through all four stages of Tuckman's model on team-building during the project lifecycle. Despite COVID-19, the project team

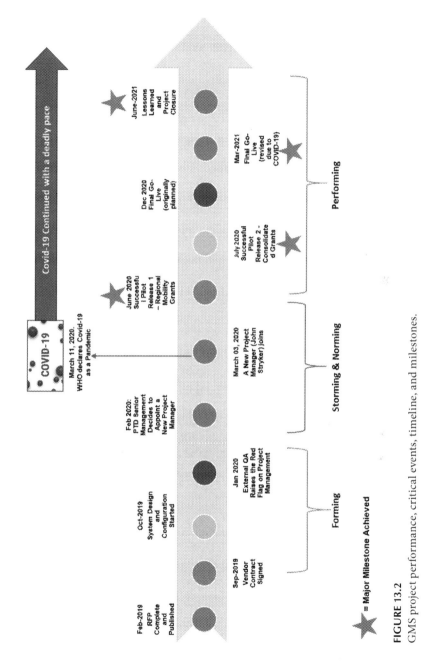

FIGURE 13.2

GMS project performance, critical events, timeline, and milestones.

was able to stick together, overcome the challenges, and deliver the project on-time, within the revised budget, and according to the scope. A summary of the project performance, critical events, timeline, and milestones are shown in Figure 13.2.

14

Lessons Learned

Executing the GMS project during a crisis such as COVID-19 posed quite a few challenges. The project team learned many valuable lessons on creating a Blue Shark (high-performance) team during the pandemic. This chapter describes the lessons learned and steps that leaders and project managers around the world can adopt during a crisis or pandemic to lead companies, teams, and projects successfully. These lessons can be applied to any crisis in the private or public sector across industries, including healthcare, IT, manufacturing, telecom, oil and gas, construction, financial services, consulting, and others.

CRITICAL SUCCESS FACTORS OF THE BLUE SHARK TEAM AT THE GMS PROJECT

The Executive Sponsor of the GMS project, Jeff Beaumont, was quite satisfied with the overall implementation of the system and said:

> "Having a talented staff with a passion for their work and a thorough knowledge of existing business processes can make an enormous contribution towards project success. While understanding the existing processes is important, it is equally important to understand everything we designed our processes to accomplish. Too much focus on the business practice will result in a new system that perpetuates the old practices. Having the ability to manage our vendor to meet our needs was our critical need. We didn't have that expertise on our staff, so we hired expert project management consultants. Our job was to produce a simple document that laid out system/business requirements for the vendor. It was not our job to tell them how to design the system to meet these requirements. The magic was

DOI: 10.1201/9781003216711-16

watching the consultant take the business requirements to the vendor and managing them to create an accessible product that efficiently met our needs."

As the Business Sponsor, Max Dillon was glad that the project was implemented successfully within the approved budget, on-time, and according to the scope. His key takeaways from the project were:

"Several months into the project, the vendor's side's lack of an implementation plan became apparent. The project's threat was real; the team needed to develop a new strategy swiftly to deal with the risk. A new better-skilled project manager was hired, and a new delivery plan, vendor management plan, and risk mitigation plan were implemented. At times when thinking of pandemic and all the challenges that we faced, I can't believe that we pulled the project away from the cliff and put it on the path to success. We certainly learned our lessons and willing to share them with others. This was teamwork and outstanding achievement."

Susan Wright of the External QA Team appreciated the overall project management, governance, risk management, and monitoring and evaluation processes that were followed ever since John took over as a Project Manager. She commented:

"The first procurement did not result in the selection of the vendor. The project sponsors then invested in bringing outside expertise to assist in this project and went back out to bid. Once there were the right people with the right skills in key roles of the project manager, business analyst, and testing analyst who were partnered with the vendor team and key subject matter experts within the business area, the project was well on its way to success. With critical processes in place, the team focused on what needed to get done one module at a time, and collaboration and cooperation to get the work done soared. Business staff saw system functionality each week, learned the system, and became more excited about how business processes would be improved."

The Blue Shark Team at the GMS project worked like a well-oiled machine after implementing Goleman's emotional intelligence model and getting through the forming, storming, norming, and performing stages of the Tuckman model. The team became highly efficient, productive, and cohesive during the performing stage. Here are the critical success factors that created the Blue Shark (high-performance) team, which led to the project's success:

1. The psychological safety of all team members was ensured by Max (the Business Sponsor), Project Manager, and Senior Management at WSDOT. All team members felt safe to talk about issues, concerns, and risks without the fear of having any negative repercussions. As Daniel Coyle said in his book, *The Culture Code*, "We have seen small signals – you are safe, we share risk here – connect people and enable them to work together as a single entity[65]." Not only did the project team perform as a single entity, but their productivity also went up during COVID-19. During a global crisis, the project team achieved what seemed impossible during normal times. It was amazing how the team came together, became a well-oiled machine, and successfully delivered the project.

2. Max Dillon and key Subject Matter Experts (SMEs) knew WSDOT's business processes profoundly well. Therefore, they knew what type of functionality they wanted in GMS, which helped with the software design and functionality validation enormously.

3. Decision-making was highly effective and efficient, which led to higher performance and productivity. Max was a quick and firm decision-maker and provided full support to the team members daily.

4. The OCIO's oversight at the Washington State was critical in managing the risks, removing bottlenecks, and getting the budget and Investment Plan approved. Chris Niceheart, from OCIO, was an outstanding professional and human being. He provided immense support and advice to the project team, which became critical success factors to the project's success.

5. The External QA Team did an excellent job of risk assessment weekly and monthly. They attended all key meetings and provided timely and effective feedback to the Project Manager and the WSDOT Senior Management. Not only did they assess the risks, but they also provided recommendations on how to mitigate them. They worked very closely and diligently with the Executive Sponsor, Business Sponsor, Project Manager, and Work Stream Leads.

6. Strong OCM support played a critical role in managing change on the project as well as across WSDOT. Linda Whiteheart (the OCM Lead) and her team did an excellent job of managing the change.

Helen Swift (a consultant from Green Tree) assisted the OCM team enormously in resolving conflicts, designing surveys, generating a monthly Newsletter, organizing Change Champions Meetings, and executing change management tasks.

7. User authentication and cybersecurity are always a major concern, especially when people work remotely during a crisis. Nick Flyer (Technology Work Stream Lead) was a certified Systems Architect. He did an excellent job ensuring that GMS complied with the State of Washington's authentication requirement, including the Secure Access Washington (SAW) protocols.

8. Team members utilized emotional intelligence elements of empathy, empathetic communication, and listening when interacting. They empathized and respected each other. There were professional differences and heated discussions, but everyone appreciated each other's opinions and valued their contribution to the project.

9. The team adopted an open communication style. Team members talked to each other directly instead of just talking to the Project Manager, team lead, or Business Sponsor. They talked to stakeholders outside the group and brought back valuable information to the team to ensure that the project was on-track and meeting stakeholders' requirements and expectations.

10. Team members looked for opportunities to help each other. The four Most Valued Persons (MVPs) on the team were: Max Dillon, Sharon Boyle, Ashley Hemmings, and Jody Foster.

11. The team went through the "storming" and "norming" phases reasonably quickly after the new Project Manager joined the team.

12. The software vendor had a strong technical team and provided good customer support. They also did a good job of training the SMEs on the software.

13. Meetings were conducted effectively and efficiently. Specific action items were generated out of the weekly and monthly team meetings. Again, Max took an active part in all weekly meetings and ensured that specific action items were generated for all issues identified during the meetings.

14. Use of the latest technology and virtual communication platforms such as MS Teams, Zoom, and others were crucial for building a high-performance team. Since in-person meetings were impossible during COVID-19, the project team quickly switched and adapted to the latest technology. Therefore, having a robust IT infrastructure, tools and technology were critical.

15. The GMS team reviewed the project schedule, milestones, and the RAID during the weekly All-Hands-On-Deck meeting, which all key stakeholders attended, including the vendor and the External QA Team.

16. Data conversion and migration was crucial, so Max appointed Larry Purpleheart as the Data Migration Lead. Larry was technically sound, had excellent people skills, and knew his job well. Both Max and John kept an eye on the data migration activities weekly and sometimes daily. A data migration scope document and schedule were created for weekly monitoring. Max, Larry, and John closely monitored all the data migration activities. Max's decision to keep Larry around and make him the Data Migration Lead paid off because he did a remarkable job with data migration.

17. Testing and Software Quality Assurance (SQA) team played a positive role in finding the bugs and issues in the system and making sure they were resolved promptly. They conducted meticulous testing and worked very closely with the vendor and SMEs to ensure that the system was free of bugs. Both Bill Hofstede and Joe Stemon did an excellent job of testing the software and making sure it was free of bugs.

18. The Business Sponsor, Project Manager, and Senior Management at WSDOT appreciated the team's efforts and held virtual celebrations at the end of each major milestone. COVID-19 prohibited in-person celebrations, so the team had to celebrate virtually.

19. Goleman's emotional intelligence model (self-awareness, self-regulation, empathy, motivation, and social skills) was implemented to create and lead the Blue Shark (high-performance) team on the project. The team also went through Tuckman's model's five stages to reach the spire and deliver the project successfully.

20. Everybody on the GMS team talked, listened to, respected each other's points of view, and contributed to the project. The following factors summed up the success of the Blue Shark team and project:
    i. Empathy
    ii. Decency Quotient (DQ) and collegiality
    iii. Mutual respect
    iv. Psychological safety for all employees
    v. Empathetic communication and listening
    vi. Heated debates (storming)
    vii. Employee recognition and appreciation

    viii. Focus and dedication of team members

     ix. Good governance, leadership, and project management

      x. Efficient meetings and timely decision-making.

LESSONS LEARNED ON CREATING A BLUE SHARK TEAM

In addition to the critical success factors mentioned above, there were general lessons learned that could be utilized to create a Blue Shark (high-performance) team to cope with any crisis. Here are the steps, not in any particular order, to develop and lead a high-performance team during a crisis such as the COVID-19 pandemic:

1. There must be some team members who know and understand the business processes very well to make effective and timely decisions. On the GMS project, Max Dillion knew WSDOT's business processes enormously well, and therefore he made very useful and quick decisions.

2. Create a well-rounded team with gender and intellectual diversity, including technical, OCM, project management, risk assessment and management, quality assurance, testing, and planning expertise.

3. Appoint a strong Project Manager with not only technical but people management skills. Someone with team-building, emotional intelligence, psychological safety, and stress management knowledge and experience should be highly desirable.

4. Create a robust IT and communication infrastructure. Several software solutions are quite effective such as MS Teams, Zoom, GoToMeeting, and others.

5. Review your contracts with the suppliers and customers. Get legal advice and try to understand the force majeure clause.

6. Conduct crisis impact assessment by finding answers to the following questions:

    a. Who is impacted? What tasks and activities would be delayed?

    b. Who is causing the bottlenecks? Identify the people, processes, and systems that are causing the bottlenecks. Create a strategy and action plan to remove the blockages on an urgent basis?

    c. What is the impact in terms of people, cost, budget, revenues, and infrastructure?

d. When will be the maximum impact on the project and organization? Monthly, quarterly, or annually?

e. Who needs help? Who can help?

f. What do we need to get through the crisis in terms of people, process, budget, and infrastructure?

g. Who will manage the communication during the crisis?

h. Who will check up on the safety and health of the team members?

i. What are the legal challenges faced by the organization?

7. Perform risk assessment and management. Conduct monthly risk review meetings and follow-up on action items.

8. Review and update the human resource, financial, and contingency plans.

9. Revise the project budget based on the risk assessment, human resource, and infrastructure needs.

10. Update the communication plan with assistance from the OCM expert on the project. If you don't have an OCM expert, hire one.

11. Re-calibrate the project schedule and update the responsibility matrix based on the ground realities. During a crisis, the situation might change daily, so you need to keep the schedule and the responsibility matrix current.

12. Create a RAID (Risks, Assumptions, Issues, and Dependencies) log and monitor it daily, weekly, and monthly. You can use tools like the SharePoint portal to create and monitor the RAID log.

13. Review and monitor the project schedule with key team members on a daily, weekly, and monthly basis. Discuss issues openly on the project status calls. Create action items for team members to resolve the issues. Don't leave issues open-ended.

14. Conduct one-on-one meetings with key stakeholders and team members weekly or more frequently if need be. Discuss all issues and provide each other candid feedback. Jot down action items and follow-up.

15. Listen, listen, and listen to your team members, especially during a crisis.

16. Practice empathy with all team members and stakeholders. And become a bridge-builder among team members and stakeholders, including vendors and customers.

17. Exercise patience and restraint through active listening.

18. Move quickly through the forming, storming, norming, performing stages of team-building. Empathy, active listening, and patience are

crucial elements of successfully creating and leading high-performance teams.

19. Create an environment of psychological safety where team members can talk freely without the fear of any negative consequences.

20. Have third-party quality assurance audits on a monthly and quarterly basis. Don't wait till the end of the year. A crisis such as the COVID-19 pandemic is an unprecedented time where we must be more efficient, diligent, and proactive.

21. Communicate, communicate, and communicate. You would rather over-communicate than under-communicate. Copy all relevant team members on emails without looking at their job titles. It's not uncommon in the public sector and large organizations to feel awkward by copying a person junior to you in rank or title. This is one of the most futile mistakes people make on projects. It hinders communication and creates silos.

22. Recognize and appreciate your team members weekly and monthly, especially in large meetings.

23. Give constructive feedback during one-on-one interactions but never in public, don't be shy of giving and receiving it. Spending most of your meeting time on exchanging pleasantries would rarely help you resolve issues and build trust. Don't try to sweep the issues under the rug. Attack the problems by openly talking about them. As a leader, I highly recommend that you go through the forming, storming, norming, and performing sessions with all team members during one-on-one meetings. This is an effective way of breaking down the silos and open communication channels with your team members. And it would help you enormously to build trust and credibility with the team members.

24. Tame your ego. Don't take constructive feedback personally. Adapt your style to make the team members comfortable, which will help you build trust with the team.

25. The Weekly Status Meetings are must. It would help if you had them, and they have to be highly organized, focused, and action-oriented. Issues must be identified, an action plan must be devised, and a sub-team be formed that would follow up and report back to the team the following week. Committing to complete tasks in front of 40+ people put enough pressure on team members to follow up and resolve the issue(s) within five business days (if not sooner). Alternatively, they come up with a concrete explanation and action plan.

Annexure A: GMS Culture Survey Results

CULTURE

 Control

 Understanding

 Leadership

Trust

 Unafraid

 Responsive

Execution

WHAT WE ASKED?

1. What is your primary role on the project?
2. How would you rate **CONTROL**? (Personal perspective – I have the authority to make the appropriate decisions that can help me get my work done. Team perspective – There is a single point of approval for most things or members of the project team feel they can make the needed changes. Frustrations are addressed and timely decisions are made)
3. How would you rate **UNDERSTANDING**? (Personal perspective – I know what we are doing, why we are doing it, and what success looks like? Team perspective – Everyone on the project team knows their role and how it fits into achieving success. Communication flows down from leaders is as needed and the team feels empowered to communicate directly at any level. The team understands how well

they are performing and feel understood, valued and that they have the opportunity to do what they do best)

4. How would you rate **LEADERSHIP**? (Personal perspective – My leaders support me and the project? As a leader, I support the team and the project. Team perspective – Does the project team feel like leadership helps eliminate roadblocks? Is the team doing things to leave a lasting impression on the organization (good) and build a healthy culture that will last beyond the project?)

5. How would you rate **TRUST**? (Personal perspective – I trust and respect the team. Team perspective – There is no "us" vs "them" mentality. We are implementing ways to develop an honest, open, and transparent environment. The team handles issues/chatter as it is brought up in a timely manner)

6. How would you rate **UNAFRAID**? (Personal perspective – I feel comfortable speaking up when I have a concern or am focused on finding a solution. Team perspective – Members of the project team speak up when there is a problem and with a solution-oriented mindset. The project team suggests solutions when raising issues. The project team does not silently resent decisions/people or fail to raise issues so they can be resolved)

7. How would you rate **RESPONSIVE**? (Personal Perspective – I respond promptly to requests. Team perspective – The team responds to requests and questions in a timely manner. Things do not fall through the cracks. The project team collaborates on work and issues effectively and feels progress is not bottlenecked with one individual or group. The organizational structure and systems for the project help and hold up the project team's ability to respond. Little things like emails, returning phone calls, etc. do not fall through the cracks)

8. How would you rate **EXECUTION**? (Personal perspective – I do what I say I will do. Team perspective – The team feels that everyone does what they say they will do when they are going to. The team is held accountable for their performance. The team members speak up and get help/work through issues when they arise. The team is not burning-out (staying late, leaving early, and one person doing the bulk of the work). The team actively protects the work/life balance of one another. The project team is engaged, collaborative, and supportive of one another.

Below are the results of the CULTURE Survey:

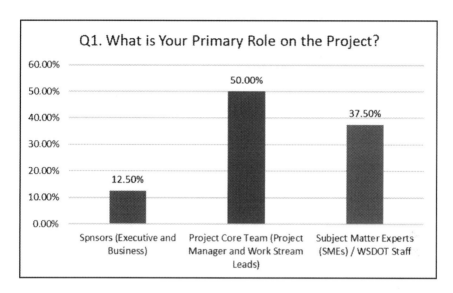

Results of the CULTURE Survey (continued.)

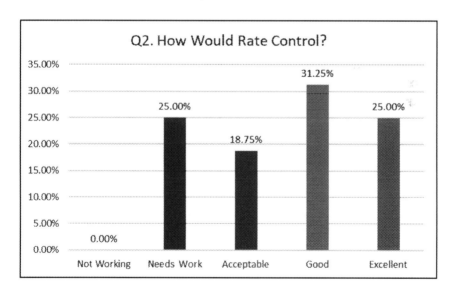

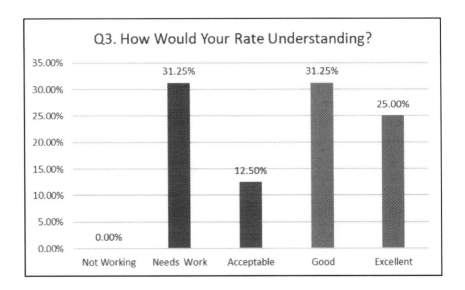

Results of the CULTURE Survey (continued.)

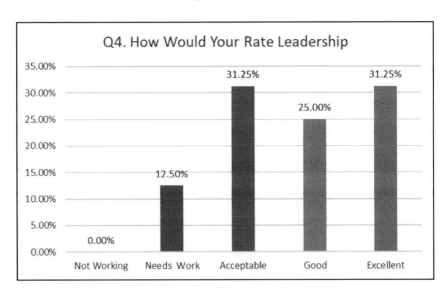

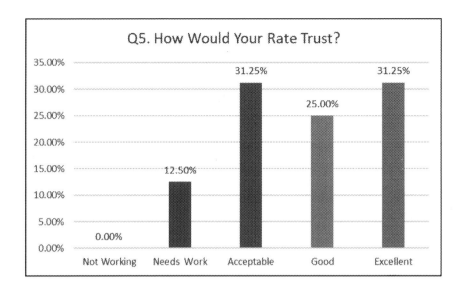

Results of the CULTURE Survey (continued.)

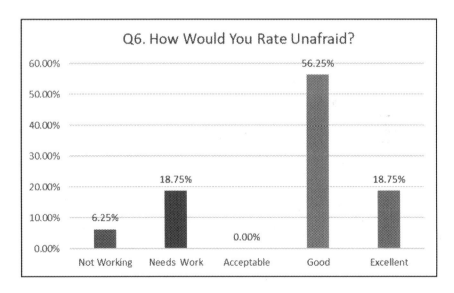

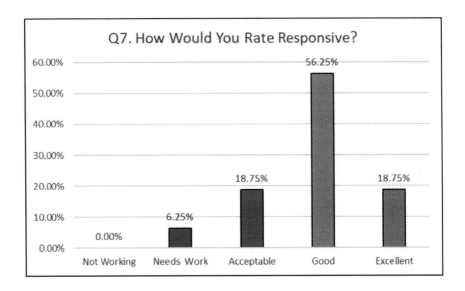

Results of the CULTURE Survey (continued.)

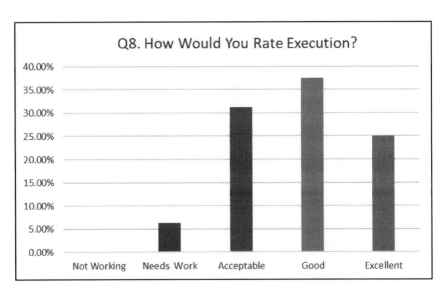

Source: GMS Project Archives.

Annexure B: External Quality Assurance Team's Monthly Report

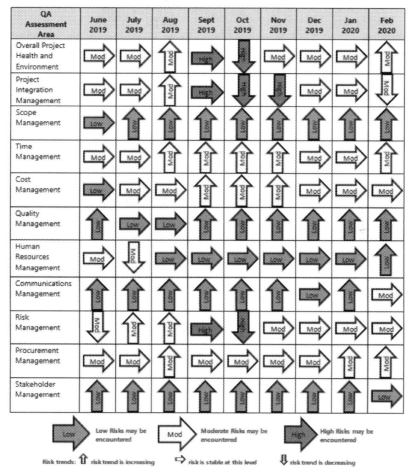

SUMMARY OF MONTHLY QUALITY ASSURANCE RISK ASSESSMENTS

QA Assessment Area	June 2019	July 2019	Aug 2019	Sept 2019	Oct 2019	Nov 2019	Dec 2019	Jan 2020	Feb 2020
Overall Project Health and Environment	Mod	Mod	Mod	High	High	Mod	Mod	Mod	Mod
Project Integration Management	Mod	Mod	Mod	High	High	High	Mod	Mod	Mod
Scope Management	Low	Low	Low	Low	Low	Low	Low	Low	Low
Time Management	Mod	Mod	Mod	Mod	Mod	Mod	Mod	Mod	Mod
Cost Management	Low	Mod	Mod	Mod	Mod	Mod	Mod	Mod	Mod
Quality Management	Low	Low	Low	Low	Low	Low	Low	Low	Low
Human Resources Management	Mod	Mod	Low	Low	Low	Low	Low	Low	Low
Communications Management	Low	Low	Low	Low	Low	Low	Low	Low	Mod
Risk Management	Mod	Mod	Mod	High	High	Mod	Mod	Mod	Mod
Procurement Management	Mod	Mod	Mod	Mod	Mod	Mod	Mod	Mod	Mod
Stakeholder Management	Low	Low	Low	Low	Low	Low	Low	Low	Low

Low — Low Risks may be encountered

Mod — Moderate Risks may be encountered

High — High Risks may be encountered

Risk trends: ⇑ risk trend is increasing ⇨ risk is stable at this level ⇓ risk trend is decreasing

Source: GMS Project Archives.

Annexure C: GMS Project Organization Chart

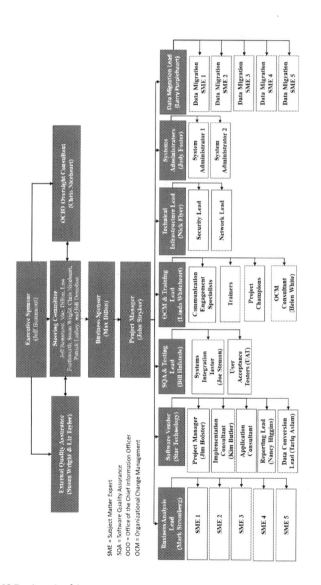

SME = Subject Matter Expert

SQA = Software Quality Assurance

OCIO = Office of the Chief Information Officer

OCM = Organizational Change Management

Source: GMS Project Archives.

Annexure D: GMS Project Team Members' Roles and Responsibilities

PROJECT LEADERSHIP/CORE TEAM

Executive Sponsor

The Executive Sponsor will:

- Provide guidance to the GMS Project Manager.
- Be ultimately accountable for the success of the new system.
- Provide strategic direction to the project.
- Provide leadership to the agency on behalf of the new system.
- Make decisions if the Steering Committee does not come to a consensus.
- Confirm decisions if the Steering Committee is in disagreement.
- Appoint members of the Steering Committee and project team as requested.
- Be willing to mandate business process alignment, where necessary.

Executive Steering Committee (ESC)

The Committee is composed of executive management and other key stakeholders who can address issues that may span multiple programs and functional areas. This Committee will:

- Represent key business areas of the agency.
- Approve and monitor the project scope, budget, and schedule.
- Secure and provide required resources as needed.
- Provide guidance on business issues, policy, and/or agency related issues.

- Address issues that may span multiple departments, programs, or and functional areas.
- Remove obstacles or roadblocks that impede progress.
- Make decisions with high impact on the project regarding policy, scope, schedule, and budget.
- Monitor results and assess project progress.
- Monitor and mitigate project risks.
- Resolve disputes between the teams regarding configuration decisions.
- Ensure the project makes good use of assets and resources.
- Monitor to ensure transparency in project management, reporting, and decision-making.
- Use their influence and authority to assist the project in achieving its outcomes.
- Ensure the project team receives adequate cooperation and support from the agency.

Business Sponsor

Represents the Executive Sponsor on a day-to-day basis; makes most of the decisions requiring Sponsor approval and will:

- Direct project activities.
- Provide final approval on the project approach and operational processes.
- Be responsible for implementation and operational support of the new system.
- Appoint members of the project team.
- Review and approve final project deliverables.
- Consider and approve Change Requests.
- Chair the Steering Committee.
- Ensure transparency in project management, reporting, and decision-making.
- Make resource decisions within the approved project budget.
- Align agency level business policies, processes, and systems, wherever necessary, to implement the new system.
- Consider and make decisions on behalf of the agency.
- Provide direction on policy, processes, or practice.
- Facilitate issue resolution.
- Direct project related activities within their specific organizational responsibility.

- Set project related priorities within approved resource levels.
- Establish and communicate the business case and its alignment to the agency's strategic goals.
- Represent the agency's project to the key external stakeholders including the vendor, other state agencies, the Legislature, the Judicial Branch, the press, other states, or the federal government.
- Own the project outcomes and results.
- Set clear expectations and accountability for meeting the approved schedule and the approach to the work.
- Identify required resources and funding.

Project Manager

The Project Manager is the person assigned to achieve the project goals, objectives, manage a quality project, deliver a product the meets the cost, time, risk, scope, quality expectations, and ultimately to the satisfaction of the customer. The Project Manager will:

- Manage the team to deliver outcomes that meet the specified project objectives.
- Review deliverables and project schedule.
- Monitor and manage project scope, schedule, risks, issues, and quality.
- Report any progress on deliverables.
- Proactively identify and document issues, risks, and change requests.
- Adhere to the established project management methodology.
- Escalate issues to Business Sponsor.
- Manage the project budget.
- Resolve issues escalated by the project team and stakeholders.
- Provide information concerning the project progress and resources, and high priority issues, risks, and change decisions as needed.
- Provide status reporting on overall aspects of the project.
- Development and management of the activity list to produce the corresponding team deliverables.
- Develop and implement mitigation strategies for relevant risks.
- Facilitate the resolution of project-specific issues and/or those relevant project issues that affect the respective teams.
- Ensure communication of project activity with the team members.
- Participate in meetings and other events.

External Quality Assurance

Quality Assurance is a neutral, unbiased party to the project that:

- Helps develop solutions and risk mitigation strategies.
- Participates as a neutral, and unbiased, party in Steering Committee and project meetings.
- Provides oversight and assessment as required by the Office of the Chief Information Officer OCIO policy.
- Assists the Project Manager with compliance with State and OCIO requirements.
- Reviews documentation, as needed, to provide advice.
- Evaluates and helps monitor risks.
- Provides additional project management expertise, as needed.
- Monitors progress of project activities.
- Prepares recurring reports on project status and risks for Executive Sponsors.

Work Stream Lead

Represents a specific business process area related to the execution of the project's deliverables and will:

- Participate in project team meetings to report Work Stream schedule, scope, risks, and issues.
- Be responsible for the delivery of the respective Work Stream deliverables by the required due date.
- Identify and report project issues, risks, and other concerns affecting project delivery to the Project Manager.
- Ensure team members adhere to the processes of the project as defined by the Project Management Plan.
- Provide input on activity list definition, sequencing, and resource assignment to the Project Manager.
- Facilitate execution of assigned work.
- Provide input and review regular project status reports.
- Act as "champions" for the project to agency team members and the broader stakeholders.

Project Team Member

A Project Team member is defined as having a regular and frequent role throughout the project lifecycle including participation throughout the project as part of regularly scheduled team meetings and other activities as required.

- Participate in project team meetings as required.
- Execute tasks as assigned.
- Provide input and subject matter expertise to project as required.
- Identify risks and issues.
- Adhere to the processes of the project as defined by the Project Management Plan.
- Review regular project status reports.
- Act as "champions" for the project to agency team members and the broader stakeholders.

WORK STREAM: BUSINESS REQUIREMENTS

Business Requirements Work Stream Lead

Lead the effort to identify, document, prioritize, and validate the functional and technical requirements for the new solution. This includes:

- Supporting the procurement of a solution that has the closest fit to the agency requirements.
- Ensuring the solution design incorporates the requirements and identifies any gaps between what is desired and what will be delivered.
- Participating in configuration, review sessions to ensure the solution being developed closely mirrors the design.
- Supporting testing efforts to ensure the solution functions as designed.
- Supporting training material development efforts.
- Ensuring the requirements are updated throughout the project to reflect the work activities and gaps identified.
- Validate that the work products delivered by the project and vendor meet the agency requirements.

Business Analysts

The Business Analysts will coordinate requirements working sessions and gather and process business requirements:

- Coordinate business requirement working sessions with SMEs.
- Produce final business requirements.
- Participate in creating test scripts and test validation.
- Act as additional project requirement resource for development and working sessions.

Subject Matter Experts (SMEs)

The Subject Matter Experts exhibit the highest level of business expertise and skill within the specific business area and support the following project activities:

- Business analysis.
- Requirements development and validation.
- Solution design.
- Testing and data validation.
- Provide input on the effect of changes proposed by the vendor.
- Assist the PM on activity list definition, sequencing, and resource assignment.

Contract Officer

Coordinate the bid, vendor selection process, and manage and vet the resulting contract.

WORK STREAM: SOLUTION IMPLEMENTATION TEAM

Delivery Manager

Coordinate overall solution and resource planning with project leadership. The primary point of contact handles day-to-day management activities.

Implementation Consultant

Works closely with the Project Team to analyze and document requirements, demonstrates and clarifies system functionality, provides software
product expertise and recommends best practices and business process
improvements. The Implementation Consultant tests the software configuration prior to delivery to WSDOT. Assists with Configuration QA,
Validation, bug triage/coordination, and deployment activities.

Integration Engineer

Defines and develops system interfaces to support integration of the
solution with external systems, provides technical assistance necessary
throughout the implementation. Provides information and recommendations on the hardware and software environments necessary to run the
application based upon the detailed requirements analysis.

Application Consultant

Configures the solution in accordance with the documented requirements
and design specification including product configuration, defect resolution, and deployment activities.

Reports Specialist

Reviews and gathers reports specifications including creation of custom reports.

Agency Configuration Specialist(s)

The configuration specialist(s) will:

- Work with the vendor during each phase to ensure that the design is
  accurately configured in the solution.
- Use the implementation period to gain a full understanding of the solution's capabilities (even capabilities planned, but not implemented).
- Be responsible for ongoing configuration of the solution following
  the implementation.
- Develop, adopt, and manage the change control process for the solution configuration.

Contract Manager

Log the completion of deliverables and incorporate into the contract management processes.

WORK STREAM: TESTING

Testing Work Stream Lead

Responsible for leading the effort to develop and execute the Testing Plan:

- Ensure that all planned testing activities occur, meet stakeholder expectations, and are sufficiently completed.
- Develop test cases designed to exhaustively test business rules.
- Ensure Entry and Exit criteria are met prior to transitioning test phases.
- Coordinate testing activities between other testing groups. This includes sequencing of testing and use of shared testing environments.
- Plan and perform System Integration Testing and User Acceptance Testing.
- Participate in Design Review sessions.
- Assist in coaching testers during System Integration and User Acceptance Testing.

System Integration Tester

Responsible for:

- Understanding the business process and business case as it relates to testing activities.
- Fully executing and evaluating test cases.
- Reporting potential issues and anomalies to the Testing Lead.

UAT Tester

Responsible for:

- Coordinating with the end users, understanding business processes, and writing test cases.
- Executing test cases in coordination with the end users.
- Reporting issues to the Testing Lead.

WORK STREAM: ORGANIZATIONAL CHANGE MANAGEMENT

Organizational Change Management (OCM) Work Stream Lead

This role is responsible for the development, management, and execution of the agency Business Process Change Management strategy & plan. This includes:

- Development and management of the Communication & Engagement Plan.
- Development and management of the change impact assessment process.
- Management of the Project Resource Plan.
  - Define resource roles.
  - Development and management of the Change Team Resource Plan.
    - Managing the team of end-users selected to lead change (champions).
    - Developing, managing, and monitoring the internal trainer program.
- Support the development of the Training Plan.
  - Facilitating the execution of the Training Plan.
    - Training material content, logistics, scheduling, attendance monitoring.
- Identification, training, support, performance monitoring.
- Development and management of the Reinforcement, Resistance, and Corrective Action Plan.
- Support the execution of the agency readiness assessments.
- Support to-be process development and identify impacts.

This role will also contribute to the project team by:

- Providing status updates on responsible tasks and agency performance against the change management activities.
- Identifying any pending risks or issues.

Communication Lead

- Execution and support of the Communication Management Plan.
  - Internal
  - External
- Leads, plans, and organizes communications and public relations efforts.
- Reviews, drafts, edit, and finalize communications materials (written, audio, online, and etcetera).
- Serves as the single point of contact for all communications with the external customers.
- Facilitates the approval processes.
- Other duties, as assigned, to support the project.

Trainer

Provides support and oversight of the vendor in the development and effective delivery of customized, process-based, training for the implementation. This may include documentation, exercises, and individual practice scenarios.

Champions

Champions support the operational transition to the new solution for their respective work groups. These groups may be organized by location, role, or department. Responsibilities include:

- Supporting the solution communication and training efforts.
- Providing immediate, on-site assistance to end-users during the deployment and support phases.
- Answering questions for end-users during the project's key phases.
- Managing resistance in a timely manner, escalating risk to OCM as needed.
- May provide support and training to new employees on the solution and business processes.

WORK STREAM: TECHNICAL ARCHITECTURE

Technical Architecture Work Stream Lead

Responsible to ensure the technical architecture for the agency is sufficient to support the new solution. Leads the work effort and coordinates with relevant team members and SMEs including:

- Network Infrastructure
  - Execution of the network infrastructure and capacity assessment.
  - Upgrades to network infrastructure to meet the assessment gaps or standards, if required.
  - Support the enterprise network team in external system connectivity, if required.
- Security
  - Adoption of project security standards and protocols.
  - Adoption of the identity management solution and related policies.
  - Adherence to the business continuity and disaster recovery plans.
  - Support other security activities where required: data classification, role management, logging, and vulnerability.
  - Work with WATech and vendors to define data flows, interfaces, and security concerns.
- Systems Platform and Infrastructure (title varies by agency)
  - Conduct a systems infrastructure assessment (e.g. desktop, kiosks, and devices).
  - Upgrade the systems infrastructure to meet assessment gaps or standards, if required.
  - Procure devices relevant to the agency requirements.
  - Install and perform device testing (if necessary).
- Application
  - Provide agency information as necessary to support the application configuration.
  - Perform agency-specific System Integration Testing (SIT) and regression testing.
- Legacy remediation
  - Examine all existing systems to find where related data is used.
  - Perform a systems gap assessment and document corresponding impacts.
  - Define the changes necessary to WSDOT systems or interfaces to replace existing or create new interfaces to enhance business value.

- Work with WSDOT, WATech, and vendor representatives to define data flows, interfaces, and security needed to meet the business needs.
- Modify internal legacy systems and interfaces to resolve the gaps identified in the impact assessment.
- Decommission legacy systems as needed.

IT Business Analyst

Provide Technology expertise, assist in identifying the business needs for the system, and provide input on changes proposed by the vendor.

The IT analysts are also responsible for ensuring the technical architecture of the agency is sufficient to support the new solution.

Key areas of focus include:

- Network Infrastructure
- Security
- Systems Platform
- Application Support
- Legacy Remediation

Source: GMS Project Archives.

Annexure E: GMS SharePoint Portal

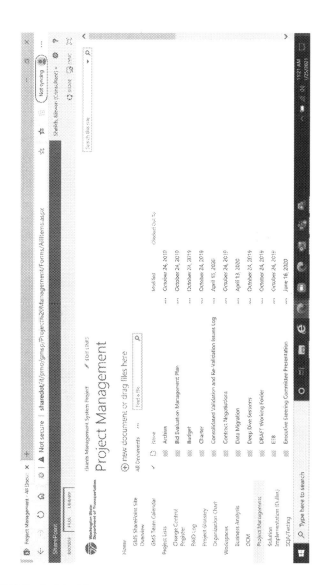

Source: GMS Project Archives.

Annexure F: RAID Log

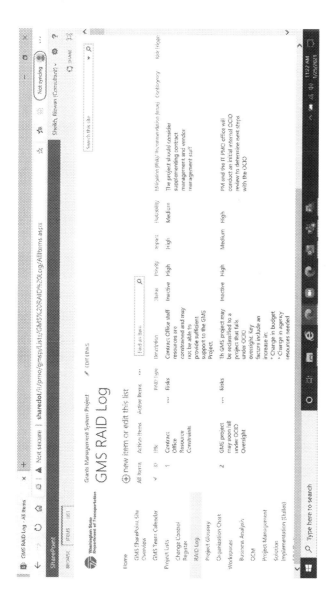

Source: GMS Project Archives.

Annexure G: Change Request Approval Process

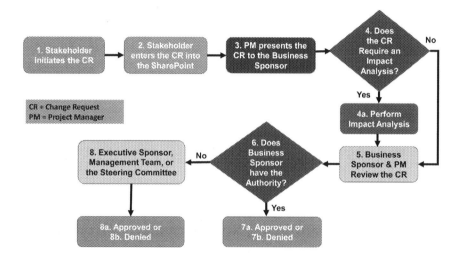

Source: GMS Project Archives.

Annexure H: Go-Live Readiness Scorecard for Regional Mobility Grants (RMG) Application Pilot Release

WSDOT Grants Management System (GMS)
Go-Live Readiness Scorecard for Regional Mobility Grants (RMG) Pilot Release

Washington State
Department of Transportation

Criterion 1 – GMS software application readiness	Criterion 2 – WSDOT application/infrastructure readiness	Criterion 3 – Data Migration readiness	Criterion 4 – Organizational / Change Readiness	Criterion 5 – Agency Business process and policy readiness	Criterion 6 – Contract activities on target and progressing as planned	Criterion 7 – Hypercare team readiness
Complete	Complete	Complete	Complete	Complete	In Progress	Hypercare is performed after Go-Live

Source: GMS Project Archives.

WSDOT Grants Management System (GMS)

Go-Live Readiness Scorecard for Regional Mobility Grants (RMG) Pilot Release

Washington State Department of Transportation

Section B Thresholds [current assessment value] • NS – not started; and/or equivalent activity is not completed yet	Criterion 1 – WSDOT software solution readiness	Criterion 2 – WSDOT application/infrastructure readiness	Criterion 3 – Data Migration readiness	Criterion 4 – Organizational Change / End-user readiness	Criterion 5 – Agency Business process and policy readiness	Criterion 6 – Cutover activities on target and progressing as planned	Criterion 7 – Hypercare team readiness
	1. 100% of the configuration items required for the end users are complete and as per the scope. 2. 100% of Functional Test cases (sub-recipients) functionally have been executed. 3. 100% of Integration Test cases that impact end users (sub-recipients) functionally have been executed. 4. 100% of End-to-End Test cases that impact end teams (sub-recipients) functionally have been executed. 5. No outstanding Critical or High priority defects that impact end users (sub-recipients). 6. 100% of profiles/UI data loaded into the GMS. This is not applicable to the Pilot Release of RMG.	1. All Office of Cyber Security and WSDOT Security standards and policies have been implemented and appropriate approvals received. [100%] 2. SaW Integration is complete 100%.	1. Subject Matter Experts (SMEs) have signed on the data mapping. This is not applicable to RMG. [100%] 2. 100% of the data migration (Organizations and People) as defined in the data migration scope document is complete, with no outstanding defects, and ready to promote to production.	1. Train-the-Trainer and End-User Training materials complete. [100%] 2. Reference materials complete. [100%] 3. System Administrators / Power users are ready and know their role in Hypercare. For RMG, Sys-Admin Support will be provided by the Vendor until WSDOT Administrators are trained. [100%] 4. End user Hypercare model is in place and roles assigned. This is not applicable to the Pilot Release of RMG. It will be read by 11/30/2020. 5. 100% of the end users (sub-recipients) trained on the RMG Application. 6. Training resources (e.g. Go-to-Meeting and Activities) are secured [100%] 7. Communications have been identified [100%] 8. 100% of RMG users report being adequately informed during the readiness survey. This was done during the End-User training, instead of a formal survey.	1. Policy and procedure updates are in final draft form and ready for the GMS team. For RMG Pilot Release, there were no changes to the policy. 2. Forms and business processes are updated to reflect new business. 3. All policy impacts have been identified and reached [100%] 4. All end-users have been informed and acknowledged the information presented [100%]	1. ✓ Cutover activities have been identified. 2. ✓ Cutover activities have an assigned resource, duration and delivery date. ✓ Cutover review sessions are occurring. 3. ✓ Cutover activities related to RMG Pilot are on schedule. ✓ No significant risk to planned activities.	1. GMS System Administrators and Hypercare roles have been identified. 2. The GMS team is ready to support the GMS system and ongoing operations are secured. 3. Hypercare resources are secured.

○ Complete = Activities to support Criterion are as complete.

✓ Green = Activities to support Criterion on target to support go-live as planned

○ Criterion = Activities to support Criterion max target to support go-live as planned

● Yellow = Activities to support Criterion max negatively impact go-live as planned

⊗ Red = Activities to support Criterion you are in a point to be as planned

WSDOT Grants Management System (GMS)

Go-Live Readiness Scorecard for Regional Mobility Grants (RMG) Pilot Release

Washington State Department of Transportation

	Criterion 1 – GMS software / solution readiness	Criterion 2 – WSDOT application/infrastructure readiness	Criterion 3 – Data Migration readiness	Criterion 4 – Organizational Change / End-user readiness	Criterion 5 – Agency Business process and policy readiness	Criterion 6 – Cutover activities on target and progressing as planned	Criterion 7 – Hypercare team readiness
Section C **Status Details**	1. All issues and bugs related to the RMG application have been resolved. 2. Testability and Ambiguity analysis completed ahead of schedule. 3. Systems Integration Testing (SIT) and User Acceptance Testing (UAT) are complete.	1. Technology Workstream Lead worked with WSDOT and WA Tech, and the Vendor to implement the SAW integration with GMS. 2. All outstanding issues related to Authentication have been resolved. 3. Testing of the SAW integration with GMS was completed on-schedule 6/5/2020. 4. Browser validation is complete (Edge & Chrome; IE not supported).	1. There is no data migration required for the RMG Pilot Release. 2. The Grantees/Sub-Recipients will enter the Organization and People data.	1. External users have been notified through meetings, seminars, training, and newsletter. 2. End-User / Sub-Recipient training for RMG is complete.	1. Policies are not changing but there are practice changes in processes regarding the functionality of the new GMS. 2. WSDOT Internal users have been trained on the RMG Application.	1. The Vendor will perform the Cut-Over activities from June 08 – June 22, 2020 and make the Production and Test Servers ready by June 23, 2020 for the RMG Release.	1. For RMG and Consolidated Applications, the Vendor will provide the Admin Support. 2. The Vendor will also provide the Escalation procedure by 6/22/2020 for this RMG Release. 3. A Hypercare Plan for the 12/31/2020 will be ready by 11/30/20. 4. M&O Plan will be prepared after the RMG and Consolidated Releases, and it will be ready by 11/30/2020.
Section D **Assessment provided by**	• Business Analyst (BA) Workstream Lead (Kyle McElfresh) • WSDOT Subject Matter Experts (Evan Olsen, Lori Barnhart, and Cherryl Steben) • SQA Workstream Lead (Adam Richards)	• Technology Workstream Lead (Terry Landes) • Data Migration Lead (Derek Lee) • WSDOT Security (Francis Diane) • SQA Workstream Lead (Adam Richards) • Business Analyst (BA) Workstream Lead (Kyle McElfresh)	• Data Workstream Lead (Derek Lee) • WSDOT Data Lead (Robert Gibson) • Business Analyst (BA) Workstream Lead (Kyle McElfresh) • SQA Workstream Lead (Adam Richards)	• OCM Lead (Debbie Ruggles)	• WSDOT Subject Matter Experts (Evan Olsen, Lori Barnhart, and Cherryl Steben) • Business Sponsor (Firas Makhlouf) • Business Analyst (BA) Workstream Lead (Kyle McElfresh) from System Perspective	• Business Sponsor (Firas Makhlouf) • Project Management (Rizwan Sheikh) • OCM Lead (Debbie Ruggles) • Business Analyst (BA) Workstream Lead (Kyle McElfresh) • WSDOT Subject Matter Experts (Evan Olsen, Lori Barnhart, and Cherryl Steben) • SQA Workstream Lead (Adam Richards) • Data Migration Lead (Derek Lee and Robert Gibson) • Technology Workstream Lead (Terry Landes)	• System Administrators (Cherryl Steben with the support of Pam Smith and Tina Ren) • WSDOT Subject Matter Experts (Evan Olsen, Lori Barnhart, and Cherryl Steben) • SQA Workstream Lead (Adam Richards) • Technology Workstream Lead (Terry Landes) • Business Analyst (BA) Workstream Lead (Kyle McElfresh) • OCM Lead (Debbie Ruggles) • Project Management (Rizwan Sheikh) • Business Sponsor (Firas Makhlouf)

Green = Activities to support Criterion

Yellow = Activities to support Criterion that negatively impact go-live as planned

Source: GMS Project Archives.

WSDOT Grants Management System (GMS)
Go-Live Readiness Scorecard for Regional Mobility Grants (RMG) Pilot Release

Washington State Department of Transportation

	Criterion 1 – GMS software / solution readiness	Criterion 2 – WSDOT application/infrastructure readiness	Criterion 3 – Data Migration readiness	Criterion 4 – Organizational Change / End-user readiness	Criterion 5 – Agency Business process and policy readiness	Criterion 6 – Cutover activities on target and progressing as planned	Criterion 7 – Hypercare team readiness
Section E **Key next steps (if any)**	1. All forms related to the RMG Application have been signed by the WSDOT Subject Matter Experts (SMEs).	1. Testing of the SAW integration with GMS was completed on 6/5/2020. 2. There are no further next steps.	1. There is no data migration required for the RMG Pilot Release. 2. The data migration activities will start 08/2020.	1. All OCM activities for the RMG Release are complete. 2. There are no further next steps for RMG.	1. There are no policy changes for the RMG Pilot Release. Therefore, there are no further next steps for RMG.	1. Cut-Over activities will be performed by the Vendor from 6/8 – 6/22/2020. 2. Both the Test and Production Servers will be ready by 6/23 for the RMG Application.	1. Sys Admin and HyperCare activities will be performed by the Vendor for the RMG Application. 2. The Vendor will provide an escalation procedure(s) for the WSDOT team to handle end-user queries and technical issues related to RMG by 6/22/2020.
Section F **Contingency Plan / Risk Mitigation (if needed)** **N/A = Not Applicable**	1. Targeted regression testing will be performed on RMG during testing for the next Release to mitigate the low risk of changes affecting this release.	1. The SOA Team tested the SAW Integration with GMS and it was fully functional. Should there be any technical issues with SAW, the vendor will be available until 12/31/2020 to resolve them.	1. N/A	1. A WSDOT / PTD Help Desk will be in place to assist the end-users / sub-recipients. 2. In addition, the vendor will be available until 12/31/2020 to answer end-user queries and resolve technical issues.	1. Should there be a need for a change in a business process or policy, it would be devised and approved by the Business Sponsor before implementation.	1. Three servers (Development, Test, and Production) will be available for development and testing of the software before implementing the changes to production.	1. In addition to the WSDOT/PTD Help Desk, the vendor will be available until 12/31/2020 to answer end-user queries and technical issues.

Complete: Activities to support Criterion are complete.

On-target: Activities to support Criterion are on target to support go-live as planned.

Green: Activities to support Criterion are on target/complete and will support go-live as planned.

Follow-x: Activities to support Criterion can negatively impact go-live as planned.

Red: Activities to support Criterion can negatively impact go-live.

Reviewed By: _____ Approved By: _____ Date: June 11, 2020

Business Sponsor   Executive Sponsor

Source: GMS Project Archives.

Annexure I: Project Schedule

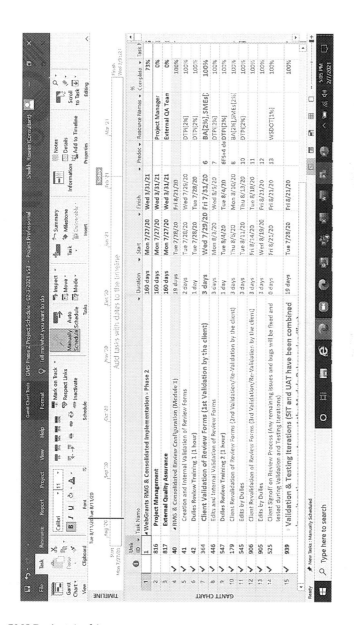

Source: GMS Project Archives.

Annexure J: Grants Management System (GMS) Monthly Newsletter

Washington State
Department of Transportation

GMS — What's next?

Some of the modules we're currently reviewing and testing:

- Application evaluation to award
- Award to appropriation to grant source
- Contracts/contract amendments
- Claims (invoices) to reimbursement
- Site visits
- Reporting
- Asset management

Watch for more updates and training opportunities in the coming months for you, the applicant/grantee!

GRANTS MANAGEMENT SYSTEM PROJECT NEWSLETTER

October 2020

PUBLIC TRANSPORTATION DIVISION   ISSUE #9

A word from our sponsor...

Hello! We've come a long way, and now we're ready to begin accepting applications through our Grants Management System. I'm excited that we'll have a more efficient method of grant management in the next year. Our staff and contractors have been hard at work to make sure the system functions as it should for all of us. My hope is that you find it a more efficient way to conduct your grant-related business with the Public Transportation Division. Thank you for your patience.

~Firas Makhlouf, Capital Programs & Business Services Manager

~ Reminder ~

Consolidated grant applications are due Friday, Oct. 30. If you have questions, you can email Susan Garber-Yonts or call 206-922-3259. You can also contact your regional community liaison.

Reminder: Public Transportation Division staff and consultants are working remotely. Nevertheless, we'll respond as quickly as possible to your calls and emails.

GMS help desk

Having issues with GMS?

Call us at 360-705-7711

Email us at PTDGMSSupport@wsdot.wa.gov

Source: GMS Project Archives.

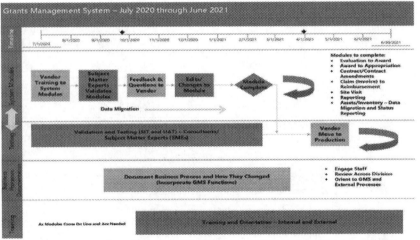

A new picture: As we continue to learn about the Grants Management System's functions, test and validate its various modules, and find out how GMS integrates with both internal and external processes, it's a good time to find a new way to demonstrate it visually. This timeline shows how various activities overlap and how they are cyclical for each module (system modules and testing). As you can see, we're moving forward with our goal of full functionality for Regional Mobility and Consolidated grants by March 2021!

Source: GMS Project Archives.

Bibliography

1. Goleman, D. (2004). *What Makes a Leader a Leader?* Harvard Business Review, January, 2–11.
2. Tuckman, B. W. (1965). Developmental sequence in small groups, Psychological Bulletin, 63, 384–399.
3. Tuckman, B. W. & Jensen, M. C. (1977). Stages of small-group development revisited. Group & Organization Studies, 2(4), 419–427.
4. Peterson, S. J., Abramson, R. & Stutman, R. K. (2020). *How to Develop Your Leadership Style?* Harvard Business Review, November–December, 1–11.
5. World Health Organization. (2020). Statement on the Second Meeting of the International Health Regulations (2005) Emergency Committee regarding the outbreak of novel coronavirus (2019-nCoV). Retrieved from https://www.who.int/news/item/30-01-2020-statement-on-the-second-meeting-of-the-international-health-regulations-(2005)-emergency-committee-regarding-the-outbreak-of-novel-coronavirus-(2019-ncov)
6. World Health Organization. (2020). WHO Director-General's Opening Remarks at theMediaBriefingonCOVID-19–11March2020.Retrievedfromhttps://www.who.int/director-general/speeches/detail/who-director-general-s-opening-remarks-at-the-media-briefing-on-covid-19—11-march-2020
7. IMFBlog. (2020). The Great Lockdown: Worst Economic Downturn Since the Great Depression. Retrieved from https://blogs.imf.org/2020/04/14/the-great-lockdown-worst-economic-downturn-since-the-great-depression/
8. World Health Organization. (2021). Coronavirus Disease (COVID-19) Pandemic. Retrieved from https://www.who.int/emergencies/diseases/novel-coronavirus-2019 on February 23, 2021.
9. World Health Organization. (2021). WHO Coronavirus Disease (COVID-19) Dashboard. Retrieved from https://covid19.who.int/ on February 23, 2021.
10. World Health Organization. (2021). United States of America Situation. Retrieved from https://covid19.who.int/region/amro/country/us on February 23, 2021.
11. Congressional Budget Office. (2020). Interim Economic Projections for 2020 and 2021. Retrieved from https://www.cbo.gov/publication/56351
12. U.S. Bureau of Labor Statistics. (2020). Current Employment Statistics – CES (National). Retrieved from https://www.bls.gov/ces/
13. USAFACTS. (2020). Coronavirus Stats & Data. Retrieved from https://usafacts.org/issues/coronavirus/
14. Kotter, J. P. (1990). *What leaders really do?* Harvard Business Review, May–June, 37–60.
15. Bennis, W. & Nanus, B. (Eds.). (1985). *Leaders: The Strategies for Taking Charge.* New York: Harper and Row.
16. House, R. J., Hanges, P. J., Javidan, M., Dorfman, P. W. & Gupta, V. (Eds.). (2004). *Culture, Leadership, and Organizations: The GLOBE Study of 62 Societies.* Thousand Oaks, CA: Sage Publications.
17. IPMA. (2007). ICB: IPMA Competence Baseline Version 3.0. In C. Caupin, H. Knopfl, G. Koch., H. Pannenbaker, F. Perez-Polo, & C. Seabury (Eds.). Njkerk, The Netherlands: International Project Management Association.

18. Sheikh, R. A. & Müller, R. (2012). The relationship between culturally endorsed leadership theory (CLT) factors and project success: a literature review. Paper presented at PMI® Research and Education Conference, Limerick, Munster, Ireland. Newtown Square, PA: Project Management Institute.

19. Drucker, P. F. (2004). *What Makes an Effective Executive?* Harvard Business Review, June, 15–21.

20. Boulding, B. (2019). *For Leader Decency is Just as Important as Intelligence.* Harvard Business Review, July, 1–4.

21. Salovey, P. & Mayer, J. D. (1990). Emotional intelligence. Imagination Cognition and Personality, 9(3), 185–211.

22. Mayer, J. D., Salovey, P. & Caruso, D. R. (2004). Target articles: Emotional intelligence: Theory, findings, and implications. Psychological Inquiry, 15(3), 197–215.

23. Van Rooy, D. & Viswesvaran, C. (2004). Emotional intelligence: A meta-analytic investigation of predictive validity and nomo-logical net. Journal of Vocational Behavior, 65, 71–95.

24. Boyatzis, R. E., Goleman, D. & Rhee, K. (2000). "Clustering competence in emotional intelligence: Insights from the emotional competence inventory (ECI)", Handbook of Emotional Intelligence, pp. 343–362.

25. Goleman, D. & Nevarez, M. (2018). *Boost Your Emotional Intelligence with these 3 Questions.* Harvard Business Review, August, 1–5.

26. Lumen Learning. (2020). The Five Stages of Team Development Retrieved from https://courses.lumenlearning.com/suny-principlesmanagement/chapter/reading-the-five-stages-of-team-development/

27. Turner, J. R. & Müller, R. (2005). The project manager's leadership style as a success factor on projects: A literature review. Project Management Journal, 36(2), 49–61.

28. Geoghegan, L. & Dulewicz, V. (2008). Do project managers' leadership competencies contribute to project success? Project Management Journal, 39(4), 58–67.

29. Dulewicz, V. & Higgs, M. (2003). Leadership at the top: The need for emotional intelligence in organizations. International Journal of Organizational Analysis, 11(3), 194–210.

30. Zheng, W. (2020). *5 Strategies to Support Your Employees Through a Crisis.* Harvard Business Review Online. Retrieved from https://hbr.org/2020/10/5-strategies-to-support-your-employees-through-a-crisis

31. Robins, M. (2019). *Why Employees Need Both Recognition and Appreciation.* Harvard Business Review Web Article, November, 1–4.

32. Kearney. (2020). Creating joyful, high-performing teams, even during the COVID-19 lockdown. Retrieved from https://www.kearney.com/covid-19/article/?/a/creating-joyful-high-performing-teams-even-during-the-covid-19-lockdown

33. Accenture. (2020). What to ask Today to be better off Tomorrow. Retrieved from https://www.accenture.com/us-en/insights/future-workforce/employee-potential-talent-management-strategy?c=acn_glb_modernhrgoogle_11312040&n=psgs_0920&gclid=Cj0KCQiAqo3-BRDoARIsAE5vnaJbikOXXlhNT4I3WlMsKV9EkBu-vN6XaojC7dXIn-SE-KrKkfOqppdAaApPUEALw_wcB&gclsrc=aw.ds

34. Fortune. (2018). Meet the CEO of the Insurance Company Growing Faster Than Apple. Retrieved from https://fortune.com/2018/11/15/progressive-insurance-ceo-tricia-griffith/

35. McKinsey. (2020). Diversity Still Matters. Retrieved from https://www.mckinsey.com/featured-insights/diversity-and-inclusion/diversity-still-matters; March 19, 2020.

36. Ludema, J. & Johnson, A. (2020). Remote Work Is Here To Stay. Three Keys To Building High-Performing Virtual Teams. Retrieved from https://www.forbes.com/sites/amberjohnson-jimludema/2020/09/16/remote-work/?sh=21d1c407197d

37. KPMG. (2020). Succeeding in the New Reality: Reaction, Resilience, Recovery, and New Reality. Retrieved from https://www.kpmg.us/insights/2020/covid-19-resilience-readiness.html

38. Southwick, S. M., Vythilingam, M. & Charney, D. S. (2005). The psychobiology of depression and resilience to stress: Implications for prevention and treatment. *Annual Review of Clinical Psychology.* 1, 255–291. doi:10.1146/annurev.clinpsy.1.102803.143948

39. Cialdini, R. B. (2001). *Harnessing the science of persuasion.* Harvard Business Review, 79(9), 72–79.

40. Psychology Today. (2020). Conscientiousness. Retrieved from https://www.psychologytoday.com/us/basics/conscientiousness

41. Viter, I. (2020). 280+ Project Managers Name Their Biggest Challenges of 2020. Retrieved from https://www.forecast.app/blog/challenges-of-project-management

42. Deloitte. (2020). Workforce Strategies for Post-Covid-19 Recovery. Retrieved from https://www2.deloitte.com/global/en/pages/about-deloitte/articles/covid-19/covid-19-workforce-strategies-for-post-covid-recovery.html

43. McKinsey Global Institute. (2021). The Future of Work After Covid-19. Retrieved from https://www.mckinsey.com/featured-insights/future-of-work/the-future-of-work-after-covid-19

44. Cybersecurity and Infrastructure Security Agency (CISA). (2020). Critical Infrastructure Sectors. Retrieved from https://www.cisa.gov/critical-infrastructure-sectors

45. World Economic Forum (WEF). (2020). How digital infrastructure can help us through the COVID-19 crisis. Retrieved from https://www.weforum.org/agenda/2020/04/digital-infrastructure-public-health-crisis-covid-19/

46. Pricewaterhousecooper (PWC). (2020). COVID-19: Four essential crisis management lessons. Retrieved from https://www.pwc.com/gx/en/issues/crisis-solutions/covid-19/four-essential-crisis-management-lessons.html

47. Wynn, S. (2020). How Can IT Infrastructure Help Your Business Prepare for Next Pandemic? BoomTech. https://www.boomtechit.com/it-infrastructure-pandemic/

48. Gartner. (2020). Gartner CFO Survey Reveals. 74% Intend to Shift Some Employees to Remote Work Permanently. Retrieved from https://www.gartner.com/en/newsroom/press-releases/2020-04-03-gartner-cfo-surey-reveals-74-percent-of-organizations-to-shift-some-employees-to-remote-work-permanently2

49. UC Berkley. (2020). Top 10 Secure Computing Tips. Retrieved from https://security.berkeley.edu/resources/best-practices-how-to-articles/top-10-secure-computing-tips

50. Norton. (2020). 10 cybersecurity best practices that every employee should know. Retrieved from https://us.norton.com/internetsecurity-how-to-cyber-security-best-practices-for-employees.html

51. Murray, E. (2020). *The Next Generation of Office Communication Tech.* Harvard Business Review. October, 1–5. https://hbr.org/2020/10/the-next-generation-of-office-communication-tech

52. Edmondson, A. C. & Daley, G. (2020). *How to Foster Psychological Safety in Virtual Meetings.* Harvard Business Review. August. https://hbr.org/2020/08/how-to-foster-psychological-safety-in-virtual-meetings

53. Kim, W. C. & Mauborgne, R. (2004). *Blue Ocean Strategy*. Harvard Business Review. October, 1–12.

54. Epstein, A. (2018). *Build Self-Awareness with Help from Your Team*. Harvard Business Review. August, 1–4.

55. Pink, D. H. (Eds.). (2006). *A Whole New Mind: Why Right-Brainers Will Rule the Future*. New York: Riverhead Books.

56. Sanchez, P. (2018). *The Secret to Leading Organization Change is Empathy* (Sanchez, Patti). Harvard Business Review, December, 1–4.

57. Zaki, J. (2019). *Making Empathy Central to Your Company Culture*. Harvard Business Review. May 1–4.

58. Lo, I. (2019). The Beautiful Truths About Being a Highly Sensitive Human, Retrieved from https://www.psychologytoday.com/intl/blog/living-emotional-intensity/201902/the-beautiful-truths-about-being-highly-sensitive-human

59. Meliones, J. (2000). *Saving Money Saving Lives*. Harvard Business Review. November–December, 1–9.

60. Delizonna, L. (2017). *High-Performing Teams Need Psychological Safety*. Here's How to Create It. Harvard Business Review.

61. Shapiro, D. (Eds.). (2017). *Negotiating the Nonnegotiable: How to Resolve Your Most Emotionally Charged Conflicts*. New York: Penguin Books.

62. Mckee, A. (2015). *Empathy is Key to a Great Meeting*. Harvard Business Review. March, 1–4.

63. Goleman, D. (2013). *Focus: The Hidden Driver of Excellence* Bloomsbury, January, 2–11.

64. Kislik, L. (2020). *Leaders, Are You Feeling the Burden of Pandemic-Related Decisions?* Harvard Business Review Online. October, 1–5.

65. Coyle, D. (2018). The Culture Code: the Secrets of Highly Successful Groups. First edition. New York: Bantam Books.

Index

Printed in the United States
by Baker & Taylor Publisher Services